THE
MEASURE
OF A
NATION

PRAISE FOR *THE MEASURE OF A NATION*

"This book does for a country what McKinsey does for companies: it compares America to the competition, on a variety of telling and transparent metrics, because facing clear facts can engender creative solutions to looming challenges. It is based on the compelling premise that while America is exceptional in many ways, all countries, including America, can learn from others' experiences. Prof. Friedman's recommendations from the data are thoughtful and stimulating, and he usefully ranks them by political feasibility. Anyone concerned for America's future needs to grasp the facts documented here."

—Michael A. Clemens, Senior Fellow,
Center for Global Development

"Howard Friedman comes neither to praise nor bury America, only to find room for improvement. If businesses can scan the competition for best practice, he suggests, why not countries? By comparing the United States against the rest of the world, he has written a thinking man's *Spirit Level*, which will stimulate and surprise readers on both sides of the pond."

—Christopher Snowden,
author of *The Spirit Level Delusion*

"Calmly and systematically, Howard Friedman scrutinizes our country's performance on the crucial tasks that confront every modern society. Friedman is an engaging guide, and his message is stark. Despite our unprecedented wealth, the United States often does not commit the resources needed to combat pressing problems. Perhaps more alarming is that, even where we spend more than other wealthy nations, we do not spend that money effectively. This book is a wake-up call to anyone who wishes our country to prosper."

—Paul Pierson, professor of political science,
University of California, Berkeley,
and coauthor of *Winner-Take-All Politics*

THE
MEASURE
OF A
NATION

HOW TO REGAIN
AMERICA'S COMPETITIVE EDGE
AND BOOST
OUR GLOBAL STANDING

HOWARD STEVEN FRIEDMAN

FOREWORD BY STAN BERNSTEIN
FORMER SENIOR POLICY ADVISER FOR THE UNITED NATIONS

 Prometheus Books

59 John Glenn Drive
Amherst, New York 14228–2119

Published 2012 by Prometheus Books

Cover image © 2012 Veer/Media Bakery
Cover design by Grace M. Conti-Zilsberger

Inquiries should be addressed to
Prometheus Books
59 John Glenn Drive
Amherst, New York 14228–2119
VOICE: 716–691–0133
FAX: 716–691–0137
WWW.PROMETHEUSBOOKS.COM

16 15 14 13 12   5 4 3 2 1

Library of Congress Cataloging-in-Publication Data

Friedman, Howard Steven, 1972–
     The measure of a nation : how to regain America's competitive edge and boost our global standing / by Howard Steven Friedman.
          p. cm.
     Includes bibliographical references and index.
     ISBN 978-1-61614-569-9 (pbk.)
     ISBN 978-1-61614-570-5 (ebook)
     1. United States—Economic policy—21st century. 2. United States—Social policy—21st century. 3. Competition—United States. 4. United States—Politics and government—21st century. I. Title.

HC106.84.F75 2012
320.60973—dc23

3 4015 07120 0420

2012004773

Printed in the United States of America

To the generations that I'll never meet, may your future be boundless.

CONTENTS

FOREWORD

by Stan Bernstein,
former senior policy adviser for the United Nations

In 1941, at a time of continuing suffering after the largest economic nose-dive in decades, Henry Luce made a strong positive declaration through his much-attended and persuasive media empire. We were living in "the American Century." American exceptionalism, rooted in our God-granted vision and democratic commitments, would increase our power and influence and serve as a beacon for global transformation. This was a heady vision for international engagement, even as a vicious war between advanced societies was intensifying and going global.

Now, seventy years later, in the face of new systemic global economic and social upheavals, many are calling for a re-examination of the American world mission. The bloom is off the rose. Arguments fly on whether we need to return to our tried-and-true advantages or adopt new approaches to success-fully engage an ever more connected and "smaller" or "flatter" world without a single dominant power. A belief in the essential superiority of American insti-tutions, perspectives, and perfectibility clashes with a nagging sense—if not an outright fear—of decline. Americans seem uncertain whether they are at the proud peak of national possibility or on the edge of a cliff.

National decline is a relative term. Are we to consider decline compared to earlier, historic national aspirations and performance levels or decline com-pared to the statuses of other countries here and now? But this question of America's relative standing when compared to our international partners seems not to elicit either passionate discussion or analytic debate. Shouldn't these issues be addressed if we as a nation are to grow, mature, and succeed as a pro-ductive international competitor? Friedman focuses on key questions that address three specific concerns:

- By what measures shall national decline or progress be judged?
- Does a nation in decline actually experience it? If so, how and on what basis?
- How does a nation respond to decline? Is progress experienced the same way?

The second concern determines the political consequences. We rarely act on what we don't experience. People do, of course, but national decision making is a far more complex process, whatever the politics of the moment.

I write this at a time of great uncertainty with regard to economic and social policy debates; everywhere one looks in America people of various political persuasions have a sense of national decline. The pundits on the "right" and "left," and the vast majority of those who don't worry about such terms, are all uneasy about America's future prospects. Pointing fingers at different elements of concern, even when they agree on what is problematic, they differ in their prescriptions because of their different perspectives.

The terms used to describe the ongoing political discussion revolve more around efforts of various parties to exercise power based on their ideologies and how they fit their quite different understandings of America's performance rather than seriously attempting to understand the current situation and envision practical, realistic alternatives.

This book takes a different tack. Its major contribution is diagnostic, and its diagnosis is framed in a novel way. The presentation reflects a core American orientation, one that reaches beyond politics. It is practical, analytic, and grounded in concrete, hard-nosed business perspectives.

Howard Friedman's *The Measure of a Nation* is an exercise in business analysis. This is the kind of thinking that Americans take pride in. And in this way it addresses the first question. To protect the perspective, he uses measures based on sources of international data that are respected throughout the world. These are, as is everything, challenged in national discussions. The politics of measurement are complex, and the technical issues are often no less daunting.

A major advantage of this work comes from its selection of the bases for comparing America with an appropriate group of competitor nations and then looking at the details of difference. Giving priority to one versus another dimension of our complex social, economic, and political world is bound to set off opposition and controversy. Here Friedman provides a sensitive and usable framework for selecting the indicators used to evaluate the competitor nations. Each chapter outlines a key issue or some basic need that converges substantially with the suggestions of such economic experts as Joseph Stiglitz, Amartya Sen, and Jean-Paul Fitoussi, who together saw the importance of addressing various interrelated aspects of human welfare and rights and of going beyond Gross Domestic Product (GDP) as a measure of national progress. Here GDP levels get you in the comparison set but don't then dominate the discussion. It is an approach that comes from business but provides business with a human face.

The attempt to measure well-being, capacity, and potential is technically difficult. The approach taken here examines key dimensions of life as we actually experience it rather than using abstract theoretical concepts that only professionals can understand. It covers a wide range of concerns, the importance of which are hard to contest: health, safety and security, education, democracy and political participation, and equity and equality (including social and economic mobility and gender advancement).

Within each of these areas Friedman's discussion is at the same time simple and complex. The simplicity comes from selecting commonly accepted (and publicly available) indicators for making the national comparisons. The complexity comes from the diversity of the aspects of each area that are selected. As would be expected from a business-oriented approach, much attention is given to how much is spent in each area and what the returns/outcomes are. This leads to challenging discussion of whether, in the United States and in the competitor countries, the returns are commensurate with the investments. But Friedman also measures the social and political mechanisms implemented in different national settings, the incentives that are offered for the performance of both institutions and individuals, and the structural differences in how politics leads to decisions and action.

The choice of social indicators is all-important when ranking or scoring national performance. But Friedman is scrupulous in not cherry picking for particular outcomes. Within each area, a wide range of issues are addressed. Despite the requirement that comparable data are required for each country, a striking diversity of issues is addressed. He measures the width, length, and depth of experience in trying to see the world in three dimensions. For example, the chapter on health references multiple measures of morbidity and mortality, compares health financing options, and considers the size and structure of groups of health workers. The security discussion richly includes both measures of domestic safety and international defense strategies. Similar diversity is explored in each of the covered concerns.

Just as the selection of topics and indicators can shape conclusions unfairly when people have an ax to grind, so can the time frame considered. The discussion is to a large extent a snapshot of the countries on these multiple dimensions. Business-like decisions must be based on rigorous assessments of current situations, but trends matter. Friedman doesn't just get three dimensions, he often adds the fourth. In times as dynamic and challenging as ours it is sensible to wonder if his current comparative assessments will prove stable. Some change will happen (it must be possible, or recommendations for action would lose credibility), but these, particularly in outcome measures, will be gradual and cumulative. In the near term, the comparative rankings, based on the best available data, will likely remain accurate. In those occasions in the discussion where trend data are available, they reinforce the conclusions from single time points.

Some may argue about whether the recommendations related to the comparison countries provide guidance to solving America's problems, based as they are on global responses to similar issues and challenges. Some suggestions are probably relevant, despite national differences, even in the face of current shortages of financial resources. But the future is the future, and leaders need to build support now and understand how their choices will create new dynamics. To Friedman's credit, his recommendations are modest and constructive. In these trying times, any recommended course of action must show evidence of having value, being affordable, and addressing existing social alignments. The recommendations offered are modest, yet cumulatively dramatic, and they could go a long way toward transforming American society as we know it.

There are no "isms" promoted here, though the vast amount of evidence found in examples from Europe and Asia (both of which are dealing with their own unique challenges) might lead to that unfair conclusion. One must go where the evidence leads based upon the method of comparison. How positive lessons were learned and whether they were sustained is the challenge this book poses.

Does *The Measure of a Nation* add up to a single, practical program of action? Could it define a "technical ticket" for an evidence-based political movement? Every reader must decide. Readers need to consider which elements reinforce each other, which are at odds, and what can be put together to make a useful outfit by "mix and match."

Politics rules. But evidence should matter. What combinations of actions or policies might work is a matter for empirical test. The constant test will lie in continuing to monitor evidence of progress and in being sensitive to the response of public opinion and the heat of political debate.

In the face of such an accumulation of evidence we are challenged to suggest what is in the analysis that we would improve. Are there important dimensions of life experience missing? Is anything that is included inappropriate or unnecessary? How can Friedman's set of recommendations for America be realized? This volume should force deeper attention to the key challenges America is too often failing to take seriously.

There are problems and there need to be problem solvers. This volume emerges from the fertile efforts of a dedicated problem solver. Any solutions to national problems will require a national perspective, but careful attention is given repeatedly to comparisons between and among America's separate states. Openness to learning from others' experiences within a country and between countries is a necessity for constructive action.

A key question posed here asks if one of the most prosperous and powerful countries in history has used its bounty advantageously. *The Measure of a Nation* assesses key areas in which America's performance lags far behind, meets, or exceeds what "business as usual" political dialog suggests. In this way Friedman forces us to think about what "business as unusual" really means. The recommendations are clear and straightforward. Whether they are correct, and whether the process to which this book should contribute represents tragedy, comedy, or just opportunity, depends on how we act and react.

Introduction

COMPETITIVE INTELLIGENCE
FOR AMERICA

When corporations find themselves stagnating or perhaps slipping in the marketplace, one of the first things they do is turn to competitive intelligence. Simply put, a corporation that finds itself in trouble will collect vital information on the performances, strategies, revenues, returns on investment, policies, procedures, and other critical data of its competition. Then the corporation's embattled management will study this data to better understand where its struggling company is excelling, where it is falling behind, and how it can improve. What it learns from this competitive intelligence will determine or at least influence the actions the company takes. The findings may include lessons learned from competitors' failures or others' best practices that the company might profitably adopt. That is why corporations regard competitive intelligence as a fundamentally strategic investment and an essential exercise for survival and growth.

IBM is a perfect example of just what competitive intelligence can do.[1] The technology giant had dominated its industry for decades and was the most admired and scientifically innovative company on the planet. But during the 1980s, IBM faltered, losing its lead in the personal computer hardware and software markets as it outsourced key elements to competitors like Intel and Microsoft. Those competitors soon became megacompanies while IBM slipped. By the end of the decade, IBM was bloated, overstaffed, and overinvested in low-margin businesses; revenue had peaked in 1990 and was declining rapidly while profit margins and the stock price were plummeting.

So what did IBM do? It studied the competitive landscape and immediately learned that its expenses were much higher than other companies' in its industry.[2] Further analysis compared IBM to the strengths and weaknesses of its competitors and drew lessons from the comparison. IBM then reinvented itself by developing a strategy to leverage its advantages and cut away many of the practices, expenses, and unproductive assets that were dragging it down. The rebirth was wildly successful. Today IBM is again a master of innovation, with more patents per year than any other American company across nearly twenty consecutive years. It is focused on high-margin software and services, and it boasts greater annual revenue than Microsoft, Apple, Intel, Amazon, or Google.[3]

If America were a corporation, it would today be the equivalent of IBM in the early 1990s—an industry giant that's failing to keep up with the times. Once a world leader, it is now in effect facing bankruptcy, lagging behind in major market segments like health, safety, education, democracy, and even equality. Around the globe, the technology of democracy has evolved, health-care systems have been developed, and the world has changed greatly since World War II, yet the United States still operates with the heavy footprints of its Founding Fathers.

Consider that those Founding Fathers were wealthy elites who set up a form of government designed to hear the voice of the people while preserving as much property as possible for themselves and their socioeconomic class. The Founders' distrust of central governments and of the masses, as well as their belief in creating opportunities for social mobility, were woven into our approach to democracy, healthcare, education, and other aspects of our society. The structure of government they created and the values it embodies still shape all areas of American society.

The countries with which America competes, however, have developed vastly different structures influenced by more contemporary values. Devastated by wars over the last century that utterly destroyed much of Europe, Japan, and Korea, these countries were forced to reconsider and renew their government structures, their social systems, and other basic aspects of society. But we in the United States have only nudged at these fundamentals, while maintaining the same basic set of government structures and laws set up in 1789.

Could there be a better time for America to embark on an exercise in competitive intelligence? Isn't it time to study the best practices of other wealthy countries so as to shape a strategy that can be adapted to the American culture? Shall we keep our head in the sand, refusing to stay current with market trends and declining to learn from competitors' advances? Or shall we study our competition, drawing lessons from what has worked for others, and then, armed with this critical intelligence, reinvent and resurrect this tired, failing national corporation?

LOOKING INWARD INSTEAD OF OUTWARD

As citizens of the most powerful nation in the world, we Americans too often feel we are above comparison with other nations. Emboldened by having the world's largest economy and military, we tend to ignore the rest of the world unless it is in our immediate interest to pay attention. Faced with domestic or international problems, the United States rarely asks "Where is this done better?" or "What can we learn from others?" in its search for solutions.

This hubris can be dangerous. The disinclination to look outward is linked to the self-perception of "American Exceptionalism"[4]—the belief that the United States is unique in its history and culture and cannot, therefore, be compared to any other country. While it is certainly true that America's situation in the world is distinct from that of other countries, that same argument can be made for every other country. Many view America's tendency to avoid comparison with other countries as indicative of either blissful ignorance or simple arrogance. Our longstanding dominance of the world's economy and military has fostered the idea that the rest of the world doesn't matter. But that is, of course, an illusion, one that is being shattered as our declining relative standing in health and education, the failures of our democracy, our rising inequality, and our waning influence on the world economy force Americans to recognize the importance of learning from others.

Whether it comes from a late-night talk show host, a prominent politician, or just a conversation around the water cooler, internal criticism of American policies, practices, or performance is often met with the dismissive rejoinder that "while it doesn't work well here, it's better than anywhere else." This may or may not be true, but all too often, the person offering the excuse has no idea what is actually happening in the rest of the world.

Whether born of ignorance or arrogance, this unwillingness to look at international best practices is a national phenomenon that needs to end soon if we are going to keep the United States from sliding dramatically off its world-leadership perch. Moreover, by failing to look outside of the American system, Americans deny themselves the opportunity to learn from other countries' valuable experiences.

THREE KEY POINTS

This book is based on three fundamental, fact-based points.

The first point is that the United States is very different from other wealthy countries. This does not mean that the United States is beyond comparison. Rather, it recognizes that so much of what Americans accept as being typical is viewed as strange or unique by the rest of the developed world. This may be human nature; after all, it is natural to assume that what is acceptable or typical locally is normal for the rest of the world. There may also be arrogance in this—an assumption that since we are the largest economy and most powerful country in the world, other aspects of our society also dominate. Hence, many Americans don't even question how we approach healthcare, education, safety, equality, or democracy. The data in this book will provide an objective assessment of which aspects of American society are similar to or different from other wealthy countries.

The second point is that when we do compare different critical aspects of society, America's approach to a particular aspect is not always the best. That is what the data show, and while it may be comforting to ignore the data and pretend that every aspect of American society is better than in all other societies, such self-enforced delusion is dangerous. After all, a company that insisted it performed with excellence in every area would soon be out of business. Companies that are willing to learn will grow and prosper while the manufacturers of black-and-white televisions and eight-track tapes become resigned to the pages of history books. Similarly, an unwillingness to recognize areas that need to be improved will gnaw at the fabric of American society and undermine the nation's future prospects. We must be willing not only to review the data objectively, but also to accept that we won't always receive the top grade.

The last point to make is that when we aren't the best, we can learn from other countries. This is the most essential purpose of competitive intelligence—for a corporation or for a nation. As the Zen proverb states, "It takes a wise man to learn from his mistakes, but an even wiser man to learn from the mistakes of others." By looking toward the other countries profiled in this book, Americans can determine which countries are leaders and which are laggards. From the leaders, Americans can identify best practices; from the laggards, Americans can learn what to avoid. Such introspection requires the humility to admit that some of the best answers to society's great questions may be waiting outside the borders of our own country.

COMPARISON DETAILS

To develop competitive intelligence for the United States, we must address some basic questions: To which countries should the United States be compared? What aspects of society will we compare and with what data?

Two selection criteria were used for entrance into the competition: (1) the competitor countries needed to be wealthy, and (2) they needed to have a reasonably large population. Of course, that still requires us to define "wealthy" and "reasonably large population."

Why only wealthy countries? It is obvious that if a country is preoccupied with trying to feed most of its people in order to stave off mass starvation, or if it is focused on constructing basic infrastructure, then it doesn't have the financial resources for such concerns as maximizing voter turnout or improving educational opportunities for all children. Comparing the health or education metrics of a wealthy country to that of poor or even middle-income countries therefore doesn't make sense; the outcomes will be massively in favor of the wealthy country. The countries in America's competitor class were required to have a mean nominal Gross Domestic Product (GDP)[5] per capita of more than $20,000, where GDP per capita is a standard (though unfortunately incomplete) measurement of wealth. The mean GDP per capita, also known as the average GDP per capita, was purposely chosen because it is the more commonly cited metric. Alternatively, the median value, defined as the value that falls in the middle when values are ordered from smallest to largest, could have been chosen. The mean value is subject to the influence of outliers. That means that when Bill Gates walks into a crowded bar, the mean wealth of everyone in the bar increases dramatically even though no one's bank account increased. On the other hand, the median wealth of everyone in the bar is virtually unchanged by the presence or absence of America's richest person. More generally, when the mean income is much larger than the median income, that indicates extreme income inequality, so using the mean value also opens up the critical discussion of equality.

The cutoff of $20,000 was chosen because above that threshold, such key statistics as life expectancy and school enrollment rates are usually independent of wealth, as will be demonstrated later. So by using $20,000 as the cutoff, the selected countries are wealthy enough to take care of the basic needs for health, safety, education, democracy, and equality of all their citizens.

What about all those small, wealthy countries like Singapore, Switzerland,

Qatar, and Lichtenstein? Is it fair to compare countries that are city-states or that have small populations with one of the most populous countries in the world? The issue is one of scale; countries with small populations do not have to deal with the issues of scale that more populous nations need to face. While there is no perfect set of selection criteria, the inclusion requirement was set so that the countries in the competitor class needed to have populations of at least ten million. This threshold selects countries in the upper one-third of national populations, eliminates city-state countries from the competition, and means also that our competitor countries are more populous than the most populous city in the United States, New York.[6]

For every decision made about inclusion in the competitor group, there will naturally be dissenting opinions. A lower threshold for wealth would let in too many countries that lack the financial strength to fully meet citizens' needs while a higher threshold for population would eliminate nearly the entire globe.

What about physical size? If each competitor had been required to mirror the physical size of the United States, our competition would be limited to Canada, China, Brazil, and Australia. This is a very small competitor class, and only one of the countries, Brazil, has a population within 50 percent of that of the United States. If each competitor country had been required to have a population within 50 percent of America's, then the competition would be limited to Indonesia, Brazil, Pakistan, Bangladesh, and Nigeria,[7] none of which could compete in terms of wealth. Simply put, there is no perfect set of criteria. No wealthy country has a population anywhere near the size of the United States, and no country with a population within half the size of the United States would be classified as wealthy.

Through these two entrance requirements of wealth and population, a set of fourteen competing countries emerged—thirteen countries and the United States. Nine of the thirteen other countries are in Europe: Belgium, France, Germany, Greece, Italy, the Netherlands, Portugal, Spain, and the United Kingdom. The non-European countries are Australia, Canada, Japan, and South Korea.[8] All of these competitor countries are members of the Organisation for Economic Co-operation and Development (OECD); the competition also includes all the members of the G7, an important economic and political group representing Canada, France, Germany, Italy, Japan, the United Kingdom, and the United States. No Middle Eastern countries make the list, since the wealthiest countries in the region (Oman, Bahrain, Brunei, Kuwait, United Arab Emirates, and Qatar) all have populations of fewer than ten million people.

The Fourteen: The Class of Competitor Countries

Australia
Belgium
Canada
France
Germany
Greece
Italy
Japan
Portugal
The Netherlands
South Korea (Korea)
Spain
United Kingdom (UK)
United States (US)

Nudging around the edges of our selection criteria by shifting the cutoffs for income or population will only slightly change the countries that are selected. For example, increasing the population cutoff to fifteen million people would have reduced our list to eleven countries—we would be forced to drop Belgium, Greece, and Portugal—but we are comforted in knowing that competitive intelligence with this smaller list of countries would draw virtually the same conclusions.

The countries selected are diverse not only in their geographic locations, but also in many other critical aspects. They range in size from the world's second largest country, Canada, to countries that could fit into a small corner of Texas. Some have comparatively ethnically homogenous populations with low immigration rates, like Korea and Japan, while others have more ethnically diverse populations with a large number of foreign-born residents, such as the United States and Canada.[9] Some, like France, the Netherlands, and the United Kingdom, have been among the wealthiest on earth for centuries while others, like Portugal, Greece, and Korea, have seen their wealth rise rapidly over the last few decades. Regardless of their history, diversity, or size, they all currently represent examples of wealthy countries that are trying to meet the needs of their people. As such, they are possible sources of best practices for America.

The competitive intelligence we'll look at for these fourteen countries focuses on five key issues that are critical to any society: health, safety, education, democracy, and equality. Societies that excel in these areas are likely to achieve stable, successful populations, while societies that fail in these areas risk internal or externally driven collapse. For example, a country that fails to keep its citizens healthy will suffer high medical expenditures, excessive loss of talent, and unnecessary pain and suffering. A society that fails to provide safety will be crippled by its people's fear and their resulting inability to thrive. A society that fails to educate its people will be destined for financial ruin. History is littered with superpowers that self-destructed either slowly or virtually overnight as they failed to meet the needs of their people, from the Roman Empire to the Soviet Union.

Our areas of focus are universal. Any development framework—from Abraham Maslow's hierarchy of needs to the framework used in the United Nations Human Development Report (a framework inspired by Amartya Sen's capabilities approach)—recognizes that basic physical needs like health and safety must be satisfied.[10] Educational investment is necessary to ensure a population is able to function in the current information age, now that the days of relying on mass, unspecialized manufacturing to generate wealth have long passed in developed countries. Democracy and its associated freedoms are fundamental to the self-definition of all the competitor countries. And the level of equality underpins many critical aspects of society, as highly unequal societies leave much of the population suffering while only a few benefit.

Of course there are countless other important subjects we could have included as points of comparison—religious viewpoints, employment opportunities, property ownership, leisure-time activities, family structures, and environmental considerations, to name just a few examples. But by deliberately limiting the scope of subjects, the statements the data make will be more meaningful.

So what data do we use? The primary data sources were the most recently published objective data that are both transparent and internationally recognized. The sources of the data are cited so readers can examine the information themselves; most often, in fact, the data come from easily accessible public websites, including those provided by the World Bank,[11] the World Health Organization,[12] the Organisation for Economic Co-operation and Development (OECD),[13] the United Nations Human Development Report,[14] and the Central Intelligence Agency World Factbook,[15] as well as peer-reviewed publications. While there will be some areas where subjective ratings are used, the more objective data are emphasized whenever possible and references have been provided for readers who want to view the original data sources.

Because the countries show a wide range of geographic sizes and populations, normalized measurements were used to make the comparisons as fair as possible. For example, infant mortality rates, high school graduation rates, and voter-turnout rates were compared rather than comparing total number of infant deaths, total number of high school graduates, or total number of voters per country.

WHY NOT COMPARE THE UNITED STATES WITH THE EUROPEAN UNION?

In any comparison, it's essential to determine the level of comparison that is of interest. For example, in looking at education, one could compare students, classes, teachers, schools, districts, or even higher levels. A statistician needs to decide which level is most relevant, most pertinent, most likely to provide insight and, possibly, most interesting. The United States is a country, and so in defining its competitors, the comparison has been defined at the level of country. The European Union is a fascinating experiment in supranational government, but it is not a country. Rather, it is an economic and political union of countries that has different systems for accountability and governance. The European Union includes twenty-seven countries and boasts a parliament, a central bank, a court of justice, and auditors, with these civic responsibilities headquartered variously in Belgium, Luxembourg, and France.

At the same time, the European Union lacks a single military. Ten of its twenty-seven members don't use the Euro as their currency. It represents different languages, cultures, religions, even climates—ranging from Arctic to subtropical. It operates under and is regulated by rules based on the Maastricht Treaty, the Treaty of Lisbon, and other agreements. Its member countries have GDP per capita positions ranging from $7,000 to nearly $70,000 and are separately represented in the United Nations and in other international governing bodies.[16]

This is not to suggest that a comparison of the United States to the European Union would not be possible or interesting and, in fact, there have been a number of good books on that subject already.[17] Rather, it's a reminder that we need to be consistent about levels of comparison. After all, we wouldn't compare New York City to the province of Quebec or to the country of Sweden just because their respective populations are of similar size. Including the European Union in our comparison would open the door to including trade blocs like the North American Free Trade Agreement (with signatories Canada, Mexico, and the United States) and the Mercado Común del Sur, or Mercosur, linking Brazil, Argentina, Paraguay, and Uruguay with other associated members. Or it might mean including currency markets like the countries of the CFA franc, used by more than fifty million people in Africa.

Again, limiting the scope of comparison to countries of similar wealth and population makes the comparisons themselves more relevant, more germane, and more meaningful.

WHERE'S CHINA?

China's tremendous economic rise over the latter two decades of the twentieth century and the first years of the twenty-first has been well documented in the media. It is now the second largest economy and the largest exporter in the world, but it is not a wealthy country. It is a middle-income country, with a GDP per capita about one-tenth that of the United States. While China has some pockets of great wealth in larger cities like Shanghai and Beijing, it also has a vast population of rural peasants and migrant workers whose lives are more similar to that of Americans of a century ago than to that of contemporary Americans. The disconnect between China's large total economy and the fact that it is still a developing country stems from its enormous population. At more than 1.3 billion people, China's population is more than four times that of the United States.[18] As a result, while some measurements of economic size may be in the same order of magnitude, the per-capita measurements express a totally different range. For example, if China's total economy reaches that of the United States over the coming decades, this will mean that its GDP per capita will have achieved a level of only about one-fourth of the GDP per capita in America. So even if the two countries reach a point where their total economies are the same size, there would still be large gaps between the two countries in terms of average standard of living and the comparable measurements that correlate with income.

If we compared any of the countries in our competitor class to China on a metric-by-metric basis, one would easily see the difference between a middle-income country with pockets of wealth and a wealthy country. China's life expectancy would be about five years below that of the lowest competitor; its measures of income inequality would be off the charts; and it would be pointless to try comparing measures of democracy with a country that is effectively a one-party state.

There is no question that the rise of developing countries like China, India, Brazil, Russia, and Mexico will change the political and economic landscape of the future, but for the purposes of competitive intelligence for the United States, we focus on countries at similar stages of development. The Human Development Report issued annually by the United Nations' Human Development Program classifies countries as being Very High Human Development, High Human Development, Medium Human Development, and Low Human Development based on wealth (Gross National Income per capita), health (life expectancy at birth), and education (mean years of schooling, expected years of schooling).[19] All fourteen countries on this list are classified as Very High Human Development while China is ranked as Medium Human Development.

THE LINGO OF COMPETITIVE INTELLIGENCE

Competitive intelligence speaks in the language of marketing and organizational strategy, and we'll do the same in ranking the fourteen competitor countries in our comparison class. In our relative rankings, countries were graded in order from best performing to worst performing. In homage to the famous matrix devised by the Boston Consulting Group, a global consulting firm, to analyze companies, we also label the top-performing countries Stars and the worst-performing countries Dogs. Countries that huddle in the middle, typically ranking between fourth through tenth in our list of fourteen countries, are labeled Middle Children, although the designation Middle Child depends on the distribution itself.

Most of our graphs display information about a single variable, such as life expectancy or homicide rate, for all of the competing countries. The countries are sorted in order from best performing, the market Star, on the left side of the graph, to the worst performing, the Dog, on the right side of the graph. The values for the Star and Dog are identified on the graph, while the values for all other countries can be estimated by observing where that country is positioned on the vertical or y-axis. A large gap on the y-axis will indicate a relatively large difference in performance. The United States is represented with the symbol of Uncle Sam's hat for easy identification.

We will look at the best practices of the Stars to identify strategies that could be adopted here in the United States. The comparisons in this book are driven by the data, yet all data is shaded with cultural nuances. For example, you will read that many competitor countries record far higher voter turnout than the United States, seemingly a signal of potential weakness in American democracy. By the same token, however, some competitor countries with higher voter turnout *require* voting; it's the law, and there are penalties for non-compliance. Mandatory voting laws simply wouldn't be acceptable in the American culture. After all, Americans hold that not voting is tantamount to a vote; it is an expression of individual will. So the comparisons driven by the data must be understood within the varied cultural contexts they represent. Nevertheless, data are data, and the comparisons communicate important differences among the competitor countries. In the discussions of these comparisons, we will mention some of the cultural influences that affect the data, but of course it is not possible to discuss in detail all the background influences affecting performance on each issue in all fourteen countries.

Chapter 1

THE NATION'S HEARTBEAT: HEALTH

Health is at the heart of human progress. It determines whether parents can work to support their families, children can attend school, women can survive childbirth, and infants can grow and thrive. Where health services are strong and accessible, families and communities flourish. Where health services are inaccessible, weak, or nonexistent, families suffer, adults die prematurely, and communities unravel.

—from the US Government Global Health Initiative Strategy, available online at http://www.ghi.gov/resources/strategies/.

Nothing else about our lives as Americans matters at all if we don't have a reasonable expectation of a healthy life. Basic safety, the enrichment of education, our entire democratic process, our own individual chance at social mobility: none of these things has any importance or interest if we cannot take advantage of them. And without health, we can't.

Maybe that's why our Declaration of Independence places life first in the list of "unalienable" rights with which we are naturally endowed. We all get just the one life, and living it in health and for as long as possible is basic to everything else that we do and everything else that affects us. So it makes sense that health should be the first comparison we look at, for it underlies all the other assessments this book explores.

But how do we measure health? So many factors determine and affect it. We have no control over many of them—gender, for example, or genes, or even the culture in which we grow up. The air we breathe, the water we drink, and other environmental realities affect our health, but these are realities we can only change immediately by moving our location. We have limited control over where we work and how much income we earn, our social status, and our education, yet all of these impact our health, as do lifestyle choices such as diet, exercise, and personal habits like smoking, use of alcohol and drugs, health practices, and coping mechanisms.

Health is a subject with which we seem to be obsessed. Wonder drugs, diet fads, and superfoods buzz around American pop culture and are regular topics on radio and television talk shows. Feats of medical practice that seem miraculous routinely lead the headlines. There isn't a newspaper or news broadcast that isn't staffed with a health columnist or physician interpreting the latest medical research results and advising us all on lifestyle choices. We thrill to the story of the child from a distant land, born with a rare ailment, who is flown here to undergo a special life-saving procedure available only in America. We read regularly about world leaders arriving in private jets for cutting-edge treatments developed by American researchers in American laboratories.

Essential to it all is our health system, the totality of medical and healthcare products, systems, services, people and resources, and physical facilities that affect us throughout our lifetime. In fact, the healthcare system starts to affect us even before our lifetime. From the moment our mothers initiate prenatal care to the debilitations of old age, and for every bruise, break, sickness, and stress in between, our healthcare system is where we go for a healthier life and more of it. So, how the system responds is central to measuring the health of our nation as a whole.

The cliché dutifully repeated by so many politicians, perhaps buoyed by the stories of those outstanding medical accomplishments, is that the United States enjoys "the best healthcare in the world." It's an oft-used phrase, its frequency of use matched only by its inaccuracy, as we will discover in separating the fiction from the facts about how the United States's healthcare stacks up against the competition.

The simplest and most compelling metric for assessing health and comparing health outcomes is life expectancy, the average number of years an individual can expect to live. On that measure, the United States does very badly indeed, registering the lowest life expectancy in our group.[1] Stunningly, that low life expectancy includes both the highest infant mortality rate[2] and maternal mortality ratio[3] in the group. Moreover, we spend per person nearly twice as much as all the other nations in our competitor group and in some cases as much as four times more. More money for the worst outcome. You don't have to be on the board of directors to know a bad return on investment when you see one.

Bottom line: as a competitor in healthcare, the United States is clearly ailing—and we the people are not getting our money's worth.

Why? How is it we can spend so much more for healthcare than our competitor nations and yet have one of the lowest life expectancies in our sector? Why are we losing so many infants and mothers in childbirth when we are supposed to be the health market leader? How have we cut our smoking rate dramatically yet seen a striking increase in obesity, a major health risk factor? How, with our world-renowned hospitals and research centers, are the vital statistics on our national health so poor?

Let's look at the data.

WEALTH MAKES HEALTH?

The inherited factors of genes and gender as well as the influences of such things as where we live, the kind of work we do, and, of course, our own behavior all affect health and, therefore, life expectancy. A positive change in behavior—for example, improving diet or exercising more—will have a positive effect on our health and can extend our lifespan. And vice versa; negative behavior can have a negative effect.

Other factors also affect life expectancy: the rate of disease at a particular time in a particular place, an individual's mental health, even the rates of crime and safety. Advances in healthcare knowledge and technology, for example, from the development of the polio vaccine to breakthroughs in cancer treatment, can increase life expectancy, while the sudden arrival of new epidemics, like HIV/AIDS and the rampant use of crack cocaine in the 1980s, can cause it to plummet.

One of the more definitive factors affecting a nation's life expectancy is wealth. The numbers demonstrate that, globally, life expectancy generally increases as a function of a country's wealth—that is, up to a certain level of wealth. In fact, looking at life expectancy data is a little like taking the rough economic pulse of a country.

The reason is simple: In poorer countries, the chances of survival are dominated by the rates of infectious diseases, infant mortality, and malnutrition; and their healthcare systems struggle to provide safe drinking water, sanitary living conditions, adequate food supplies, and basic health services. Indeed, the poorest countries on the planet have life expectancies in some cases of less than fifty years, with few resources to fight infectious diseases like AIDS, malaria, tuberculosis, and measles.[4]

In the developed world, however, where sanitation, sufficient food, and basic healthcare are givens, mortality is driven mostly by noncommunicable diseases such as heart disease and cancer, diseases affected by lifestyle, nutrition, environmental factors, and genetics. In these wealthier countries, there are no infectious diseases in the top eight causes of death,[5] and life expectancy, which has increased dramatically in the past century, can average seventy-five years or more as the rates of infectious diseases and infant mortality have declined. In the United States, in fact, the average lifespan increased by more than thirty years in the twentieth century.[6] In some sense, therefore, comparing the health of today's wealthy nations to today's poor nations is like comparing the health of today's wealthy nations to the health of those same countries several generations ago, when they struggled to fight polio, smallpox, and other infectious diseases.

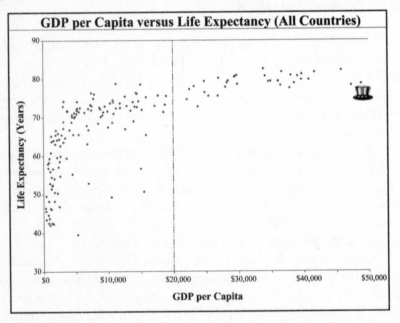

The relationship between health and wealth can be clearly seen in the global life expectancy curve. This graph includes all countries in the world for which data were available; each data point represents a country's life expectancy and GDP per capita. At the lower left-hand corner of the graph, the point at which GDP per capita is the lowest, life expectancy is also the lowest. Moving to the right, we see that life expectancies rise very sharply with wealth—until we reach around the $4,000 level. As the average wealth improves, so do health services, sanitation, and the supply and availability of safe drinking water. The provision of those basics produces a dramatic spike in people's health, and they live longer, thus raising average life expectancy. Above the $4,000-per-capita point, although life expectancy continues to rise, it does so at a slower rate. And when per-capita GDP exceeds $20,000, the life expectancy curve becomes an almost completely flat line. This flat-lining tells us that above a certain threshold of national wealth, the nation's finances are sufficient to meet its citizens' medical needs, and therefore other factors become more important in predicting life expectancy.

As often happens, the exceptions to this prove the rule. South Africa is a negative outlier: with one of the world's highest rates of HIV/AIDS, average life expectancy is some twenty years lower than in countries of similar wealth. By contrast, Vietnam and Nepal are positive outliers that enjoy life expectancies much higher than countries of similar wealth.

THE COMPETITORS

So, which countries are best at keeping their citizens alive? And where does the United States, the richest country on earth, stand in the rankings? Take a look:

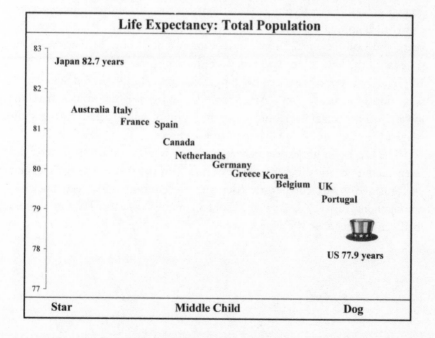

As in our other competitive intelligence graphs, the Star appears on the left side of the graph and the Dog appears on the right. In our competitor set of countries, the United States is the clear market Dog in life expectancy, falling more than one year shorter than the next closest competitor, Portugal.[7] The market segment Star, Japan, has the highest life expectancy, nearly five years longer than in the United States and more than one year longer than any of the other competitors. Other stronger performers like Australia, Italy, France, and Spain all have life expectancies that are more than three years longer than in the United States.

Perhaps equally striking, we've come down in the world. Back in 1987 only seven other countries had longer life expectancies. Today we're not even in the top twenty![8]

As with many other aspects of American society, life expectancy varies greatly from one population subgroup to another, reflecting fundamental disparities between ethnic groups, socioeconomic groups, and geographies. One striking example: there is a difference of about twenty years of lifespan between Asian American women and African American urban males.[9] On a state level, the diverse set of states with the longest life expectancies (Hawaii at 81.5 years, Minnesota at 80.9 years, California at 80.4 years, and New York at 80.4 years) average at least five years longer than the states with the shortest life expectancies (Mississippi at 74.8 years, West Virginia at 75.2 years, Alabama at 75.2 years, and Louisiana at 75.4 years). It is important to observe that the eleven states with the lowest life expectancy are all in the South.[10]

Nearly universally, women live longer than men. In the United States, both sexes do rather badly: both American men and American women have the lowest life expectancy in our competitor group, while Japan registers the longest life expectancy for both men and women.[11]

The US-Japan life expectancy comparison is affected by vast genetic differences, but genetic differences are not sufficient to explain America's lagging performance versus competitor countries with more similar gene pools—among them Australia, Italy, France, and Spain. Other factors must be at work in affecting American life expectancy.

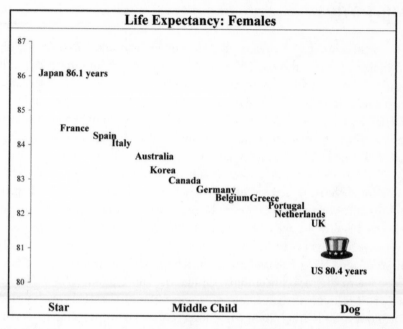

Life Expectancy: Females

Japan 86.1 years

France
Spain
Italy
Australia
Korea
Canada
Germany
BelgiumGreece
Portugal
Netherlands
UK

US 80.4 years

Star   Middle Child   Dog

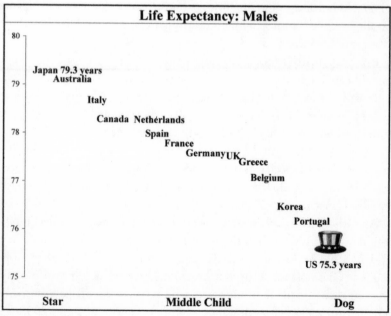

Life Expectancy: Males

Japan 79.3 years
Australia
Italy
Canada   Netherlands
Spain
France
GermanyUKGreece
Belgium
Korea
Portugal

US 75.3 years

Star   Middle Child   Dog

WHO'S DYING?

The infant mortality rate is defined as the number of deaths of infants one year or younger per one thousand live births. It is a critical measure because the death of a young child has a greater impact on a population's life expectancy than does a death from disease or injury in the middle or later stages of life. In the developing world, infant mortality tends to be a result of pneumonia, diarrhea, tetanus, and congenital malformation. In the developed world, it is typically associated with low birthweight or extremely premature births.

We don't usually think about infant mortality in the United States. We associate it with the developing world or with the distant past. During the Industrial Revolution, for example, the percentage of children born in London who died before the age of five decreased from 74.5 percent to 31.8 percent over a span of sixty years.[12] The introduction of clean drinking water, sewage disposal, and greater attention to personal hygiene dramatically reduced death rates due to diarrhea, pneumonia, diphtheria, and typhoid fever during the early part of the twentieth century. The post–World War II era saw vaccines, antibiotics, and other life-saving interventions contributing to further declines.[13] Globally, in just the brief period between 1960 and 2001, infant mortality declined from 126 infant deaths per one thousand live births to 57 per one thousand live births.[14]

It is particularly stunning to note that today the United States has the highest rate of infant mortality of any of the competitors while Japan, the competitor with the longest life expectancy, has the lowest.[15] In the United States, the most common causes of infant mortality are congenital malformations and disorders associated with low birthweight and short gestation.[16]

The fact that the United States is the market Dog in infant mortality is not because of a lack of specialists or facilities for neonatal births; on the contrary, we have more neonatologists and neonatal-intensive-care beds per person than Australia, Canada, or the United Kingdom.[17]

As with other health metrics, our relative performance is declining. In 1960, the United States had the twelfth-lowest infant mortality rate in the world. By 1990, we had dropped to twenty-third, and we sank to thirty-fourth in 2008.[18] Our most recent decline in ranking has been accompanied by a relatively stagnant infant mortality rate, which remained virtually unchanged from 2000 to 2005 before declining slightly between 2005 and 2006. That stagnant mortality rate was accompanied by an increase in the percentage of very preterm births[19]—that is, births happening at fewer than thirty-seven weeks of gestation, an occurrence cited by the Centers for Disease Control and Prevention (CDC) as a key risk factor for infant mortality. By 2005, the start of a slight decline in the infant mortality rate, preterm babies accounted for 69 percent of all infant deaths. Although data comparing the rate of preterm births are not readily available, the key contributing factor to our high rate of infant mortality appears to be our rate of low-birthweight newborns, which is one of the highest among our competitor nations.[20]

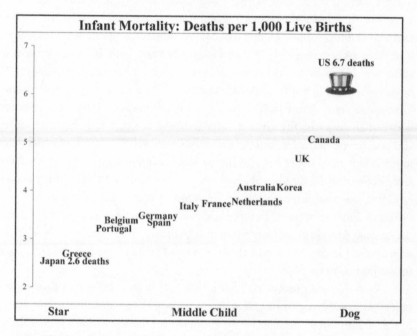

Our high infant mortality rate evidences the economic, ethnic, and racial disparities referred to earlier. For example, in 2005, African American infants suffered a death rate of 13.63 per one thousand births, more than twice the national average.[21] The CDC's 2004 world rankings indicate that an African American baby would have a better chance of survival if born in Russia or Bulgaria than in the United States. Low-birthweight incidence explains some of the racial inequality. Low-weight births, defined as newborns weighing less than 2,500 grams or approximately five pounds, are about twice as common among African Americans as among (non-Hispanic) Caucasian and Hispanic babies,[22] occurring at a rate of 13 percent among the former and at a rate of only 6.5 percent among the latter. Among the factors contributing to these lopsided out-comes are disparities in prenatal care, nutritional supplementation for pregnant women, and inadequate social welfare. Yet even if we eliminate this racial disparity and compare only the infant mortality rate of the United States's Caucasian population, our ranking versus the competition is unaffected.[23]

Could our relatively high infant mortality rate result from the fact that Americans are less likely to selectively abort? Whether motivated by religion, politics, or some other perspective, a choice not to abort an impaired preg-nancy raises the percentage of births with congenital malformations, and some argue it is this choice that raises our infant mortality rate. It isn't at all obvious that this claim is supported by facts. We are able to compare the overall abor-tion rates across countries, but we lack insight into whether the decision to abort was driven by social reasons, economic pressures, or concerns about the health of the mother or fetus in each country. When we do examine the overall US abortion rate, defined as the number of abortions per one thousand women between the ages of fifteen and forty-four, we see that it is higher than in Canada, Belgium, the Netherlands, and the United Kingdom, all of which have lower infant mortality rates and higher life expectancy rates.[24] The abortion *ratio*, defined as the number of abortions per one hundred known pregnancies, is higher for the combination of the United States and Canada than for northern Europe, western Europe, and western Asia.[25] There is thus no evi-dence that American women show a disinclination to abortion, so selective abortion tendencies are not likely to be a valid explanation for America's high infant mortality rate.

The childbirth process itself has historically been risky, and maternal mor-tality—women dying while giving life—cuts to the very core of the concept of health. Measured as the number of women who die in or after childbirth for every one hundred thousand live births, maternal mortality ratios are affected by a number of contributing factors: nutrition, the quality of the birthing and prenatal care, access to quality emergency obstetric care, the mother's age, the number of previous pregnancies, and genetics all may play a role. In the early 1900s, maternal mortality ratios in developed countries were around one thou-sand per one hundred thousand live births, but improvements in all those con-tributing factors have steadily decreased those rates to a point where today they are some one hundred times lower.[26]

One important caveat about data on maternal mortality: some of the intercountry variance may be due to variations in the way different countries interpret and apply the World Health Organization's definition of a maternal death and may not, therefore, reflect true differences in the safety of delivering a baby. Against this background, nevertheless, the United States has the highest maternal mortality ratio in our group of competitors, nearly four times higher than in Greece, Italy, and Belgium. Moreover, the rate in the United States has been increasing, although some have suggested that this trend is due to more accurate measurements.[27] A troubling ramification of this higher maternal mortality rate is that, combined with the significantly higher fertility rate in the United States than among competitors,[28] the lifetime risk of an American woman dying of maternal causes[29] is much higher than in any of the other countries.

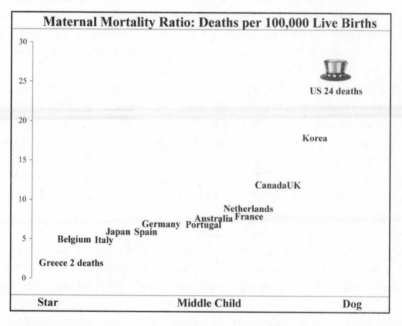

Two key factors likely contributing to maternal mortality are obesity[30] and teenage pregnancy, both often associated with poverty. During the 2008 presidential election, the very public teenage pregnancy of Bristol Palin, the seventeen-year-old daughter of Republican vice-presidential candidate Sarah Palin, an advocate of abstinence-only sex education, placed the issue in a political context. Yet the reality is that teenage pregnancy and its attendant problems typically occur in families without the economic support and access to healthcare that the Palins enjoyed at the time. In 1998 in the United States, the teen birth rate was nearly double that of the United Kingdom, the next highest country, and nearly twenty times higher than that of Korea, the country with the lowest rate.[31] Pregnant teenagers and their infants face significantly greater health risks than pregnant women in their twenties; in the developing world, the maternal mortality rate for these young women is five times higher than for women in their twenties.[32] While it is comforting to know that the teenage pregnancy rate in the United States has declined by about 40 percent from its 1990 peak of 116.9 teenage pregnancies per one thousand women ages fifteen to nineteen to a rate of 71.5 as of this writing, this is still an extremely high rate compared to the rest of the developed world.[33]

The United States' high teen pregnancy rate is really a sociological issue that affects health outcomes, rather than a direct indicator of the nation's health, and sex education plays a powerful role. Since education is administered by states and localities, the content of sex education varies widely,[34] especially when it comes to such issues as birth control and infection prevention.

A component of sex education that may affect our teenage pregnancy rates is the popularity of abstinence-only education programs, despite their demonstrated ineffectiveness.[35] In western European countries, sex education programs are far more comprehensive and teenage pregnancy rates are far lower. The Long Live Love program in the Netherlands, which includes material on sexuality, negotiation skills, and contraception, is credited with helping the Netherlands achieve one of the lowest teenage pregnancy rates in the developed world.[36] No wonder UNESCO has praised it as the gold standard in sex education,[37] a model for the world.

A final factor that may be contributing to America's relatively low life expectancy is our rate of amenable mortality, defined as deaths before age seventy-five that were potentially preventable through timely and effective healthcare. In a study of nineteen countries, including the United States, fourteen western European countries, Canada, Australia, New Zealand, and Japan, the United States placed last—dead last, we might say. Ranked as of 2002–2003, our rate of amenable mortality was 109.7 deaths per one hundred thousand people—more than 50 percent higher than the best-performing countries of France (64.8 deaths per one hundred thousand), Japan (71.2 deaths per one hundred thousand), and Australia (71.3 deaths per one hundred thousand).[38] Another way to view this is to recognize that even if the United States had the lowest infant mortality in the competition, it would still have the lowest life expectancy.[39]

**The Catch-22 of US Health Insurance:
A Common Nightmare**

Natavidad lived in Texas, worked as a bookbinder, and never had health insurance. As the *New York Times* reported on October 25, 2006,[40] at the age of fifty-one, she was diagnosed with liver cancer. Her economic status qualified her for Medicaid so she applied for federal disability. She was placed on a waiting list, along with thousands of others, for a liver transplant. Without the transplant, said her doctors, Natavidad could expect to live only from six months to two years. While on the waiting list, she received approval of her federal disability application, but the disability payments spiked her income enough to make her ineligible for Medicaid, so she was taken off the waiting list for the liver she needed to survive. Under the disability rules, she could qualify for Medicare but would have to wait for months for the coverage; only when it kicked in could she get back on the waiting list for the liver transplant, and she would go back to the end of the line. This "death by paperwork" is a nightmare echoed in the lives of the millions of Americans living without health insurance.

WHAT IS SHORTER LIFE EXPECTANCY COSTING AMERICANS?

With the contributing factors already discussed, with American women experiencing the lowest life expectancy in our competitor group—"hitting the glass basement," as one woman executive put it—and with a correspondingly last-place life expectancy outcome for American men, it's clear that we Americans simply live shorter lives than our counterparts in other wealthy countries. Naturally, it raises the question of whether we're spending enough on healthcare. Perhaps people in other countries live longer because they spend more on their health.

Our relatively low life expectancy costs us on average nearly **twice as much**

as and, in some cases, up to four times *more* per capita than our competitors spend on health.[41] That's the upshot of a healthcare system dominated by for-profit insurance companies, driven by unregulated pharmaceutical drug prices, and encumbered by a huge population of uninsured people whose care all tax-payers eventually pay for in other ways. Looking at the data another way, we see that the United States spends 16 percent of its GDP on health while the next closest competitors spend only around 11 percent.[42] The numbers are there to see in black and white, and no amount of detailed analysis can refute the over-whelming bottom line—namely, that **Americans are spending much more on their health than people in other countries and are getting a far worse result: we live shorter lives than those who spend less.**

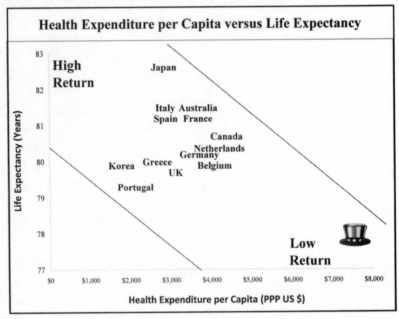

Age might be a mitigating factor. If the average American is older, then the higher costs per capita wouldn't be surprising. We know that, all things being equal, older people have more medical needs and incur more expenses for healthcare. But the average American is not older; in fact, just the opposite is true. With an average age of 36.9 years, the United States is the youngest com-petitor country,[43] while Japan, Germany, Italy, Greece, Belgium, and Spain all have average ages of forty or more. Only 13 percent of the American popula-tion is over sixty-five, compared to more than 20 percent in Belgium, Canada, Germany, Greece, Italy, Japan, the Netherlands, and Spain.[44]

If average age provides no explanation, why do we spend so much more on healthcare yet die so much younger? Let's start analyzing the overspend by looking at our healthcare budget and seeing how and where our spending differs from that of our competitors.

OVERSPENDING ON WHAT?

This isn't the first time it has been pointed out that Americans spend too much on health. A 2008 report from the McKinsey Global Institute[45] estimated that the United States spends $650 billion more on healthcare than might be expected for a country with our cost of living. That's approximately $2,000 more per person. Where do these excess billions go?

Roughly two-thirds of this excess spending pays for outpatient care: visits to physicians, same-day hospital treatment, emergency-room care, and the use of expensive diagnostic tests like MRIs by fee-for-service practitioners. One reason for this excessive outpatient care is health insurance coverage policies. Doctors weighing whether or not to perform a test or procedure, or considering which one to perform, will look to see what's covered by health insurance. When a given procedure is not covered by insurance, doctors may order a more expensive procedure that is covered.

A hint of the role insurance policies play in this comes from dental care, which is rarely included in insurance plans and is not covered by Medicare. In fact, most Americans pay about one-half of their dental care as out-of-pocket costs, yet those costs are more in line with what the McKinsey report considers expected. It's reflective of a simple reality that when we open our wallets, we tend to be much more careful and deliberate about spending, though out-of-pocket financing of health has its own issues, including a tendency to underspend on preventive medicine.

Another cause of the excess spending is defensive medicine, defined as "the practice of ordering medical tests, procedures, or consultations of doubtful clinical value in order to protect the prescribing physician from malpractice suits."[46] In Canada, for example, malpractice insurance typically costs only 10 percent of the corresponding specialty in the United States. The reason is that Canada imposes caps on malpractice jury awards,[47] giving Canadian physicians less motivation to practice defensive medicine. Americans, by contrast, are more likely to be subjected to a battery of tests simply because their doctors and hospitals are afraid of being sued.

Fifteen percent of American overspending for healthcare is linked to pharmaceuticals. Americans use on average about 10 percent fewer drugs than our comparison countries and 40 percent fewer branded drugs, yet we pay 50 percent more for comparable products than patients in the United Kingdom, Germany, Spain, France, and Italy. Why are Americans paying so much more for the same drugs?

To find the answer, we simply have to follow the money. The beneficiary of America's high drug prices is the pharmaceutical industry. When American citizens cross the border into Canada to buy prescription drugs, they often purchase the very drugs their own country has just exported. The Canadian price for the drugs, negotiated by the government, is dramatically lower than what is available to Americans. This phenomenon of reimportation is ongoing, despite lobbying by Big Pharma (as the pharmaceutical giants are collectively known) for legislative efforts to stop it. For those Americans able to cross the border, it's the free-market system at work.

Yet in 2006, when Medicare coverage was expanded to include prescription drugs, a provision of the new law *specifically prevented* the US government from negotiating on drug prices, thus further distorting the US drug pricing market. Just contrast the prices paid for drugs by the Veterans Administration (VA), which negotiates the prices of drugs, and Medicare. Of the twenty medications most frequently prescribed for seniors, all were less expensive for those on the VA plan. In fact, the median price difference was about 50 percent less and in the case of some drugs as much as ten times less.[48] This law benefits only drug companies at a direct cost to taxpayers by defeating the concepts of purchasing power and the ability to negotiate in a free market.

Instead, the American "free market" for pharmaceuticals is being influenced by more than Adam Smith's "invisible hand," the self-regulating forces of supply and demand, competition, and self-interest. Direct-to-consumer advertising (DTCA) for prescription drugs, which is only legal in the United States among competitor countries, is not a public service announcement. The ads are designed to prompt viewers to pressure their doctors into prescribing more products. "Ask your doctor," the ads say, and many patients obediently rush to the doctor. "I saw this drug on TV," the patient tells the physician. "Can you prescribe it for me?" Knowing that patients can comparison shop and switch doctors, a physician may be all too willing to prescribe a possibly unnecessary drug to appease the patient. The result is a commoditization of prescription drugs, which act as products in a consumer marketplace in which uncontrolled prices can rise as high as the market will bear in order to cover what pharmaceutical companies claim is the steep cost of researching and inventing new drugs. In those countries in which DTCA is not permitted, and where drug prices are, therefore, not as subject to market manipulation, that cannot and does not happen.

Next, 14 percent of America's overspending on healthcare is associated with health administration and insurance. As we will discuss later, the US healthcare system is a fragmented combination of many systems, and this fragmentation results in significant administrative costs. For-profit insurance companies charge rates that allow them to recoup not only the costs of providing care but also the costs of marketing, internal administration, and additional charges to buffer their profit margins.

Finally, nearly 10 percent of the overspending goes for the salaries of medical professionals. Physicians' salaries—specialists' salaries in particular—are much higher in the United States than in most developed countries. Nursing salaries in the United States are 50 percent higher than the GDP per capita compared to 10 percent higher than the GDP per capita in other OECD (Organisation for Economic Co-operation and Development) countries. Some of the pay differential is attributed to differences in the cost of attending nursing and medical schools as well as to differences in malpractice insurance costs, which are typically passed on to the patient. French physicians, for example, are reimbursed at far lower rates than American physicians; French medical school costs, however, are paid for by the state, and French malpractice insurance premiums are only a tiny fraction of what they are in the United States. Even within the United States, medical malpractice premiums vary greatly by specialty and location. For example, in 2003, obstetrician-gynecologists paid more than $200,000 annually in Florida and less than 10 percent of that in Minnesota[49] for comparable insurance.

While pharmaceutical giants, for-profit insurance firms, and many medical professionals are benefiting from the US healthcare system, those of us whom the system is supposed to serve are not doing very well. Certainly, as the data make clear, we are not doing nearly as well as the populations of our competitor countries. It's time to look at our healthcare system.

HEALTHCARE SYSTEMS 101

The first thing to look at is how healthcare systems are organized. I'll use the four main categories of health system financing and coverage identified so eloquently by T. R. Reid in his *The Healing of America*.[50]

The **Bismarck model** uses a universal coverage insurance system in which the insurance companies are nonprofit. It's usually financed jointly by employees and employers. Insurance for the unemployed, for self-employed retirees, and for students is typically covered by the government. This system is found in Germany, Japan, France, Belgium, and the Netherlands and is similar to the system many Americans obtain through their employers, except that in the United States, the insurance companies are for-profit and universal coverage is not mandatory.

In the **Beveridge model**, healthcare is provided by the government and financed through taxes. Medical treatment is a public service: many hospitals are owned by the government, doctors may be either government employees or private physicians who receive fixed service fees from the government, and patients often don't receive a medical bill. Since government is the sole payer, costs and services are strictly controlled. This system is found in Britain, Italy, and Spain. In the United States, a similar system exists for Native Americans, military personnel, and veterans.

Healthcare providers in the **National Health Insurance model** (NHI) work privately, but a government-run insurance program strictly negotiates prices and limits services. Universal insurance programs tend to be less expensive thanks to the single-payer savings associated with lower-priced services, drugs, and operating costs. On the downside, this model sometimes results in lengthy waiting times for patient care. The NHI system is found in Canada and South Korea. The United States's Medicare system, which covers American adults sixty-five years and older, operates in a similar fashion.

Finally, there is the **Out-of-Pocket model**, in which patients are almost entirely responsible for medical costs with little to no insurance coverage or government plan. This is more commonly found in poorer countries. For example, 91 percent of total health spending is out of pocket in Cambodia, 85 percent in India, and 73 percent in Egypt.[51] In the United States, 17 percent of healthcare spending is out of pocket—either because of lack of insurance or because of health policy limitations.

The United States's system of healthcare financing is a hodgepodge, especially compared to the simpler financing modalities and coverage strategies of our competitor nations. It's like an incomplete jigsaw puzzle with lots of different sizes, shapes, and colors of healthcare financing and coverage. The result is greater inefficiencies, higher administrative costs, and yawning gaps in coverage for the working poor, students, and the unemployed.

The Patient Protection and Affordable Care Act (PPACA) of 2010, reforms of which are due to start in 2014, is aimed at closing some of those gaps, although the legislation remains under attack in both the courts and Congress. Even if implemented, millions will still be uninsured and the reforms may have only minimal, if any, impact on cost containment. In the meantime, the costs of our healthcare continue to skyrocket, with outcomes lagging far behind.

THE HIGH COST OF THE UNINSURED

Uninsured Americans make fewer visits to physician offices[52] than those with health insurance, but they visit emergency rooms about twice as often. To be sure, severe health conditions may require ER visits. Still, for many uninsured Americans, an ER is their only recourse—the one place where they can be fairly sure of obtaining some sort of healthcare. In an emergency, physicians are legally required to stabilize a patient, although they are not required to treat the condition comprehensively.[53] Frequently, the uninsured receive substandard healthcare and can be turned away altogether if circumstances are deemed non-life-threatening.[54] Since emergency room visits are astronomically more expensive than office visits, this excessive use of the ER by the uninsured spikes healthcare costs for all of us.

Moreover, precisely because they receive poor healthcare support, the uninsured are at a higher risk for compromised health. Compounding this issue is the fact that for-profit health insurance companies prefer to deny coverage to applicants with "health issues" since they will likely be less profitable, a deadly catch-22.

With less preventive care and less healthcare support, uninsured ill people get diagnosed at more advanced disease stages, and once diagnosed, they tend to receive less therapeutic care. Consequently, the uninsured have significantly higher mortality rates than comparable insured individuals.[55] Studies estimate that the number of preventable deaths among uninsured adults in the twenty-five-to-sixty-four age group is about twenty-two thousand deaths annually, exceeding the number of annual deaths from diabetes within the same age group.[56] Uninsured cancer patients are 1.6 times more likely to die within five years of diagnosis than are insured patients—even after controlling for age, race, sex, and income.[57]

The Anxiety of the Uninsured

Don is a sixty-two-year-old longtime marketing executive. Two years ago he was made redundant by his company when it went into Chapter 11 bankruptcy. Too young for retirement and with too many assets to qualify for Medicaid, Don is stunned and scared. Now that his Cobra continuation coverage has run out, he is uninsured. Don's father died of prostate cancer, and he is terrified by a lump he identified in a self-exam. He knows an emergency room won't do the clinical work he needs, and he doesn't have the cash to pay for tests out of pocket. He also knows that if he pays out of pocket for a diagnosis, he may make himself uninsurable by identifying a "preexisting" condition. Don simply doesn't know what to do . . .

The bottom line of this lack of timely therapeutic treatment and adequate maintenance medicine for the uninsured is that the United States has a higher rate of hospital admissions than other wealthy countries for chronic conditions such as asthma or diabetes complications.[58] That, too, adds to the overall national cost of healthcare.

And it isn't only healthcare costs that rise for us all because so many Americans are uninsured. Lost productivity takes a tremendous financial toll on the nation as a whole, and plenty of productivity is lost when folks without insurance work through an illness or at less than peak effectiveness.

Why are so many Americans uninsured? There is little doubt that the answer is the exorbitant cost of health insurance. Since 1999, health insurance premiums have increased 131 percent for employers, while employee spending for health insurance coverage increased 128 percent between 1999 and 2008.[59] For small firms in particular the skyrocketing costs of health insurance premiums make it financially prohibitive to offer health insurance coverage. While the average annual increase in inflation has been around 2.5 percent, health insurance premiums for small firms have escalated an average of 12 percent annually.[60] Even if employees are offered employer-based coverage, many people can't afford their portion of the premium. If you're earning $30,000 a year as a secretary and you pay $1,200 monthly for rent, that doesn't give you much wiggle room to pay the hundreds of dollars required for your employee contributions to health insurance—plus the various copayments and deductibles.

Yet while the premium costs can seem overwhelming, the impact of a major medical bill can be utterly devastating. One in three low-income households without coverage report that medical bills have a major financial impact on their families,[61] and it is no secret that unexpected medical bills are a major reason for foreclosures and bankruptcies.

The uninsured versus the insured: it sets up a fundamental inequality in health services and outcomes. A closer look at who is uninsured shows even more inequality. The uninsured in America are most likely to be Hispanic, for 32.8 percent of this group is uninsured versus the significantly lower rates of 15.8 percent uninsured among non-Hispanic African Americans and 10.2 percent uninsured among non-Hispanic Caucasians.[62] This coverage difference may be related to such issues as culture and language barriers, but one of the most critical factors is economics. The median earnings in the United States for Hispanics are 12 percent lower than for African Americans, 31 percent lower than for Caucasian Americans, and nearly 37 percent lower than for Asian Americans. Hispanics are simply less able to pay the high costs of health insurance.[63]

A final assessment of the US healthcare system can be found in the WHO's 2000 rankings.[64] Here the United States ranked thirty-seventh in the world overall and second to last in our competitive group, topping only Korea. Competitors France, Italy, Spain, and Japan ranked first, second, seventh, and tenth, respectively, in the world. This ranking is more subjective than the objective measurement of life expectancy, but it is telling that it concurs in the assessment that the United States is far behind the leaders. The United States received comparatively low ratings for fairness in financial contribution but had a top rating for responsiveness—defined as meeting a population's expectations of how it should be treated by providers of prevention, care, or nonpersonal services. The overall low ranking is further evidence, as if more were needed, that the mix of public and private healthcare spending isn't working for much of America.

HEALTHCARE PROFESSIONALS: DELIVERING HEALTHCARE

Obviously, if you're going to have good health, you need skilled healthcare professionals to diagnose ailments and provide therapies and cures. Data on the density of physicians rank the United States as average. Our 26.7 physicians per ten thousand people puts us far behind Greece and Italy but well above Canada, with 19.1 physicians per ten thousand.[65] The same is true for nurse and midwife density, where the United States is about in the middle.

As it turns out, there is no obvious relationship between the overall density of healthcare professionals—that is, doctors, nurses, and midwives—and life expectancy in our competitor nations. This is likely a reflection of the fact that physical access is not an issue for the vast majority of people living in wealthy countries; those who need medical help can either reach the services or the services can reach them.

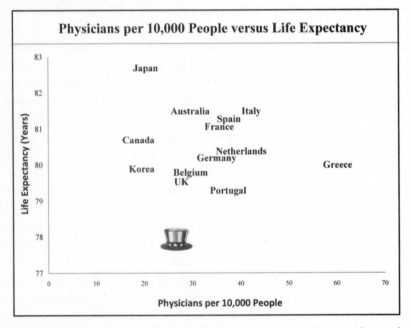

One interesting point related to physician density is who is authorized to write prescriptions for drugs in these different countries. In the United States, prescriptions can be written by physicians, dentists, podiatrists, and physician associates; a limited set of drugs can also be prescribed by clinical psychologists and optometrists. In much of the United States, the restrictions on nurse practitioners prescribing medications are greater than in other nations—such as the United Kingdom, for example, where nurse practitioners, acting as the first line of patient interaction, can do so readily. This capability tends to make physician density a less critical issue.

Nevertheless, the number of healthcare professionals is not particularly pertinent for understanding the overall picture of health in wealthy nations like the United States and our competitors.

HOW SICK ARE WE?

Since the density of healthcare professionals isn't critical, it is important to understand how Americans die.

In general, people die of either disease or injury. We can readily understand and track deaths associated with injuries sustained in car accidents, accidental falls, or even homicides. Disease mortality is more complicated. Diseases are usually divided into two categories: communicable and noncommunicable. Communicable diseases are those transmitted from one individual to another, either by direct contact or through blood, saliva, and semen. Examples of communicable diseases include respiratory infections, influenza, pneumonia, and AIDS. Noncommunicable diseases are not infectious and tend to progress more slowly than communicable diseases. Cardiovascular disease, cancer, stroke, asthma, diabetes, chronic kidney disease, and osteoporosis are examples.

In reviewing the data on causes of death, we need to adjust for the age of the population, since, all things being equal, a fifty-year-old is less likely to die than a seventy-year-old. Using age-standardized mortality rates, countries with older populations, like Japan, can be fairly compared to countries with younger populations, like the United States and Korea. These mortality rates reflect both the incidence rate as well as the effectiveness of the health system in early detection and effective treatment.

The largest of these categories, noncommunicable diseases, shows the United States with the highest mortality rate, about 50 percent higher than that of the leader, Japan, and more than 20 percent higher than in other strongly performing countries like Australia, France, Italy, and Canada.[66]

This comparatively high rate of noncommunicable disease is not surprising given that noncommunicable diseases are the biggest killers in developed countries. For example, according to the CDC, in 2007 the biggest causes of mortality in the United States were, in descending order: cardiovascular disease, responsible for about 25 percent of all deaths; cancers, causing 23 percent of deaths; stroke, responsible for 6 percent of deaths; chronic lower respiratory diseases, responsible for 5 percent of American mortality; and accidents, causing 5 percent of deaths—with other specific causes each making up less than 3 percent each.[67] These statistics tells us two important things immediately. First, we learn that nearly one-half of the deaths in the United States are associated with the two leading killers: cardiovascular disease and cancer, neither of which are communicable. Consequently, any comparison of life expectancy and mortality needs to pay particularly close attention to those two diseases. Second, we learn that communicable diseases and accidents together are relatively minor causes of mortality in the United States, although it is still important to review the relative rate. Medical errors are also culpable; errors are estimated to cause between forty-four thousand and ninety-eight thousand additional hospital deaths annually.[68]

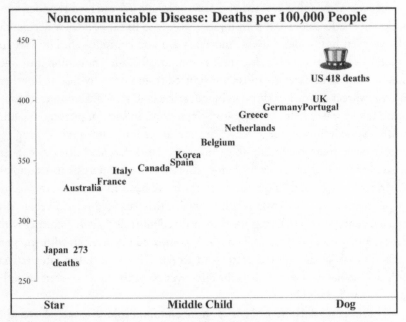

Within the class of noncommunicable diseases, cardiovascular diseases are the dominant killers. The United States has a comparatively poor performance in the rate of deaths from cardiovascular disease for both men and women, outperforming only Germany and Greece for men and topping only those two plus Portugal for women. A number of factors, including lifestyle decisions about exercise, diet, smoking, alcohol and drug use, and, of course, genetics play a role in the rate of heart disease.

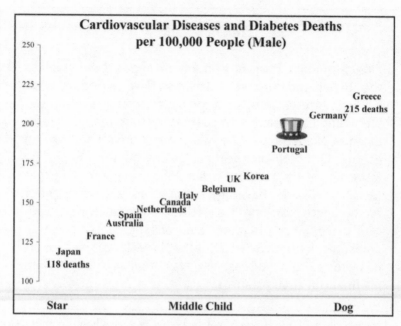

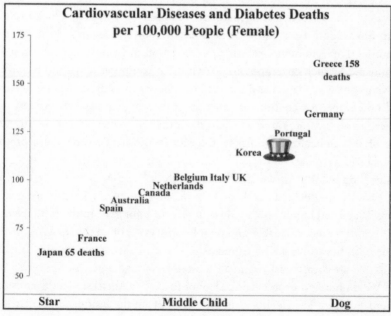

Out of Breath

John, fifty-eight, is an African American gas station worker with high blood pressure and asthma. Two years ago, he let his insurance lapse because he simply couldn't afford the premiums. Last year he paid a local doctor out of pocket for a health exam because he was short of breath and low on energy. It turned out he had lesions on the lungs. The lesions may be cancerous, but John can't afford further tests. His children have urged him to go to an emergency room facility, but John is skeptical about receiving proper care there. Since his father died of lung cancer and was uninsured, John is not hopeful that he will get the support he needs to fight a disease as devastating as cancer—not in his financial circumstances.

One reason the United States may be below average when it comes to cardiovascular health is the rising incidence of obesity, which plays a major role in heart disease and stroke rates. Obesity has been on the rise in most developed countries thanks to higher-calorie processed food and more sedentary lifestyles dominated by such couch-potato "activities" as computer usage and television viewing. But while Japan and Korea show obesity rates of less than 5 percent, and no competitor country has an obesity rate higher than 25 percent, the American obesity rate tips the scale at more than 30 percent,[69] a truly stunning rate of this unhealthy condition. Obesity is another leading cause of preventable death in the country, indirectly resulting in thousands of excess annual deaths[70] via induced strokes and heart disease.

Obesity is usually a result of lifestyle choices, and it is tied to poverty. Prepackaged and highly processed fast foods are among the most affordable and least healthy choices available, and their low prices are often the result of government subsidies to particular segments of the agricultural community. But the foods that are cheap today eventually cost us all in higher healthcare costs.

We do not as a people drink alcohol to excess; American adults consume some 10 percent less alcohol than typical adults in the European countries on the list.[71] In 2007 it was estimated that less than 5.2 percent of American adults were heavy drinkers,[72] which should be to America's health advantage, since excessive alcohol use can increase the risk of liver disease and injuries related to drunkenness and drunk-driving accidents. While studies have demonstrated that moderate alcohol consumption may have some positive health effects,[73] it is unclear if this plays a significant role in national cardiovascular disease rates.

Another factor that may affect cardiovascular health and that appears to be on the rise in the United States is drug use, which is a concern also for its direct health threats—namely, drug overdose deaths, now the second leading cause of accidental deaths, behind only automobile accidents.[74] Unintentional fatal drug overdoses nearly doubled from 1999 to 2004, with much of the rise attributed to overdoses of cocaine and prescription sedatives. The very public deaths from prescription medications of Heath Ledger and Michael Jackson highlighted this alarming trend. Cocaine use, which has been closely related to strokes, heart attacks, and a variety of other cardiovascular complications,[75] is significantly more common in America. A seventeen-country study by the WHO found that more than 16 percent of American adults had used cocaine, more than four times as many as in any other surveyed country, including our competitor nations of Spain, Belgium, France, Germany, Netherlands, and Japan.[76]

For the next largest cause of disease mortality among Americans, cancer, the biggest killers are, in order: lung cancer, prostate cancer, and breast cancer, with lung cancer accounting for more American deaths than breast and prostate cancer combined and for more than 50 percent of the total cancer deaths in the United States.[77] When we compare the age-standardized mortality rates for these largest killers, we see that America's rating is average compared to the competition for all cancers but one; we show the highest mortality rate for lung cancer in women. This may be one reason that the overall cancer mortality rate for women is comparatively poor, outperforming only Canada, the Netherlands, and the United Kingdom. By contrast, the cancer mortality rate for men is one of the best in our competitor group. One positive trend in American health is that both the incidences and the mortality rates for all cancers combined are decreasing for both men and women.[78]

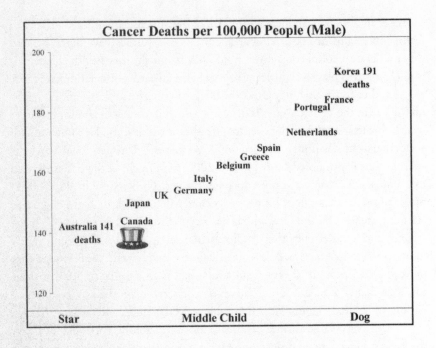

Cancer Deaths per 100,000 People (Male)

Korea 191 deaths
France
Portugal
Netherlands
Spain
Greece
Belgium
Italy
Germany
UK
Japan
Australia 141 deaths
Canada

Star   Middle Child   Dog

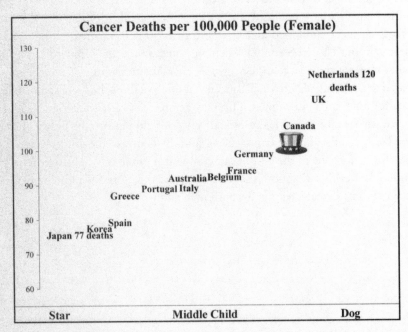

Cancer Deaths per 100,000 People (Female)

Netherlands 120 deaths
UK
Canada
Germany
France
Australia Belgium
Portugal Italy
Greece
Spain
Korea
Japan 77 deaths

Star   Middle Child   Dog

Certainly, smoking and exposure to secondhand smoke are major risk factors for lung cancer, a relationship that was identified by the early twentieth century and quantified by midcentury.[79] And as the data show, America has the highest age-specific lung cancer mortality rate for women and an average age-specific lung cancer mortality rate for men. This relative difference in performance is likely related to the fact that American women have roughly an average smoking prevalence, while American men have the lowest smoking prevalence among our competitors.[80] Unfortunately with lung cancer, as elsewhere, inequality plays a role. African Americans have significantly lower survival rates from lung cancer than Caucasian Americans; the reason is detection rates, which are worse for African Americans.[81] Overall, however, lung cancer mortality rates for men are much higher than for women. In the United States, for example, men are 1.8 times more likely to die of lung cancer than women while in Spain, men are more than ten times as likely to die of lung cancer than women.

Tobacco smoking causes a staggering 87 percent of lung cancer deaths—90 percent of lung cancer deaths in men and almost 80 percent of lung cancer deaths in women[82]—so it is heartening that smoking rates continue to decline in the United States. Today, the American-adult smoking rate is the lowest of any of the competing countries; only 16 percent of the population over fifteen years old are daily smokers.[83] Smoking dropped by half between 1965 and 2006,[84] and by 2004, nearly one-half of all Americans who had ever smoked had quit, although the lagging effects of smoking on cancer rates still affect these former smokers' health. But if the decline continues—not unlikely for a generation that has never had a beer in a smoke-filled bar or traveled on an airplane with a smoking section—the incidence of lung cancer as well as chronic obstructive pulmonary disease will likely decline as well.

Prostate cancer is the second leading cause of cancer mortality in America. Despite an incidence rate more than twice that of European countries, except for Belgium, our prostate cancer mortality rate ranks as average in our group. The higher incidence rate may suggest genetic predispositions among American men or the influence of lifestyle choices. Thanks to aggressive screening programs and, therefore, earlier detection, our survival rate is higher than that of Europe.[85]

How can America have average mortality rates and very high survival rates? A look behind the statistics suggests what's actually going on. For prostate cancer, as for a number of diseases, survival rates are often measured as the percentage of patients alive within five years of detection. Imagine two patients: Neil, an American, and Hans, a German. At age sixty-five, thanks to aggressive screening procedures, American Neil is identified with early-stage prostate cancer. His physicians adopt a wait-and-see approach for two years before beginning treatment when Neil is sixty-seven. He lives for four more years before dying of the disease. Hans in Germany is identified as having prostate cancer at age sixty-seven and also lives four years before dying of the disease. Both men began treatment at the same age and died at the same age, so the age-specific mortality is the same, yet statistically, Neil survived more than five years from the time the disease was detected.

There are certainly benefits to the early detection of diseases, but every preventive measure carries a cost as well as a benefit, and an optimal frequency of testing precludes testing everyone every year for every possible disease. Excessive screenings don't just drive up costs; they may result in a high incidence of false positives that can lead to unnecessary and costly treatments, not to mention to emotional anguish. In the United States in 2009, both the American College of Obstetricians and Gynecologists and the United States Preventive Services Task Force revised their guidelines in order to reduce breast cancer overscreening using mammograms. In October 2011, the United States Preventive Services Task Force recommended that healthy men should no longer receive a blood test to screen for prostate cancer; the task force asserted that these screenings do not save lives, are costly, and often lead to unnecessary treatments. The impact of these official recommendations is not yet clear, since both physicians and patients with comprehensive health insurance like screenings.

Let's summarize: for the largest category of killers—noncommunicable diseases—the United States has the worst performance in its competitor group, a poor showing that is driven by comparatively high mortality rates due to cardiovascular disease and cancer in women. How does America fare in the other categories of mortality?

The United States has a comparatively high mortality rate from communicable diseases, besting only Portugal, Japan, and the United Kingdom.[86] The biggest killers among communicable diseases in the United States are chronic lower respiratory diseases, influenza, and pneumonia. As you look at the chart of communicable disease deaths, note that its scale is about one-tenth the scale for noncommunicable diseases. For example, the age-standardized mortality rate for noncommunicable diseases in the United States is about twelve times higher than the rate for communicable disease. In real terms, this means that the last-place performance by the United States in noncommunicable diseases is more relevant to its overall health performance than its fourth-to-last-place finish in communicable diseases.

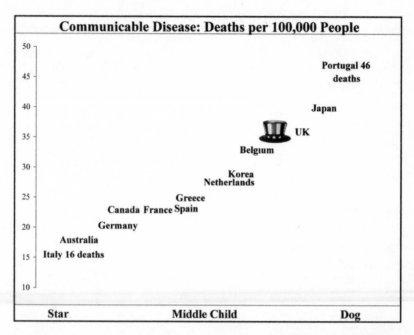

Communicable Disease: Deaths per 100,000 People

Portugal 46 deaths

Japan

UK

Belgium

Korea
Netherlands

Greece
Canada France Spain

Germany

Australia

Italy 16 deaths

Star   Middle Child   Dog

Finally, how does the United States rank on mortality from injuries—including deaths from vehicle collisions, falls, accidental poisonings, drug overdoses, or from such deliberate actions as homicides and suicides? In our comparison countries, injury-related deaths occur at similar rates to those of communicable diseases and at rates that are about one-eighth that of noncommunicable diseases, reinforcing the point that noncommunicable diseases are the main causes of death in these countries.

The United States has the highest rate of injury-related deaths by far.[87] Only Korea comes close. Of all unintentional injury deaths in the United States, about one-third are due to motor vehicle accidents, one-quarter to accidental poisonings, and one-fifth to accidental falls.[88]

America's road-traffic accident mortality is higher than average for both men and women.[89] In developed countries in general, road-traffic accidents are the sixth-largest source of mortality, according to the latest figures from 2001.[90] But the United States evidences a positive trend: the percentage of motor vehicle deaths as a fraction of the total US population has been declining steadily and is now about one-half the rate it was in 1980.

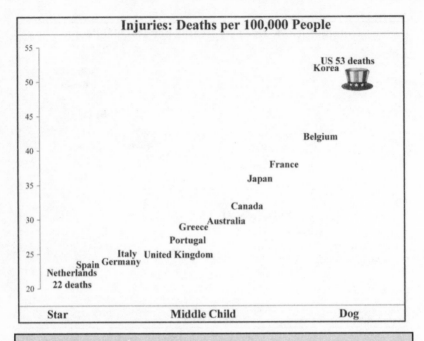

Injuries: Deaths per 100,000 People

55

US 53 deaths
Korea

50

45

Belgium

40

France

Japan

35

Canada

30   Australia
      Greece

Portugal

25
        Italy   United Kingdom
    Spain Germany
Netherlands
20   22 deaths

Star   Middle Child   Dog

The Price Increase Heard Round the Company

Steve is a thirty-five-year-old business executive with comprehensive health insurance partially subsidized by his employer. His annual checkup includes a physical exam, full blood screening, eye exam, hearing tests, and diet consultation. The hearing test, using a newly purchased, computerized acoustic instrument, flagged a problem, and Steve's physician referred him to a hearing specialist. With no information about Steve's medical history or even the reason for the referral, the specialist concluded that Steve simply needed ear wax removed, but she offered to run an MRI to determine the source of the wax buildup. When Steve questioned the need for the MRI, the specialist conceded that the chance that a tumor caused the buildup is "extremely small, so if you don't want the scan, which happens to be fully covered by your insurance, sign this legal waiver." Since it didn't seem to cost anything extra, Steve agreed to the scan, which came up clean. The next year, health insurance costs for all company employees increased by 15 percent.

WHAT ABOUT MENTAL HEALTH?

A difference in life expectancy of almost twenty-five years separates the mentally healthy from those with mental illnesses,[91] so it would seem critical to any competitive intelligence on health to examine the differences in mental health. Unfortunately, by its very nature, mental health is difficult to measure. The frequencies of depression, mania, schizophrenia, and other mental illnesses by country are not readily available and are highly dependent on cultural definitions.[92] Furthermore, comparing the use of depressants, stimulants, and antipsychotic medications in different countries is equally influenced by culture, patient behavior, and the national healthcare systems. We do know that physical health, life activities, and changes in life events are important variables in supporting, or detracting from, mental health, but these factors are decidedly individual and have varying impacts.

Two available measures are happiness, a survey-based measure,[93] and suicide rate. Both measures are heavily influenced by culture. On the happiness metric, culture affects the willingness to express that one is happy and the meaning of the word. For suicide, culture affects the society's attitude toward and acceptance of it and even the accuracy of the data on suicide rates. Because of these concerns about the objectivity of these metrics, it is sufficient simply to state that the United States has an average rating for happiness and that the rating has not changed significantly in the last sixty years. The suicide rate in the United States is also average, at 11.3 suicide deaths per one hundred thousand Americans.[94] Japan ranks highest in suicide rate in the group, but since the rate is less than 3 percent of all deaths in Japan, it has little impact on national life expectancy.

"BEST MEDICAL CARE IN THE WORLD"?

Despite the inequities in our healthcare system, we adhere to the notion that America excels in research, innovation, and specialty care so that for those who can afford it, the best medical care in the world *is* available.

The "best" of anything is hard to measure; assessments tend to be subjective. It is certainly the case that our great medical schools—Harvard University, the University of Pennsylvania, Johns Hopkins University, and Stanford University, among others—draw some of the world's most talented medical students. Many of these medical schools, along with other laboratories and hospitals and the National Institutes of Health, develop leading-edge medical research that extends and improves the lives of people around the world, supported by more than $100 billion in federal, state, and local government aid to biomedical research.[95]

The research itself may stir other innovations. While there are no perfect measures of this, the World Intellectual Property Indicators filings show that the United States, Japan, Korea, and Germany have the highest rate of patent filings per person as well as the highest rate of patent filings per GDP.[96] Narrowing our analysis to medical patents from 1996 to 2000, the United States had more than twice the number of patent filings (with the United States Patent and Trademark Office) per person than any of its competitors.[97]

Measuring hospitals objectively is even more difficult, since such assessments depend very much on the specialty of care provided and the criteria used to define "best." It is safe to say that for many specialties, such hospitals as the Mayo Clinic, Johns Hopkins, Memorial Sloan-Kettering Cancer Center, Massachusetts General Hospital, and the Brigham and Women's Hospital are world-class, setting or exceeding the standards of excellence also provided by many outstanding hospitals in other countries.

Such achievements make our poor national health record more disturbing. The idea that momentous advances are being made here and that our population as a whole is not reaping the benefits of these advances is dismaying, to say the least. We cannot even say that if you can find and can afford the best care, then you can get it and live a healthy life—that is, that good health is available to "the elite." For example, the disease rates for diabetes, hypertension, cancer, and heart disease are higher in the United States than in Great Britain for all educational levels. The most educated Americans have higher disease rates than the most educated British; the wealthiest Americans are sicker than the wealthiest Brits.[98] Even more shocking is that Americans in the top education and income levels have similar rates of diabetes and heart disease to those in Great Britain's *lowest* education and income levels.

THE FINAL ANALYSIS: THE UNITED STATES, THE DOG OF THE MARKET

The data leave no room for doubt: America's healthcare ranking is sick. We have the lowest life expectancy in our group of competitor nations despite spending nearly twice as much, and for some countries up to four times more, on healthcare per person—an extremely poor return on investment. Our population has the highest rate of infant and maternal mortality. A large percentage of our population lacks insurance or access to adequate healthcare. The system is riddled with inequities of race, gender, and socioeconomic condition. These inequities drive the central paradox of healthcare in the United States, namely, that we have some of the finest medical research facilities and hospitals in the world, yet our public health metrics are vastly below those of most wealthy countries.

The American experience with one infectious disease in particular, the HIV/AIDS epidemic, is emblematic of much that is wrong with our healthcare system. At the highest end of the medical spectrum—that is, in research and innovation—the United States excels; researchers here helped to identify HIV's role in AIDS,[99] and they developed HIV-antibody tests and the use of AZT as HIV therapy, thus leading the world in the battle against this deadly virus. Yet, at the same time, our own public health response was inadequate and slow, costing lives and deepening suffering. We were late in offering the kinds of needle-exchange programs initiated in the Netherlands in 1984 and, in fact, we banned federal funding of these programs from 1988 to 2009.[100] Public discussion of the issue was absent early on in the epidemic: AIDS was only first mentioned by President Reagan in September 1985, and it wasn't until 1986 that then Surgeon General C. Everett Koop published a report calling for sex education. Yet another two years would pass before a national mass-media campaign was implemented. Meanwhile, the persistence of ineffective abstinence-only programs, driven by ideology rather than by the facts on the ground, exacerbated the epidemic. The distance between scientists finding the cause and a treatment for this disease and political leaders unwilling to use the word "condoms" is illustrative of both the strength and weakness of our healthcare—enormous capabilities that are simply not reaching the people most in need.

Surely, there is much we can learn from the healthcare market Stars like Japan and France.

RECOMMENDATIONS

The data suggest four recommendations that would improve our healthcare and extend our life expectancy. Three are as much cultural and social as anything else, but they lead unequivocally to a fourth recommendation, structural in nature, that would change our system fundamentally and potentially provide the greatest payback in terms of the health of our citizens.

First, *diet*. We are what we eat, and the average American diet is far less healthy than is good for us and than our agricultural wealth can make possible. We can learn from our competitors. The Japanese diet, for example, based on fish and rice, is far lower in calories. In fact, Americans eat more than one thousand calories per day *more* than the Japanese; the excess is roughly the number of calories found in two Big Macs®. Japanese cuisine is also far lower in saturated fats, which predominate in the American way of eating. Not surprisingly, Japan enjoys an obesity rate that is nearly ten times lower than the American rate.[101] This lower obesity rate in turn contributes to lower rates of cardiovascular disease, prostate cancer, and breast cancer, among other causes of mortality.

In France, where the content of the diet is closer to standard American fare than Japanese cuisine, obesity levels are nevertheless some three times lower than in the United States. In fact, Americans consume more calories per person than in any other country anywhere, including every competitor country. It is difficult to enjoy life and liberty and to pursue happiness when weighed down, literally, by obesity and by the health risks it confers.

Fast food is a major culprit in advancing the high-calorie, high-fat diet that is killing Americans, and government subsidies enable fast food. A study by the Physicians Committee for Responsible Medicine,[102] for example, found that from 1995 to 2005, almost 75 percent of federal subsidies for food production went for dairy and meat while less than 0.5 percent supported the growing of fruits and vegetables. In a price-comparison study, the Bureau of Labor Statistics noted that, compared to 1978 prices, sodas, butter, and beer are all cheaper relative to prices in the rest of the economy while vegetables and fruits are in excess of 40 percent *more* expensive. Government subsidies of healthier foods would support national health, as would federal legislation requiring fast-food companies to publish calorie content information, a move that some local areas have already initiated. The latter could be an important consumer tool. Right now, ordering a healthful-sounding salad in some fast-food places can turn out to be an act of self-sabotage. At one well-known chain, for example, the chicken Caesar salad has more calories than the double cheeseburger and is loaded with saturated fats and sodium.[103] If that information were there to see, health-conscious consumers might either say, "Hold the toppings!" or go elsewhere.

Second, *drugs and tobacco*. Illegal drug use has been estimated to cause seventeen thousand deaths annually in America,[104] and the War on Drugs and exploding incarceration rates for drug offenders show little promise of reducing

America's high rates of addiction. The federal government has recently set a goal of reducing diseases and deaths caused by drug addiction,[105] but it has set goals related to drug abuse many times before with little positive impact.

Although Americans have made exceptional progress in reducing cigarette smoking, tobacco taxes in the United States are generally lower than in Europe, and smoking by some groups—notably teenagers—is no longer declining.[106] The evidence is clear that higher cigarette prices reduce overall cigarette consumption, especially among the young, minorities, and low-income smokers, but tobacco taxes are established by the states, and the disparities can be stunning. Tobacco-growing states, for example, add less than $0.70 a pack while others add more than $2 a pack in taxes.[107] The tobacco industry remains powerful in the United States, but the dangers of smoking are so severe and so well documented that tobacco-industry economic interests should not be allowed to prevail over the long-term health benefits of reduced smoking.

Third, *violent crime*. The sixth-most-common cause of mortality for African Americans and the seventh most common for Hispanics in the United States is homicide. Our homicide rate is about ten times that of Japan and triple that of France. We'll discuss this issue more in chapter 2, "Locking Our Doors," but it's worth noting it here. It also bears repeating that both of the market Stars in health, Japan and France, have strict gun-control laws while America has some of the most lax regulations. Japan, with one-tenth our homicide rate, has some of the strictest gun-control laws in the developed world.

Finally, and most importantly, *paying for healthcare*. At the very core of our dismal market performance in health is this central fact: US healthcare operates as a for-profit business. That is the most fundamental difference between our healthcare system and the systems of our competitor nations, all of which, without exception, regard healthcare as a basic right—like public education or voting or the right to live where you like. In fact, healthcare is seen as the right that enables all those other rights.

"The for-profit model enables the law of supply and demand to operate effectively," argue the free-market evangelists, "which will ensure that in time costs and prices will come down." But every economist knows that this argument doesn't hold when demand is inelastic. And healthcare is the perfect example of a realm in which demand is inelastic. What do we mean by inelastic demand? Simple. If there is a life-saving drug that can cure your illness, or perhaps your child's illness, you will pay whatever it costs to have that drug. You will mortgage your home, sell all your assets, indenture yourself into servitude if you must to get the drug.

This is precisely the way the for-profit health market has worked in the United States. The reality of inelastic demand for health services and the unarguable political clout of Big Pharma and the healthcare industry, both of which every year between 1999 and 2011 spent more than any other industry on lobbying,[108] make a powerful combination. For instance, the health-insurance lobby successfully scuttled healthcare-reform legislation in 1994 with its massive "Harry and Louise" ad campaign. When we recognize that those industries have a collective self-interest in keeping things just as they are, then it is clear why America remains trapped in the for-profit model of healthcare.

Every competitor country, each of which has a longer life expectancy and lower costs of healthcare than we do, has exactly the opposite—a model in which healthcare is a guaranteed right, not a commodity to be manipulated by colluding industries and cooperating politicians, and with care auctioned off to the highest bidder.

Japan, the Star of the health market, applies the Bismarck model in which the health-insurance system is financed jointly by employees and employers. First, Japan requires that insurance plans must cover everyone. All Japanese are required to enroll in an insurance plan, either employee health insurance or, for the self-employed and students, national health insurance. All elderly persons are covered by government-sponsored insurance. In all these programs, patients are free to choose their physicians and their treatment facilities.

Both insurance companies and hospitals in Japan are nonprofit entities. (France and Germany, also health Stars, require private health insurance to be nonprofit.) For-profit corporations may neither own nor operate hospitals in Japan.

This universal, nonprofit coverage results in effective preventive medicine, complete prenatal care, and an appropriate use of emergency medical services. In addition, Japanese employers are required to offer a free annual checkup, thus reinforcing a culture of basic healthcare and shared responsibility for public health.

The picture this paints could not be further from the fragmented and incomplete coverage found in the United States or from the poor health outcomes that result. The great irony is that the nonprofit model of Japan and other countries is far less costly than our own array of for-profit plans. America has models of nonprofit, "socialized" medicine as well—in Medicare and in the military and for veterans. Those systems also deliver better health outcomes more efficiently and much more cheaply than the private, for-profit insurance plans available to other Americans. In a report by the National Committee for

Quality Assurance, the United States Veterans Health Administration (VHA) has been rated higher in patient management "in every single category" of performance measure than such world-famous non-VHA hospitals as Johns Hopkins, the Mayo Clinic, and Massachusetts General.[109] And the patient-monitoring software the VHA developed has been adopted in Finland, Germany, Egypt, and Nigeria.[110]

The United States is the only country in the competition with a significant percentage of its population uninsured. There's an irony in that as well. Back in 1948, America codrafted and signed the Universal Declaration of Human Rights, which includes the statement that all people have a right to basic health and social services, so there's a sense that denial of coverage violates our basic values. What is certain—what this chapter has shown conclusively—is that the presence of the uninsured is a huge cost to all of us. We all pay for the lost productivity and the ever higher costs of medical care to cover all those emergency room visits, not to mention the human costs of limited and shortened lives and the loss felt by family and friends. The Patient Protection and Affordable Care Act (PPACA) includes provisions that will achieve near-universal coverage, but it still leaves millions uncovered—it's a first step toward ameliorating the high cost of our uninsured, although it remains to be seen what impact these provisions will have.

The healthcare reform debate that raged during 2010 heard many loud and articulate political voices argue in favor of maintaining America's for-profit health system. Behind those voices is an array of formidable forces including the pharmaceutical industry, health insurance companies, medical staff, malpractice lawyers, and, of course, lobbyists. It's unrealistic to think that these forces will let up in their efforts to maintain America's for-profit healthcare system; the stakes for them are very high.

Big Pharma spends lavishly in both money and influence to maintain the status quo of how Americans buy drugs. No wonder. The world's two largest pharmaceutical companies, Johnson & Johnson and Pfizer, together brought in profits of $20 billion in 2008, with about one-half of their revenue earned in the United States, where, as we have seen, pharmaceuticals cost about 50 percent more than comparable products abroad. Banning direct-to-consumer advertising, which is illegal in competitor countries, would liberate American physicians from patient requests for drugs they've been "informed" about in ads. Instead, doctors could prescribe cheaper and equally efficacious generics, and Big Pharma could put some of that marketing money into research and development.

The world's five largest healthcare companies by annual revenue—

UnitedHealth Group, WellPoint, Aetna, Humana, and Cigna—are all based in the United States and enjoy huge profit margins through high premiums, selective coverage of services, and denial of coverage to applicants with preexisting conditions. It's a great business: consistently raise premiums for what people consider a necessity and make sure you rarely have to pay out benefits by, as much as possible, covering only people with few or no health needs. Denial of coverage for preexisting conditions will be illegal under the PPACA, but it remains to be seen how effective the law will be.

Doctors and nurses earn considerably more in the United States than in comparable countries, and specialists get an even greater pay boost. The American Medical Association (AMA) uses its considerable power to protect physician earnings and will likely continue to do so, despite widespread criticism from both the right—notably by Nobel laureate Milton Friedman, the prominent conservative economist[111]—and left ends of the political spectrum.

Malpractice lawyers and malpractice insurance companies also benefit greatly from our for-profit healthcare system. Steadily increasing malpractice costs and the costs of defensive medicine have driven some hospitals to close maternity wards[112] and childbearing centers, while lawyers are kept busy defending doctors against malpractice suits. Of the forty-six thousand members of the American College of Obstetricians and Gynecologists, 76 percent have been sued at least once and 41.5 percent have been sued three times or more. Yet about one-half of these malpractice suits were dropped, dismissed, or settled without payment.[113] Where payment is awarded, the majority of jury awards exceed $1 million, and the average award is around $5 million.[114]

All of these forces—Big Pharma, the healthcare giants, the AMA, and the malpractice industry—have their own lobbyists who have cultivated close ties with politicians. In fact, many current lobbyists once served in Congress and now reap the rewards of leveraging their political connections.[115] Between 1998 and 2011, the health industry spent about $2.2 billion[116] on lobbying—not including campaign contributions. Since 1989, the AMA has donated more than $26 million to campaigning politicians while the American Dental Association, the American Hospital Association, and Blue Cross/Blue Shield have all given more than $16 million. That an affordable care bill was passed at all seems almost a miracle against such odds, but, of course, passage of the bill seems to have been only a starting point for the fight to keep for-profit healthcare. The fight has moved to the courts and to state legislatures, and now the US Supreme Court has agreed to review the new healthcare law. It seems clear that the proponents of for-profit healthcare will not go away quietly.

There are signs, however, that people are beginning to see what our health Star countries have long known. In May 2011, the Vermont state legislature enacted a bill that set in motion the first single-payer healthcare system in the country. In signing the bill into law, Governor Peter Shumlin declared that the aim was "to have health care that is the best in the world that treats health care as a right and not a privilege, where health care follows the individual not the employer."

Chapter 2

LOCKING OUR DOORS: SAFETY

> They who can give up essential liberty to obtain a little temporary safety deserve neither liberty nor safety.
>
> **—Benjamin Franklin, 1705–1790**

I n his 1941 State of the Union address, President Franklin D. Roosevelt articulated the four fundamental freedoms that he asserted people "everywhere in the world" ought to enjoy: freedom of speech and expression, freedom of worship, freedom from want, and freedom from fear.

By freedom from fear, Roosevelt meant the ability to enjoy life with confidence in one's personal safety, with a reasonable expectation that injury, danger, and loss were not a natural part of one's daily life.[1] Fear of such occurrences is, of course, basic to human nature; it is the ancient and inherent survival instinct that protects us by triggering our fight-or-flight mechanism.

When individuals come together in a community, the issue is the extent to which citizens fear for their safety collectively. What do they believe is their risk? Is the risk they perceive grounded in reality—in the crime rate, for example? And then there is the question of response. How do different nations respond to those responsible for crimes? What justice is handed out to those committing crimes?

The formula of fear, reality, and response works for a nation's external relations as well, in whether and how the nation perceives it is at risk of attack. It is reflected in how nations protect themselves through laws and policies and with military force. Here, too, the question is how well the perception tracks with the actual risk of the nation being attacked. And, finally, what is the national response to an attack and how do nations handle their safety issues internationally?

71

Those are the questions we'll explore in this chapter. We will focus on physical safety, looking first at such issues of internal safety as weapons, crime, and incarceration. Then we'll look at an external mirror image of those issues, exploring how a nation deals with external safety issues by examining the role of the military, investments in defense, and overall assessments of national safety. In this way, we'll try to assess the current state of each competitor country's safety, both internally and externally, as well as how each country responds to the risks.

On the external front, there is a big difference between the subject of safety and all the other subjects this book is looking at, and that difference is the role of the United States. When we compare our countries in terms of health, for example, or education, or democracy, each stands on its own with minimal impact on the others. The educational system or healthcare system of Australia has minimal, if any, direct influence on that of the rest of the competition. When it comes to external safety, we have a different situation. For in today's world, a single superpower, the United States, is the major determinant of safety, and its actions profoundly affect the external security of many other countries, including all of our competitor countries. So in the case of external safety, rather than focusing on market Stars and Dogs, we will need to keep in mind the fact that military policies and actions taken by the United States can—and often do—affect and even sometimes determine the decisions taken by other countries. In this instance, after reviewing the data, we will ask whether there are other options for ensuring world safety.

THE DARK FIGURE OF CRIME

First, a word about the kinds of crimes we'll look at in exploring internal safety. Criminologists use the phrase the "dark figure of crime" to describe the amount of crime that goes unreported or undetected.[2] It represents the gap between the true crime rate and the rate found in official reports.

A number of things have to happen before a crime shows up in official statistics: it must be determined that a crime has occurred; the crime must be reported; and the police or other official agency must include this occurrence accurately in its crime statistics. At each step along the way, factors may intervene to influence the report of the occurrence and, thus, of overall crime statistics. Victims' tendencies to report crimes vary by the crime type, the victim's age, the relationship to the criminal, and the victim's confidence in law enforcement, not to mention the accessibility of local policing. The accuracy and fidelity of official reporting are affected by the practices the police use to report statistics and by legal definitions of the crime, which may vary by locality.

The inconsistent reporting rates that result create an enormous challenge in comparing crime data. To supplement officially reported crime rates, criminologists conduct surveys by polling citizens to ask if they've been victims of a crime. Such surveys—like the British Crime Survey[3] (BCS) in the United Kingdom and the National Crime Victimization Survey[4] in the United States—provide a more complete picture of the true crime rate. For example, the BCS for 2009–2010 shows a crime rate that is about twice as high as the officially recorded crime rates for that time period;[5] this represents a vast improvement over levels from fifteen years earlier, when fully 80 percent of crimes went unreported. The Australian Bureau of Statistics notes that assault is the "most common crime against a person, yet it is the most widely under-reported offense to police."[6] In the United States it has been estimated that fewer than 39 percent of all rapes and sexual assaults are reported to law enforcement.[7]

The point is that the issues underlying reported crime data may diminish the usefulness of the data in illustrating safety. For that reason, our analysis of internal safety will focus exclusively on homicide data. In the case of a homicide, the victim's willingness or unwillingness to report the crime has been eliminated as a factor; homicide data are thus more reliable than other crime statistics. While there may still be variations in the way police report homicide rates, this is a more accurate metric than other crime rates. It therefore constitutes data we can rely on the most.

AMERICA THE VIOLENT

That America is a violent country is hardly an original thought. The United States came into being through violent revolution, later fought a civil war of almost unfathomable carnage, and has a long history of both external and internal conflict. What is important for our purposes, however, is that America is much more violent than all of our competitor nations. This violent tendency is not a new phenomenon: back in 1916, for example, Chicago's homicide rate, which was typical of large American cities, was about ten times higher than that of London, Europe's most populous city at the time.[8]

Today, from its passionate gun rights activists to its propensity for capital punishment to its massive military, the United States holds positions with respect to safety that are very different from the rest of the competition. Part of this distinctive American world of safety derives from historical influences, but some of it is simply a reflection of real-world politics. The "crime card" was aggressively played in the Nixon campaigns; and certainly ever since the Willie Horton ad campaign proved to be such an effective political weapon, as wielded by George H. W. Bush in his 1988 presidential run, the accusation of being "soft on crime" or "not tough enough on security" has been used in countless political races. Even the most conservative elected officials, those favoring spending cuts and small government, find it prudent and often rewarding to beef up the budgets for police, prisons, or the military establishment. One example was the 2011 public union-busting initiatives of Wisconsin governor Scott Walker, which pointedly exempted police and fire unions, offering no justification for making those exceptions. The bottom line in competitive terms is that while so much of the US government is relatively smaller than that of other countries, budgets for police, prisons, and the military are significantly higher than in the competitor countries.

What are these beefed-up budgets buying?

- The US homicide rate is more than twice that of our closest competitor.
- The incarceration rate in the United States is more than four times higher than in our next closest competitor.
- The United States budgets more of its GDP to the military than other wealthy countries, yet the percentage of the population in the military is about average. In practice, the US military often protects the interests of other wealthy countries through its NATO alliance and its historical relationships with Japan and South Korea.

If America were a corporation, two facts would be clear about its investment in safety. First, its policies on safety are not working. Second, the current situation is unsustainable, both for the nation's wallet and for the lives of its citizens.

Yet surveys show that in response to such questions as "Do you think most people try to take advantage of you?" "Do you think most people can be trusted?" or "How much do you trust people you meet for the first time?" Americans have an average level of trust compared to people in our competitor group.[9] Since trust and fear are highly related, it is reasonable to assume that Americans do not feel greater fear for their safety than do their counterparts in competitor nations.

GUNS, GUNS, AND MORE GUNS

Few people can explain America's obsession with guns. Foreigners marvel at it. Whether it is our classic westerns glorifying the gunfighter's showdown, the latest action film, or this year's politician photographed in hunting gear, America and guns seem almost synonymous. Attempts to ban assault rifles have failed,[10] and, while the Brady Handgun Violence Prevention Act finally passed in 1993, there are still major gaps in the gun laws—including no restrictions on sales of handguns by unlicensed individuals—as well as large differences in the gun laws in different states.

Yes, guns are a big business in the United States, with some iconic brand names that figure prominently in popular history—Colt, Winchester, Remington, and Smith & Wesson. Between 1986 and 2005, the US firearms industry produced between three million and greater than five million guns annually, with handguns outpacing shotguns and rifles. The three largest firearms manufactures, Remington, Sturm Ruger & Co., and Smith & Wesson, owned more than one-third of the market in 2005.[11] But the economic value of the industry does not begin to shed light on the important role guns play in our society and their hold on our history.

Gun advocates argue that gun ownership is a basic right enshrined in the Second Amendment to the Constitution, which reads: "A well regulated militia being necessary to the security of a free State, the right of the People to keep and bear arms shall not be infringed." The amendment, protecting citizens' right to bear arms, stems from the eighteenth-century colonists' reaction to British attempts to disarm and embargo firearms, parts, and ammunition,[12] and it expresses their distrust of government and desire for self-defense through the formation of militias.[13] On the basis of that right, and backed by the formidable and deep-pocketed National Rifle Association, legislatures and the courts have continued to protect gun ownership and obstruct limitations on it. It is therefore not surprising that America's rate of civilian firearms ownership, defined as the number of civilian-owned firearms per person, vastly exceeds that of other countries. It is more than twice that of the next closest competitors, France and Canada, and it is orders of magnitude higher than our Asian competitors, Japan and South Korea.[14]

What does the right of gun ownership have to do with safety? The correlation between the presence of guns and the murder rate is too strong to dismiss. If it is true, as gun owners often repeat, that "guns don't kill, people kill," then the data are equally clear that guns make it a lot easier for people to do all

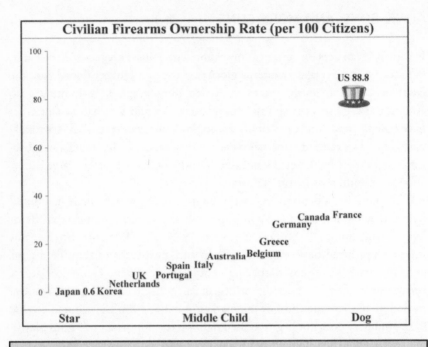

Dying to Learn

On April 16, 2007, Virginia Tech senior and English major Seung-Hui Cho killed thirty-two people and wounded twenty-five others in the largest and deadliest shooting incident by a single gunman in US history. Cho was armed with two semi-automatic weapons and carried out the attacks in two phases separated by about two hours. He killed himself with a shot in the head approximately ten minutes into the second attack. As with other gun incidents in the United States, gun-control supporters and opponents immediately took their familiar positions. Supporters of gun-control legislation pointed out that Cho, a mentally unsound individual, should not have been able to purchase the weapons; opponents of gun control argued that Virginia Tech's gun-free "safe zone" was to blame for so many students and faculty being unable to defend themselves. While school shootings become an almost monthly event in America, no solution is in sight for keeping our students safe.

that killing. For example, in the United States in 2006, firearms were used in 68 percent of murders, 42 percent of robbery offenses, and 22 percent of aggravated assaults nationwide.[15]

The data strongly suggest that guns intensify crime situations and increase the likelihood of the outcome being more violent or lethal.[16] For example, in a family or intimate assault, death is twelve times more likely if a gun is present than if another weapon is used.[17] Analysis shows that an estimated 41 percent of gun-related homicides and 94 percent of gun-related suicides would not have occurred under the same circumstances had no guns been present.[18]

The correlation between rates of firearm-related deaths and gun ownership is etched even more sharply by the fact that countries with the lowest rates of civilian firearms ownership, like Japan and South Korea, have the lowest rates of firearm-related deaths. The United States, with its widespread presence of guns, has by far the highest rate of firearm-related deaths;[19] in 1998, about one-half the deaths were suicides. The low rate of firearms-related deaths in the United Kingdom is undoubtedly a reflection of that country's 1997 ban on private handgun ownership.[20]

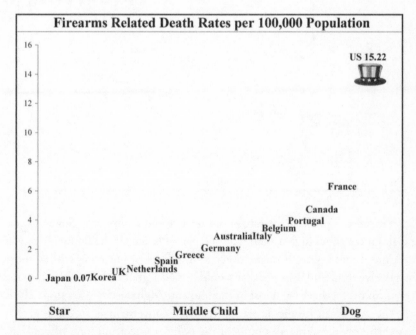

Our violence is not limited to the streets and to ordinary citizens. We even have a higher rate of political assassination than most other countries—all by guns. Four American presidents out of forty-four, as of this writing, have been assassinated while in office,[21] and two others were severely injured in assassination attempts.[22] Japan and Spain are the only competitors that have seen a similar level of political violence against heads of state; in both countries, four prime ministers have been assassinated since 1870.

The correlation between the presence of guns and personal safety comes into sharpest focus when we look at murder rate. In 2009, firearms were the cause of 67 percent of all homicides in the United States—by far the majority of these deaths.[23] At the same time, the intentional homicide rate in the United States is much higher than that of other countries.

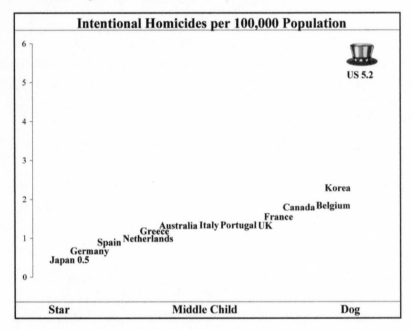

It is more than twice the rate of our next closest competitor, South Korea, and about ten times higher than that of Japan.[24] In fact, if the homicide rate in the United States were brought down to the level of our competitors, more than twelve thousand lives per year would be saved; that is about twice as many American lives as have been lost in the Iraq and Afghanistan Wars since 2001.

The American homicide rate is clearly a concern; it is so extreme that thoughtful people along all points of the political spectrum have offered different suggestions for the cause—from high degrees of inequality[25] to issues of gun ownership laws, drug wars, organized crime, and gang violence.[26]

As enormous as the American homicide rate is compared to other wealthy countries, it actually declined by 43 percent from 1991 to 2001. Economist Steven Levitt has posited that the decline was due to the increasing numbers of police officers, the rising incarceration rates, the receding epidemic of crack cocaine use, and the legalization of abortion.[27]

It is also important to note that even in the case of murder, racial inequality characterizes the US figures: The homicide rate of African American men in 2006 was 7.5 times higher than that of Caucasian men; it was 3.5 times higher for African American women than for Caucasian women.[28]

THE RESPONSE TO CRIME: INCARCERATION

Arrest and incarceration constitute perhaps the most obvious and common response to crime, and here, too, the rates are higher in the United States than in other countries. The data show that there are more US arrests and convictions and that sentences tend to be longer, more widely applied, and harsher than in our competitor countries. Perhaps the most telling case in point is the death penalty. It has been banned in all the competitor countries except the United States, Japan, and South Korea. And with South Korea having carried out no executions since 1997, it is by now considered to be abolished in practice. In 2010, a year in which only 21 of the 192 member states of the United Nations carried out executions, only the United States and Japan among the competitor nations did so.[29]

We begin our analysis of the response to crime where it begins—with police hauling citizens in for questioning or arresting them on suspicion of having committed a crime. While it is difficult to accurately measure the baseline crime rate in different countries because of varying levels of reporting bias, the data do show that the chances of being brought into formal contact with the police are significantly higher in the United States than in other countries. In fact, the number of people brought into contact with the police is higher in America (more than four thousand per every one hundred thousand in the population) than in every competitor nation except Korea.[30]

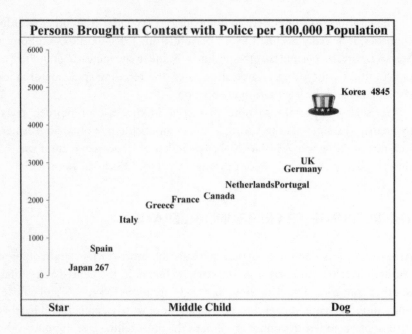

But it is America's incarceration rate that is off the charts compared to other countries. The rate of greater than seven hundred people for every one hundred thousand is more than three times higher than for the next closest competitor and more than ten times higher than the rate in Japan.[31] To put this rate in perspective, it is close to the incarceration rate that the Soviet Union was estimated to have had in 1979 when its notorious gulag system was in effect.[32] It's important to note that the incarceration rate in the United States varies greatly by state, with rates in many of the Southern states—such as Louisiana, Mississippi, Texas, Alabama, and Georgia—being two to three times higher than rates in Northern states.[33]

The United States did not always have so high an incarceration rate. Rather, this rate has been growing steadily over time and is now almost four times what it was in 1980. This is a reflection of changing policies on sentencing, especially with respect to drug laws. Evidence of this may be seen in the astronomical rate of increase in the number and percentage of prisoners incarcerated for drug crimes: from 8 percent of the prison population in 1980 to 26 percent by 1993 to more than 50 percent of the federal prison population by 2009.[34]

Some people have surmised that the large number of noncitizens in the United States is responsible for America's extraordinarily high incarceration

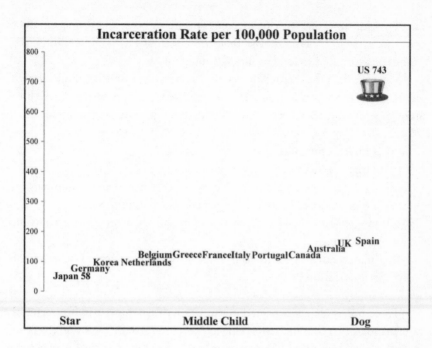

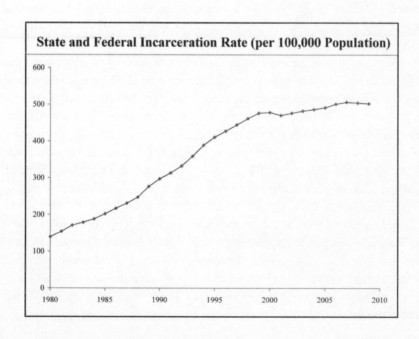

rate, but as it turns out, only 6.4 percent of state and federal prisoners in 2005 were noncitizens.[35] This means that the enormous US incarceration rate cannot be attributed to legal or illegal immigrants.

So where does the soaring incarceration rate come from? Breaking it down, we see that it is due to a combination of a number of factors that work as a hierarchy in which the levels are inextricably tied to one another, as follows:

(a) a higher crime rate,
(b) a higher rate of reporting committed crimes,
(c) a greater likelihood that police will interview and arrest criminals,
(d) a higher rate of incarceration for convicted criminals,
(e) longer sentences for convicted criminals than in most other countries,[36] and
(f) higher rates of recidivism (repeat offending) for those criminals released from prison.

Three policy changes enacted in the 1980s drove this rise in incarceration rate: mandatory minimum sentencing laws, "Three Strikes" laws, and the criminalization of drug usage. The Sentencing Reform Act of 1984 spurred the mandatory minimum sentence laws that followed; Three Strikes policies were enacted into law in the 1990s in twenty-three states; and federal laws like the Anti-Drug Abuse Act of 1986 and the 1988 Omnibus Anti-Drug Abuse Act criminalized drug usage.

Mandatory minimum sentencing laws were established with the positive goal of eliminating judicial bias so criminals convicted of the same crime would get reasonably similar sentences regardless of race, income, or other factors. As it turned out, these laws were largely used for drug and weapons offenses and, according to one lawyers' group, served as a powerful bargaining chip "in order to obtain guilty pleas and cooperation from defendants."[37] Whether intended or not, one result was more guilty pleas; in 2002, for example, an astounding 97.1 percent of charged offenses resulted in guilty pleas and, thus, in increased incarceration.[38]

Three Strikes laws, also known as habitual offender laws, both in the United States and elsewhere, have succeeded in costing huge amounts of public money to incarcerate low-level criminals. It's also important to note that these are state laws, currently enacted in twenty-five states, which leaves twenty-five states without such laws, and that the laws vary from state to state. Again, it's a mark of America's federal system that there is not uniformity on every issue across the nation.

Canada repealed its habitual offender law after a review by the Law Commission found that the application was erratic and often being applied against nonviolent offenders.[39] Similar results were observed in California, which passed a Three Strikes law in 1994 and saw a majority of those incarcerated under it to be nonviolent offenders; it is why voters approved Proposition 36 in 2000, providing for drug treatment instead of life in prison for most of those convicted of possessing drugs. Because drug treatment programs are far cheaper than prison sentences with no chance of parole, Proposition 36 was estimated to have saved taxpayers $2.50 for every $1 invested.[40] But even a shift to drug treatment programs was not enough to reduce California prison populations for the US Supreme Court, which, in a 2011 decision, held that prison overcrowding in California was unconstitutional and mandated a prisoner-release program.[41]

Three Strikes—and Really Out

In 2000 Gary Ewing was arrested for shoplifting three golf clubs worth a total of about $1,200. He was convicted of felony grand theft and, based on his previous convictions for burglary and robbery with a knife, received a sentence of twenty-five years to life under California's Three Strikes law. In fact, the sentence he received for shoplifting golf clubs was the same as what Mr. Ewing might have received had he been convicted of rape or murder. He challenged this conviction as being grossly disproportionate to the crime. The US Supreme Court ruled that his sentence was not excessive. Writing for the majority, Justice O'Conner asserted that the Three Strikes law represented a policy decision to isolate career criminals; the dissenting judges claimed Ewing's sentence violated the Eighth Amendment's restrictions on cruel and unusual punishment, but this position did not prevail.

Several other factors need to be mentioned in connection with the rise in incarceration rates, although none are directly related to crime. One factor is the US Census Bureau's policy of counting the incarcerated residents in the town in which the prison is located. Since census data are used to draw con-

gressional and state legislative district lines, a prison can be a boon of disproportionate representation, especially to smaller, rural communities, many of
which have been in a rush to build prisons. As it turns out, in twenty-one counties in the United States, at least 21 percent of the population consists of prison
inmates.[42] In New York State, where forty thousand New York City residents
were housed in prisons outside the city and were being "counted" as residents
of the prison towns,[43] the legislature finally passed a 2010 law banning prison-
based gerrymandering to combat the misrepresentation. But in many other
states, prison building continues to be a desirable mechanism for funneling
public funds into an area and, it is hoped, thus spurring economic growth. And
prisons need to be filled.

The other factor is the trend toward private prisons, which have become
big business. The Corrections Corporation of America (CCA), owner-
operator of sixty-five facilities with more than eighty thousand beds, and the
GEO Group, with sixty-one facilities with a capacity of forty-nine thousand
offender beds, thrive as the prison population expands. The idea of running
prisons for-profit is not a new one. Jeremy Bentham, the innovative designer of
prisons in the eighteenth century, sought not only to create optimal prisons but
also to reap profits from constructing them.[44]

But for at least two reasons, the trend toward for-profit prisons is a troubling one. For one thing, these corporations step over the line in their lobbying
and substantial financial support for laws that would expand criminal judgments and incarceration; there, they are playing with public policy for private
profit. One example is Arizona's Bill 1070, passed in 2010, the highly contro-
versial anti-immigrant law in the drafting of which CCA was involved.[45] Or,
in a more egregious example, Pennsylvania judge Mark Ciavarella was convicted of taking more than $1 million in kickbacks from a private company
that built and maintained a local youth detention facility.[46] The judge "earned"
this kickback by sending kids to juvenile detention and, upon judicial review,
hundreds of his juvenile convictions were overturned.

Even more fundamentally, there is no evidence that the for-profit companies
provide better service for less money, as their marketing campaigns claim. In fact,
the nonpartisan General Accounting Office (GAO) conducted a metastudy of
prisons in five states and found that there is no clear evidence that private prisons
demonstrate cost savings or higher quality compared to public prisons.[47]

Perhaps most troubling of all is another for-profit trend in prisons—the
fortunes being made by using prisoner labor. For pennies an hour,[48] with no
fear of workers striking and no need to pay benefits, companies get cheap

prison labor that they don't have to worry about laying off during a business downturn or a recession. Prisoners are the perfect "just-in-time" laborers and have actually displaced manufacturing and even unionized public sector jobs in some locations[49]—most notably when US Technologies sold its plant in Austin, Texas, and opened production in a Texas prison. Prisoners work at jobs ranging from manufacturing to data entry; in eight states, they have access to social security numbers and are thus handling sensitive personal information that could potentially be used for identity fraud.[50] Prisoners themselves barely profit from their labor. After allocations for federal, state, and local taxes, for room and board payments to the state, for federal victims funds and other costs, most prisoners keep less than one-half of what they earn.

One more point about the prison population in the United States: it is impossible to ignore the racial and class profile of those in jail. Nationally, African American men experience nearly seven times the incarceration rate of Caucasians and more than twice the rate for Hispanics; African American women experience nearly four times the incarceration rate of Caucasians and more than twice that of Hispanics.[51] In fact, African Americans have a higher incarceration rate in all fifty states than Caucasians while in some states, like Florida, Arkansas, Georgia, and Louisiana, Hispanics experience lower rates than Caucasians.[52] One analyst has noted that by the mid-1990s, "roughly one in three young black men were under the 'supervision' of the criminal justice system—that is, in a jail or prison, on probation or parole, or under pretrial release."[53] Unfortunately, the tendency for minority groups to have higher incarceration rates is not restricted to the United States; the United Kingdom, Canada, and Australia have experienced comparatively high rates of incarceration for minority groups as well.[54]

The racial makeup of inmates reflects arrest rates and sentencing rates; it is less clear that it reflects real crime rates. For example, 94 percent of inmates sentenced for drug crimes in New York are African American or Hispanic while surveys indicate that Caucasians are involved in narcotics at similar rates.[55] Presumably, Caucasians involved in narcotics are not caught or prosecuted as frequently, or they have better legal representation. Sentencing laws also played a clear role in this racial bias. From 1986 to 2010, the sentencing guidelines for defendants caught with five hundred grams of powder cocaine received the same punishment as defendants convicted of possessing only five grams of crack cocaine, a form of cocaine more associated with African Americans than with Caucasians.[56] This disparity was partially addressed with the Fair Sentencing Act of 2010, which eliminated the five-year mandatory minimum sentencing for crack cocaine possession and reduced, but did not eliminate, this disparity in sentencing between cocaine users and crack users.

Finally, in spite of this incredible investment in prisons, Americans' confidence in their police and justice system ranks only average in our competitor group.[57]

TO ATTACK OR BE ATTACKED

When we turn our attention to external safety issues, it's important to note that for our competitor group as a whole, many of the international political structures and security arrangements that determine how they deal with the external world were established in the aftermath of World War II and the Cold War. Many of the nations in our group were battlefields of the war. Since that time, our competitors have not been invaded or attacked by other nations, and only South Korea, which is technically still at war with North Korea, is under the presumed threat of attack. At the same time, many of the countries in our group have been involved in military engagements through either the United Nations or NATO, although the fighting has been on the soil of other countries.

In short, except for South Korea, our competitor group has been relatively free from the risk of invasion or attack by other countries. Still, many have been plagued by terrorist threats—especially the United Kingdom, with its Northern Ireland situation; Spain, with its Basque terrorists; France, with the Algerian terrorists who carried out the 1995 Paris metro bombings; Italy, with its political "revolutionaries" who were responsible for the kidnapping and killing of Prime Minister Aldo Moro; Japan, with the sarin gas attack in Tokyo; and the United States, with the Oklahoma City bombing. More recently, there has been the wave of large-scale terrorist attacks, most notably, of course, the attacks of September 11, 2001, that killed nearly three thousand people, the 2004 commuter-train bombing in Madrid, and the 2005 London bombings.

The success of these terrorist attacks is a function of the skill and intensity of the attackers as well as the quality of the defense. These attacks and the precautions nations take to counter them have affected daily life in countries around the world—from lengthy airport security checks to bomb-sniffing dogs in malls to bag checks in museums, at sporting events, and at amusement parks. By contrast, 9/11 was the trigger for unleashing the massive American war machine in Afghanistan, and it later became an excuse for invading Iraq.

The post–World War II structures like the United Nations and the NATO alliance that have linked our competitor countries together militarily with the United States nevertheless leave the lead role to America. We serve as the primary arsenal, the main fighting force, and the self-proclaimed protector. That leadership is evidenced in America's prominent position in NATO, its nuclear weapons program, one ongoing war (as of this writing), its leading role in the recent Iraq War and subsequent occupation, and its decades-long troop commitments around the world.

In some specific cases, the protection is partially spelled out. Following defeat in World War II, for example, Japan was occupied by the United States, which imposed a constitution that forbade the country from maintaining a standing army or waging war. Since the end of the occupation, a series of treaties have further secured America's military presence, consisting, as of 2009, of 35,688 military personnel in eighty-five facilities, plus 5,500 civilians.[58] For this large military expenditure, Japan provides compensation, the "sympathy budget." It's not unlike what a mercenary does; that is, the United States provides protective services for a negotiated price, though in this case the negotiations should be more transparent.

South Korea is another US "protectorate." American soldiers comprised the largest single element of the United Nations force supporting the South in the Korean War of the 1950s, and we have continued to maintain a major presence on the southern side of the Korean Demilitarized Zone that still divides North and South Korea. That force comprises some twenty-five thousand troops,[59] and their presence was formally recognized in 1978 with the establishment of a Combined Forces Command. An American four-star general commands the combined US and Republic of Korea forces.

All the other competitor countries are members of NATO, the North Atlantic Treaty Organization, except Australia, for obvious geographic reasons, although it is a contact member of the alliance.[60] NATO's military operations are directed by the chairman of the NATO Military Committee and are split into two strategic commands, both headed by a senior US officer assisted by staff drawn from across NATO. The chairmanship of the alliance rotates every three years, the position typically being filled by very senior military officers of the NATO countries.[61] This alliance has huge ramifications for any comparison of military forces and expenditures.

Evidence that European countries may be showing a willingness to assume more of the responsibility for their own defense is Eurocorps, a multinational standing army of sixty thousand troops under the control of the European Union. Eurocorps was deployed in Bosnia, Kosovo, and Afghanistan.

Still, the US war machine gets a lot of practice. In just the beginning of the twenty-first century, our military was involved in major conflicts in Afghanistan starting in 2001, Iraq starting in 2003, Haiti in 2004, and Libya in 2011. No other country on our list has had anywhere near the same level of military engagement in foreign conflicts. The only one that comes close is the United Kingdom, which has fought alongside the United States in Iraq and Afghanistan, and which maintains forces in Kenya, Germany, Canada, Brunei, Belize, Cyprus, Gibraltar, Northern Ireland, Sierra Leone, Pakistan, and the Falkland Islands. French forces have been involved in the last decade on a much smaller scale in conflicts involving former colonies (Chad, the Ivory Coast, and Haiti). Australia has sent small forces to support US-led efforts in Iraq and Afghanistan, but in the last decade it has played a major role only in INTERFET, the United Nations force in East Timor, a former colony of Portugal, which also maintains a force there. Many of the countries on our competitor list have had minor roles in NATO, in UN deployments, or in such US-led conflicts as Iraq and Afghanistan, but few of the competitor countries maintain major forces or have had other large conflicts outside of these events. By contrast, American troops in NATO countries alone number some eighty thousand.

This activist military role is nothing new for the United States. In 1823, the Monroe Doctrine, articulated fewer than ten years after America's second war with the British ended, stated that any attempts by European powers to colonize in the Western Hemisphere would be considered an act of aggression against the United States. So the nation has never been shy about taking up arms, even when the United States isn't directly threatened.

Given its active war machine and dominant position as the world's sole military superpower, it is little surprise that the United States has a much higher rate of military expenditure per GDP than its competitors. In absolute terms, the numbers are astounding: the US military budget is more than the military expenditures of all its competitors combined in spite of the total population in the competitor countries being nearly twice that of the United States.[62] This massive American military budget represents about 43 percent of all military spending worldwide. Enormous as it is, the budget doesn't include such other defense-related spending as FBI counterterrorism efforts, State Department foreign arms sales, Energy Department defense-related projects, NASA and satellites, veterans benefits, and the interest being paid on debt associated with military expenditures. Nevertheless, the influence of the military can easily be seen in the fact that the six largest recipients of US government contracts in 2008 and 2009 were all in the defense industry.[63]

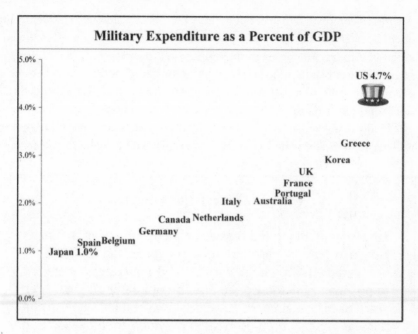

In comparative terms, the United States spends a higher percent of its GDP—4.7 percent—on military expenditures than any of the competitors. This current rate is significantly higher than the 3 percent America spent in 2000,[64] a reflection of the costs of the ongoing war in Afghanistan and increased troop deployments in the Middle East.

WHERE DOES THE MONEY GO?

Since the US military "protects" much of the rest of the world, it makes sense to examine what its huge budget is paying for.

The first cost, of course, is to support its troops. Like most of its competitors, the United States has an all-volunteer army. Mandatory military service among competitor nations is limited to Greece and South Korea; Germany, Italy, Portugal, and Spain eliminated conscription early in the twenty-first century. Of the twelve competitor countries with volunteer enlistment, the United States has the second highest percentage of its population in active duty, behind France, while its overall military enrollment rate (active duty, reserves, and paramilitary) is slightly higher than the average competitor.[65] As with so many aspects of American society, race plays a role in military service as well. African

Americans comprise 17 percent of military personnel[66] although they represent only 12 percent of the total US population. While some view this overrepresentation of African Americans in the military as a positive, since the military is often a sponsor of education and is an educational institution itself, others see it as a negative reflection that African Americans, having fewer career and educational options than others, are being steered toward military service.

In any case, the fact that America spends so much more per GDP on the military than its competitor countries isn't explained by the higher percentage

When Is a Citizen Not a Citizen?

Yaser Hamdi identified himself immediately as an American citizen when he was captured in Afghanistan in 2001. He was detained at Guantanamo Bay and then later transferred to prisons inside the United States. For nearly the first three years of his detainment, no charges were filed against him nor was any legal representation provided, thereby violating both the United States Constitution and the Geneva Convention. The Supreme Court ruled in *Hamdi v. Rumsfeld* that his rights, along with those of the other non-American detainees, had indeed been violated and ordered due process for determining that detainees are enemy combatants.[67] Hamdi was released in 2004 after agreeing to renounce his American citizenship, to be deported to Saudi Arabia, and to limit his travel. Most important for America, he agreed never to sue the government over his years of illegal detention. Other competitor countries faced with terrorist attacks or inhabited by terrorist cells—including Germany, France, Spain, and the United Kingdom—have relied on police investigations, arrests of suspects, and trials to bring suspects to justice.

Guantanamo Bay continues to represent an embarrassing black eye to America's claim to be a leader in pursuing justice, although in 2008 the US Supreme Court finally ruled in the *Boumediene v. Bush* case that detainees are entitled to the rights of habeas corpus guaranteed in the Constitution.[68]

of its population serving in the military. Rather, the major expense differential is due to military research and development. The Pentagon spends about $28,000 per soldier per year on research and development, about four to five times the amount spent by Europeans.[69] This massive investment has resulted in the development of the first atomic bomb, the first hydrogen bomb, and inventions with direct civilian application like Global Positioning Systems and the Internet.

The United States exports a significant amount of military equipment. In 2010, it exported more than the rest of its competitor countries combined, a reflection of America's economic size, defense industry technology, and its vision of the defense role it sees itself playing in the world. While the second-largest exporter, Russia, is not on our competitor list, other major exporters are on our competitor list; Germany is the world's third-largest exporter and France is the fourth largest. The largest defense importers on our list are Australia, the world's fourth-largest importer, and South Korea, the fifth-largest arms importer, although all competitors were vastly outstripped by the world's largest defense importers, India, Pakistan, and Singapore.[70]

The United States was the first country to develop nuclear weapons, in cooperation with Canada and the United Kingdom, and it is the only nation to have used them on another country, having bombed Japan's Hiroshima and Nagasaki during World War II. It maintains a nuclear stockpile today of some 8,500 weapons, greatly reduced from the more than 32,000 nuclear weapons maintained at the height of the Cold War.[71] The only other countries on our list with nuclear weapons are France, with 300, and the United Kingdom, with 225 nuclear warheads.[72]

As with other aspects of US military operations, the reach of its nuclear weapons spreads to many of the competitors in the group. American nuclear weapons were stored in and deployed from Canada until 1984, Greece until 2001,[73] and are currently stored in "shared arrangements" with Belgium, Germany, Italy, and the Netherlands—as well as with a noncompetitor, Turkey. This shared arrangement enables those countries to practice handling and delivering the nuclear bombs and to adapt their warplanes to deliver nuclear bombs while still qualifying as nuclear-free because the weapons are officially US property.[74] Among our competitor nations, only France supports continued deployment of US nuclear weapons in Europe, while three competitors currently hosting American nuclear weapons—Germany, Belgium, and the Netherlands—as well as the United States itself all support the removal of the American nuclear weapons from Europe.[75]

In addition to its direct military forces, the United States employs large numbers of mercenaries for its overseas work. These contractors are estimated to cost up to six times more than an average soldier and so provide no cost savings.[76] Their "advantage" is their ambiguous legal status: they can act with immunity from prosecution by the host country to which they have been deployed and will not be charged with crimes by their client, the CIA. In 2011, the State Department announced that 5,500 mercenaries would be hired for a protection force in Iraq from Triple Canopy and Global Strategies Group in contracts worth more than $2 billion for five years.[77]

ALL WE ARE SAYING IS GIVE PEACE A CHANCE

So, is the vast expenditure and the US-led protection of the safety of nations achieving its goal? That's hard to answer. World peace, a universal and pretty constant goal of humankind, may be more difficult to measure than to achieve. One organization, however, has set itself that task.

The Global Peace Index (GPI),[78] the brainchild of Australian entrepreneur Steve Killelea, seeks to measure just how peaceful nations are in relation to one another. A product of the Institute for Economics and Peace, the index uses data from the International Institute of Strategic Studies, the World Bank, various UN offices and peace institutes, and the Economist Intelligence Unit[79] to measure a group of twenty-three indicators—namely:

Level of organized conflict	Armed services personnel
Weapons imports	Military expenditure
Number of conflicts fought	Jailed population
Deaths from conflict (internal)	Potential for terrorist acts
Level of violent crime	Political instability
Military capability/sophistication	Disrespect for human rights
Number of homicides	UN Peacekeeping funding
Number of heavy weapons	Number of displaced people
Neighboring country relations	Weapons exports
Deaths from conflict (external)	Violent demonstrations
Access to weapons	Perceived criminality in society
Security officers and police	

The GPI rating is subjective in its weightings and selection of indicators, many of which are open to broad interpretations. It is instructive nevertheless that the United States rates worse than any of the countries on our competitor

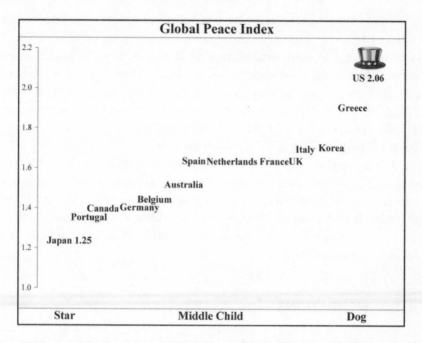

Global Peace Index

2.2	
2.0	US 2.06
1.8	Greece
1.6	Italy Korea / Spain Netherlands France UK
1.4	Australia / Belgium / Canada Germany / Portugal
1.2	Japan 1.25
1.0	

Star   Middle Child   Dog

list while Japan rates the best. The major components in this poor rating are America's high incarceration rate, high potential for terrorist attacks, access to weapons, and disrespect for human life.

Equally instructive is the index's breakdown of states within the United States. According to the GPI, the most peaceful states are Maine, New Hampshire, Vermont, and Minnesota, while the least peaceful are Louisiana, Tennessee, Nevada, and Florida. These state-level rankings correlate closely with economic opportunities, education, and health and are independent of the party in power in the separate statehouses and state legislatures.[80] Incarceration and homicide rates in the most peaceful states are roughly one-fifth the rates of the most dangerous states and are close to the rates found in the European competition.

The bottom line is that the United States is by far the least safe of the competitor nations in terms of both internal security and external conflict. Internally, the homicide and incarceration rates are off the charts compared to the rest of the competition. Externally, the United States spends more on defense than all its competitor countries combined.[81] The conclusion is inescapable that both the internal lack of security and the vast spending on external safety are unsustainable.

While there is no question that America plays a unique role in the world's balance of military power, it simply cannot continue to spend on external defense more than twice what it spent in 2000 and about 20 percent of its entire federal budget and hope to remain fiscally solvent. America needs to pare back its overseas military operations, to partner more effectively with allies, and to gain control of the military-industrial complex that President Eisenhower warned of in 1961, the behemoth that continues to encourage America's military excesses and profits from them.

It is ironic that Japan, one of the aggressors of World War II, has enjoyed under US protection an era of minimal internal and external violence that has enabled it to reduce its military expenditures and to institute policies and laws that make it a safer place to live than the United States. Indeed, that is true of all the competitor nations the United States "helps" with defense, and there are lessons to be learned from it.

RECOMMENDATIONS

How can Americans be safer and more secure? The data drive five recommendations, three having to do with internal security and two having to do with our external defense.

Gun control tops the list of changes that would make a difference in Americans' safety. Few aspects of American society are more out of line with the rest of the world and certainly with our competitor group than our protection of gun ownership. There is zero chance of a constitutional change or of wholesale legislation to ban guns, but it is not unreasonable to demand that all gun users be licensed and, as is true in Canada, that license applicants must pass a firearms safety course.[82] We do it for drivers' licenses and for many occupations considered dangerous, and we should do no less for gun owners.

It also makes sense to require background checks on all would-be gun purchasers, not just those buying from licensed dealers, and to halt the legal sale of assault weapons. There is only one reason to buy an assault weapon: to kill human beings. Those nostalgic for the days of the Boston Tea Party notwithstanding, there are other ways in our democracy to overturn government actions. The Second Amendment does not empower citizens to build nuclear bombs in their backyards and it similarly need not sanction gun owners acting like infantry personnel in their neighborhoods.

In addition, the United States should develop a national database for tracking guns, gun parts, and ammunition. All the European Union countries on our list do so under EU Directive 2008/51/EC, and this provides a common basis for laws affecting gun ownership.

Second, *put justice back into the prison system*. The Three Strikes laws and the criminalization of drug offenders have resulted in an explosion in the American incarceration rate. The majority of these prisoners are nonviolent offenders whose damage to society is far less than the costs of imprisonment. In Michigan, prison costs are 20 percent of the state's general funds,[83] and the state spends more on prisons than on higher education. This is one reason why Michigan, like Texas, has begun supporting community approaches for drug offenders rather than prison sentences.

The Three Strikes laws need to be dramatically modified to distinguish between violent and nonviolent offenders. For one thing, the practice is inhumane. For another, the return on investment for twenty-five-year sentences for nonviolent criminals is negative. Nationally, states need to recognize what Canada learned decades ago—that simply locking away habitual lawbreakers will crowd our jails with nonviolent offenders.

The criminalization of drug offenders is not just costly, it is also ineffective. The United States continues to have a rate of marijuana and cocaine use that is two to four times higher than most other competitor countries,[84] so clearly the criminalization of drugs is not having its intended effect. In fact, at every level, it is difficult to find a better example of a failed policy than America's drug policy. At the same time, the argument that legalization will lead to greater drug usage is not consistent with the facts.

Portugal is a competitor country that offers an intriguing alternative. In 2001, Portugal decriminalized the use and possession of heroin, cocaine, marijuana, LSD, and other illicit street drugs and focused on treatment and prevention rather than incarceration. The net result was a decline in overdoses and in new HIV infections related to heroine usage. This may be one reason why Europe is more broadly moving away from the criminalization of drug use and toward prevention and treatment policies for some drugs including marijuana.[85]

Third, we need to *remove the perverse incentives* that exist for expanding the prison system—namely, prison gerrymandering and the for-profit prison business. Prison gerrymandering both falsifies representation and provides a financial incentive to increase the prison population. The for-profit prison business is rife with conflicts of interest and the potential for subverting the public good for private profit. Considering that the for-profit prison model is by no means more cost-effective, there seems little reason to pursue or replicate the model.

Externally, we need first to see a *strategic and operational drawdown* of fortress America as the world's watchdog. The United States cannot and should not be the primary defense mechanism around the world, a hired set of mercenaries looking for opportunities to leverage its strength either for direct gain or in response to requests. A model exists for a first step toward this, and that is the NATO intervention in Libya in 2011. There, the United States was neither the perceived initiator of the intervention nor the first to pull the trigger. It acted rather as one among equals, one player in a partnership of allies. The Libya multilateral response model could serve as an exemplar of a more balanced approach to the world's safety and world peace.

In addition, given the economic scale of the European Union, the time has come for that entity to make a significantly greater contribution of finances and troops to NATO so that the United States can reduce or even withdraw from its European commitments. At the same time, we need to rethink our commitments in Japan and South Korea. If we are operating as a protector of these countries, then the financial terms should be explicit; we should evaluate the costs of our deployments and bill those nations appropriately. If the two countries are not willing to pay for our protective services, then we need to rethink why we are spending billions of dollars there.

Lastly, for its own fiscal solvency, the United States needs to *reduce military expenses by operating more efficiently*. As of this writing, the United States is trying to fight a war in Afghanistan, has recently pulled out of Iraq, and also has scattered more than one hundred thousand troops across Europe and Asia. To repeat: this expense comprises 20 percent of the federal budget and represents nearly one-half of the world's expenditures on defense.

Among the steps that could be taken to operate more efficiently is to eliminate no-bid contracting in which there is no competition to keep costs down, a process that undermines the free-market system and virtually guarantees that the government will be overcharged. No-bid contracting flies in the face of all business best practices; no private corporation worth its salt would ever indulge in it as a regular habit. Instead, standard operating procedure should be to issue a request for proposal (RFP) to competing suppliers and review from among three or more to select the best quality product/service at the lowest price.

At the same time, we need an updated version of the Truman Committee to investigate waste and cost overruns[86] and to answer President Roosevelt's demand that there must not be "a single war millionaire created in the United States as a result of this world disaster." That 1941 investigation by a then little-known US senator from Missouri saved billions of taxpayer dollars and reformed the national defense program. Today the scale can only be greater while the outsourcing of services for security, logistics, and even food and transportation to private companies is troubling. For one thing, there is no logical reason why the US armed forces cannot meet its military, security, and even logistics needs within its own budget. Can't our military supply its own food services and transportation without relying on private companies, most of which are staffed by former military personnel?

In addition, outsourcing can lead to overbidding and price gouging. We have seen how the extensive use of contractors like Xe, formerly Blackwater, is far more expensive than seeing the operation through within the structure of our armed services. The contractors also undermine the US role and create legal ambiguities that could haunt the nation as a whole, as was certainly the case with Blackwater's mercenaries.

Chapter 3

THE RIGHT TO THE THREE RS: EDUCATION

If a nation expects to be ignorant and free, in a state of civi-
lization, it expects what never was and never will be.
—Thomas Jefferson (1743–1826)

Education is fundamental to the success of any country. It isn't simply that higher levels of education correlate to better health and greater wealth everywhere across the globe. It is also that education underlies the growth potential of a society and creates the foundation upon which cultural and economic achievements are constructed. As developed countries move from manufacturing economies to technology-driven economies, the importance of education continues to rise; the best-educated countries are optimally positioned for economic success while the least educated must resign themselves to fading global importance. Among the competitor countries on our list, the last few decades have seen rapid changes in education performance; some of the countries in the group have made vast improvements while others have stagnated. Those improving are well positioned for future economic strength; those falling behind clearly are not.

Education is so critical to development that it is one of only three factors used to compute the Human Development Reports compiled annually by the United Nations Development Program. Launched in 1990, the Human Development Reports track the extension of human capabilities in countries at all stages of development, from the poorest to the wealthiest, measuring that progress in terms of education, health, and wealth. The reports use two education measurements: the mean years of schooling (defined as the average number of years of education received by people twenty-five and older[1]) and the expected years of schooling (defined as the number of years of schooling that a child currently of school-entrance age can expect to receive[2]).

99

These two metrics enable comparisons of educational performance in terms of time committed to the educational experience. This discussion will also look at the length of time spent in learning, but we'll bring a particular focus to that measure and will introduce measures of quality as well.

First, since education naturally divides into separate phases, from preprimary to primary to secondary to tertiary to graduate education, we'll do the same. Our discussion will be split, however, into two parts. One will focus on preprimary, primary, and secondary education—all of which except preprimary are usually the responsibility of the public education system. The other part will be dedicated to tertiary education. Because so much government effort and research have been focused at the lower levels of education, there is far more data available there than for tertiary education. Since graduate education (education following an undergraduate degree) is the exception, not the norm, for most students in all countries, it will not be examined in this discussion.

Second, whenever possible, we will try to avoid using total population measures, focusing instead on metrics that represent the most recent educational accomplishments, which naturally reflect the most current state of the educational system. The reason is that if we measure the entire population's educational level, we include not only the generation that is currently being educated but older generations as well. That gives us an outdated and somewhat skewed picture. Because this book aims to see where America is right now versus competitor nations, we'll put more emphasis on the expected years of schooling rather than the mean years of school, concentrating on today's students, not on total population.

When we examine the mean years of schooling for current total population in our competitor group, the United States and Germany are the leaders, with Portugal lagging far behind. But remember: this metric reflects the educational accomplishments of adults over the age of twenty-five, many of whom completed their education decades ago. If we turn to the other metric used by the United Nations, the expected number of years of schooling, reflecting the experience of a child entering school now, we find a very different story. The United States is now a laggard, along with Germany, Portugal, and Japan, far behind leading countries like Australia and South Korea.

The two different results tell us something fundamental about American education. While today's older Americans were generally better educated than the competition, this advantage has dissipated. The advantage enjoyed by older Americans was generated by the fact that, as late as the 1930s, "America was virtually alone in providing universally free and accessible secondary education"[3]

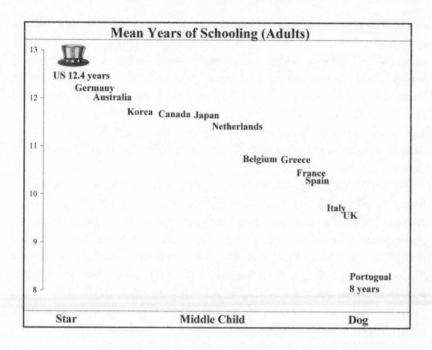

Mean Years of Schooling (Adults)

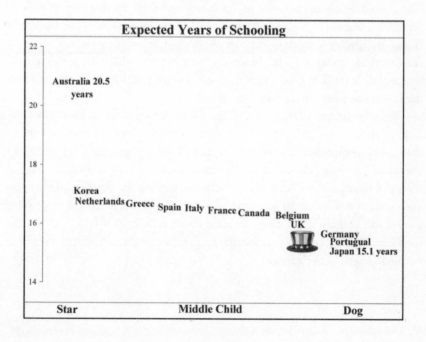

Expected Years of Schooling

and by the aggressive support of higher education provided by the G.I. Bill following World War II. (The G.I. Bill, also known as the Servicemen's Readjustment Act of 1944, provided college or vocational education for returning World War II veterans and was later extended to veterans of conflicts including those in Korea, Vietnam, Iraq, and Afghanistan.) Other countries have caught up to America's educational advantage, and some have now surpassed it. US high school graduation rates confirm this conclusion; the rate rose from less than 10 percent in 1910 to about 77 percent in 1970—and has remained at or near that level ever since![4]

Why? What has gone so wrong in these past decades that the United States has slipped from being the world leader to being passed up by other countries so that it must now play catch-up with its competitors—and isn't doing a very good job of catching up. It is no secret that the United States is struggling with education. *A Nation at Risk*,[5] the landmark 1983 report by the National Commission on Excellence in Education, concluded that America has "squandered the gains in student achievement made in the wake of the Sputnik challenge. Moreover, we have dismantled essential support systems which helped make those gains possible. We have, in effect, been committing an act of unthinking, unilateral educational disarmament. Our society and its educational institutions seem to have lost sight of the basic purposes of schooling, and of the high expectations and disciplined effort needed to attain them." By 1989, President George H. W. Bush announced an educational goal for American students—namely, ranking first in the world in math and science by the year 2000. The goal was not achieved—not even close. Clearly, our students and our nation have fallen far short!

The comparative data in this chapter offer an explanation for the decline in US educational performance. The data compare American performance to that of our competitor countries in terms of both the quantity and quality of the education being delivered in school. As throughout this book, a range of metrics identifies the discrepancies between the United States and its more successful competitors; in so doing, the data point us toward the important lessons the United States needs to learn about education if it is to create the workforce it will need for every individual's fulfillment and for the future economic strength of the nation.

EDUCATIONAL QUALITY

We'll measure quality in two ways: first by looking at the level of education attained, then by comparing how well students at various levels have learned—that is, how much knowledge they have absorbed as measured by international academic tests.

We'll start by looking at the rates of secondary school graduation.

When we do so, we see that the United States has an above-average rate of people with at least a secondary education (about 88 percent of adults ages twenty-five to thirty-four); Korea and Canada lead the way on this, and Portugal falls far behind the other countries.[6] (It should be noted that there are no data on this metric for Japan, one of the leading countries with regard to educational performance.) How does that above-average rate of secondary education translate into educational quality? In other words, how much do American students know compared to the students in other countries?

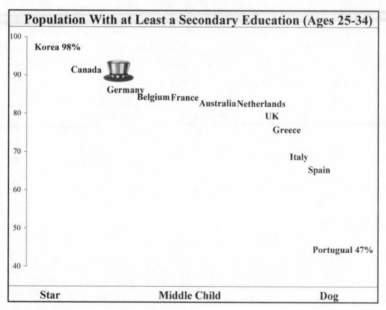

There are many international tests given to compare student performance. This discussion will draw on three, with a major focus on one in particular, the Programme for International Student Assessment (PISA). This is a worldwide evaluation of fifteen-year-old pupils' scholastic performance in math, science, and reading. It is administered in more than seventy countries, including all the countries on our competition list, and it tests only students in school, so dropouts and home-schooled students do not affect outcomes. The most recent PISA as of this writing was in 2009.

The Trends in International Mathematics and Science Study (TIMSS) test is an international assessment of the mathematics and science knowledge of fourth and eighth graders in forty-eight countries, including about one-half the countries in our comparison (Australia, Germany, Italy, Japan, Korea, the Netherlands, the United Kingdom, and the United States took some part of the exam; Australia, Italy, Japan, the United Kingdom, and the United States took all parts of the exam). The last TIMSS assessment for which figures are available was in 2007.

Finally, the Progress in International Reading Literacy Study (PIRLS) administers tests to fourth graders in thirty-five countries, including about one-half of the countries in our comparison (Belgium, Canada, France, Germany, Italy, the Netherlands, Spain, the United Kingdom, and the United States). The most recently available data is from the 2006 PIRLS exam.

While there is a strong correlation among the results from all three of these data sources, PISA is the most relevant for our purposes because it covers all the countries on which we seek to gather competitive intelligence and is the most comprehensive in terms of subjects covered.

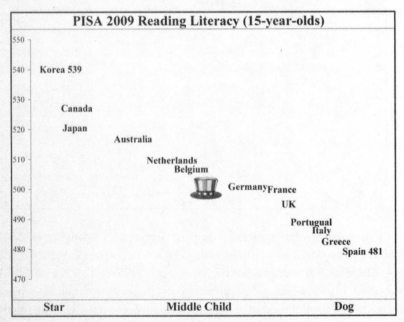

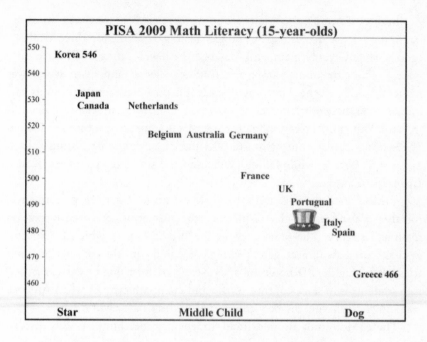

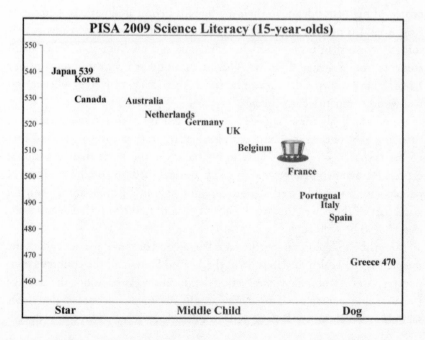

In the PISA tests, the results are consistent across all measures—reading, math, and science: Korea, Japan, and Canada ranked in the top three in all categories while Greece, Spain, and Italy had the lowest rating in all three categories.[7] The correlation among the reading, science, and math scores was higher than 88 percent. The United States is depressingly consistent in its performance on these tests, ranking seventh in reading, ninth in science, and tenth in math. When the average of all three scores is computed, we see the United States in tenth place out of fourteen countries, besting only Portugal, Italy, Spain, and Greece, while falling far behind the top three countries, Korea, Japan, and Canada.

TIMSS confirms this average-to-below-average American performance; fourth-grade and eighth-grade American students performed about average on math and science. The same goes for the PIRLS test, in which US fourth-graders scored about average in reading compared with the competitor countries also taking the PIRLS exam. This average performance by current American students is in stark contrast to the mid-twentieth century when America was known for having the best-educated workforce in the world.[8]

The TIMSS study also measured student attitudes. Students were divided into groups according to their level of confidence in their math skills—low, medium, and high confidence. Thirty-one percent of American students expressed high confidence in their math ability, compared with 10 percent of Korean and 6 percent of Japanese students. Yet the American students performed worse than both the high-confidence and medium-confidence math students from Korea and Japan.[9] This isn't unique; many other points of our research have shown a disconnect between America's perceived excellence and real-world competitive intelligence.

One thing all these knowledge scores tell us is that our students are spending a lot of time in school with less return on their investment—or that of the taxpayers—certainly a far lower bang for the buck than we should expect. Remember that we score above average in terms of the number of people with a secondary education. So a lot of young people are spending a good part of their lives in school without obtaining the knowledge and skills they should be acquiring.

But the PISA scores in particular tell us a good deal more. They reflect the inequalities in wealth distribution in the United States and the country's high poverty rate. As noted by the National Education Association, the average PISA reading score in the United States for higher-income schools—that is, for schools in which fewer than 10 percent of students receive a free or reduced-price lunch—exceeded that of all our competitor countries. Meanwhile, the average PISA reading score for lower-income American schools, those in which more than three-quarters of students receive a free or reduced-price lunch, was far lower than any of our comparison countries. It is not surprising to learn that wealthier students outperform poorer students, but this extremely large disparity in performance among American students is of great concern because of what it implies about social mobility, which we will discuss in greater detail in chapter 5. More critical to this discussion is the fact that the PISA scores by American students were highly influenced by their parents' backgrounds. The influence was not just greater than in all our competitor nations, but it was also greater than in every single OECD country. American students who move up one socioeconomic level would earn on average sixty points more in science, while students in Japan, Italy, Canada, and Korea who did the same would gain fewer than forty more PISA points.[10]

Educational performance inequalities have also been identified in terms of race. On the PISA reading scores in the United States in 2009, Asian American students averaged higher than students of every other country, while non-Hispanic Caucasian Americans scored the equivalent of second in the overall ranking, just below Korea. By contrast, the average scores for Hispanics and African Americans were significantly lower than in the lowest country on our competition list. Nor is disparity in performance as a function of race limited to the PISA scores. On the National Assessment of Educational Progress (NAEPP), African American and Hispanic twelfth-graders scored about the same as Caucasian American eighth graders![11] This massive difference in performance by race is reflected in such other aspects of education as the attainment of college degrees.[12] President Obama has described these race and class-based differences as "morally unacceptable and economically untenable."[13]

The disparity in educational outcomes as a function of economics and race is mirrored also in geography. An excellent resource, *The Measure of America*, an undertaking of the American Human Development Project of the Social Science Research Council, charts the performance of different sections of the United States in education, health, and income.[14] It has been found, for example, that residents of Massachusetts and Connecticut are about twice as likely to have an undergraduate or a graduate degree as residents of Arkansas and West Virginia. It is sometimes possible to drill down and see these disparities even between different districts of the same city. For example, about 20 percent of the people living in the Fourth Congressional District in Chicago have an undergraduate degree, compared with about 50 percent in the Tenth

Congressional District only a few miles away. The Fourth District is more than 70 percent Hispanic, while the Tenth is about 80 percent Caucasian. Nationally, about 31 percent of Caucasians have undergraduate degrees, compared with 18 percent of African Americans, 13 percent of Hispanics and Native Americans, and nearly 50 percent of Asian Americans.

CAN I BUY AN A?

What are Americans spending, relative to other wealthy, developed nations, to achieve this unexceptional educational performance rating for our primary and secondary education? As it turns out, the average cost per student for primary and secondary education in the United States is considerably higher than in our competitor countries, and, adjusted for inflation, the spending per student has more than doubled from 1970 to 2007.[15] In 2010, the average cost per primary school student in the United States was $10,229—24 percent higher than in the next most expensive country, the United Kingdom.[16] At the same time, the average cost per secondary student in the United States was $11,301—10 percent higher than in the next most expensive country, the Netherlands.[17] This spending has been ramped up over time with an inflation-

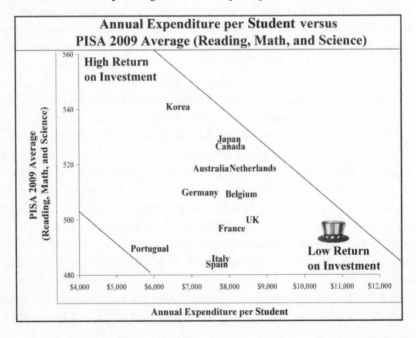

adjusted 73 percent increase in public spending per student between 1980 and 2005. As in the health sector, the issue is not that Americans don't spend enough on education; rather, the issue is that the money doesn't appear to be spent well. If we think of the PISA score as a measure of the return on the investment in primary and secondary education, we would conclude that the United States has by far the worst return on investment of any of the competitor countries and that Korea has one of the highest.

Public spending on education in the United States is 5.5 percent of the nation's GDP, a figure that is higher than all but two other countries on our list: Belgium and France.[18] Another metric on education expenditure, the percentage of all government expenditures that go to public education, shows the United States to have the second-highest rate, topped only by South Korea.[19]

As with so many of the topics discussed in this book, the state-to-state differences in per-pupil expenditure can be dramatic. New Jersey and Connecticut, for example, spend more than twice the amount per student as Utah, the lowest spending state. But state-by-state variations in spending don't by themselves explain educational outcomes. Utah and West Virginia, for example, record similar educational outcomes despite the fact that West Virginia spends about twice as much per student.

The bottom line, therefore, is that despite generous public investment in education, we are achieving only average performance at best in our primary and secondary education. That's an unacceptable return on investment, as is widely known and much discussed. One key discussion was that of the global management consulting firm McKinsey and Company. The McKinsey report, *How the World's Best School Systems Come Out on Top*,[20] cited three critical factors in successful school systems: (1) recruiting high-quality individuals into the teaching profession, (2) developing these individuals into effective teachers, and (3) ensuring that the system is able to deliver the best possible education for every child by starting education early and making it a major part of the day, by defining standards and establishing quality checks, and by targeting funding.

BRINGING IN TOP TEACHERS

When it comes to recruiting top talent for the teaching profession, South Korea, the education market Star, has set a standard that is tough to match. Prospective college students must take a national College Entrance Exam (like

America's SATs), and any students who want to be trained as primary school teachers must score in the top 5 percent! This means that Korean primary school teachers are the academic elite, who later go on to educate Korea's youngest, most impressionable children. The supply of primary school teachers is carefully managed so that graduates easily find jobs after completing their training.

For teachers in secondary education, Korea is less selective than for primary education. But its massive overproduction of teachers leads to fierce competition for finding secondary school positions. There are typically some twelve applicants for every secondary school position in Korea.

Another factor that can't be ignored in exploring the high quality of Korean school teachers, especially primary school teachers, is their elevated social status. Status draws more top talent so it is not surprising that in Korea, teaching is the most popular career choice among young Koreans.

Funneling top students into teaching is not specific to Korea. In three of the top school systems in the world—Singapore, Finland, and Korea—100 percent of candidate teachers come from the top third of students. In America, only 23 percent of new teachers come from the top third, and only 14 percent of the teachers in high-poverty schools came from the top third. In fact, nearly one-half of America's teachers come from the bottom third of college classes.[21]

There have been several attempts to change this ratio and turn top students into teachers in the United States—notably through such programs as Boston Teacher Residency, New York Teaching Fellows, Teach for America, and Chicago Teaching Fellows. Yet these programs, geared to graduates of so-called elite colleges, contribute in only a minor way to the overall American teacher population. Moreover, they suffer from high attrition rates and are not generally seen as a way to train a new generation of permanent teachers. For example, more than 80 percent of Teach for America recruits have left teaching by their fourth year[22] compared with attrition rates of from 40 to 50 percent over a similar time span for new teachers recruited from more traditional routes.[23] Even a 40–50 percent attrition rate is high and adds billions of dollars to the cost of training replacement teachers. Teacher attrition rates are not random; the rate is about 50 percent higher in poor schools than in wealthy schools.[24]

Of course, while status is important in attracting and retaining top talent, compensation is probably even more important. We originally used the national GDP per capita, defined as the ratio of the value of goods produced in a country by the population, as one of the two selection criterion for our competition. Within a country, workers who earn much more than the national GDP per capita are the better-compensated people in the country, while those earning less than one-half of the median income are usually considered to be below the poverty line. In 1970, the average American teacher made about 175 percent of the national GDP per capita, making the teaching profession a relatively well-compensated profession. By 2008, teachers earned roughly the same as the national GDP per capita, less than one-half that of lawyers and about one-third that of doctors.[25] Just look how this compares to the market Star, Korea: it pays its experienced primary school teachers about twice the national GDP per capita, while America's experienced primary school teachers earn slightly less than the national GDP per capita.[26] It's much the same at the secondary school level: experienced secondary school teachers in Korea make about twice their national GDP per capita, while in America they earn about the national average. With these comparatively low levels of compensation, it is not surprising that nearly 50 percent of new teachers in America leave the profession in the first five years, commonly citing low pay as a chief reason.[27]

In Korea, by contrast, the financial remuneration and the cultural respect accorded teachers help that nation maintain a teacher turnover rate (the per-

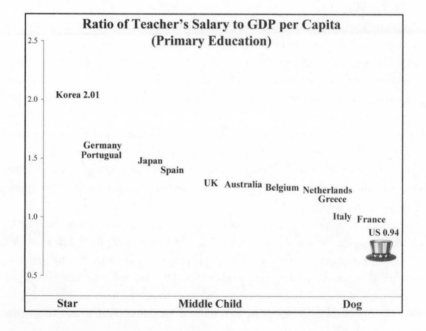

centage of teachers who are replaced annually) of 1 percent; in the United States, the rate is about 14 percent overall and 20 percent in the high-need schools.[28]

STARTING EARLY

It has been shown time and again that preprimary school enrollment is important to delivering the best possible education.[29] American students who participated in preschool education were 31 percent less likely to repeat a grade and 32 percent less likely to drop out of high school.[30] Moreover, the states with the highest rates of preprimary school enrollment—New Jersey, Massachusetts, and Connecticut, for example—also have some of the highest rates of adults with college educations. The state-by-state range of preschool enrollment rates is wide, from 28 percent in Nevada to 67 percent in New Jersey. Nevada, with the lowest rate of preprimary school education, also has the lowest rate of public high school graduation—only 52 percent. Preschool enrollment is also very often a function of parents' income, with US preschool enrollment rates being about 20 percent higher for children of parents earning more than $50,000 a year than for the children of parents earning less than $15,000 a year.[31]

Preschool offers other advantages besides its demonstrated benefits on the long-term education of children. For example, it has a major impact on projected crime rates. Nobel Prize–winner James Heckman has shown in a number of studies that investment in the early education of babies and young children from low-income communities yields a higher return on the investment than later schooling or job training.[32] American children who were randomly chosen from a low-income neighborhood to attend preschool were one-fifth as likely to become chronic criminal offenders as the matched control group.[33] Given the vastly cheaper costs of preschool over the costs of likely incarceration later, the investment in preprimary education is not only sensible but also cost-effective.

In addition, preprimary education appears critical in leveling the playing field among the different socioeconomic classes, a playing field that starts off slanted downward for the economically disadvantaged and shifts further and further downward as students grow older. For example, by age three, the average child of professional parents has a vocabulary about twice as large as the average child of parents on welfare.[34] This correlation is not surprising

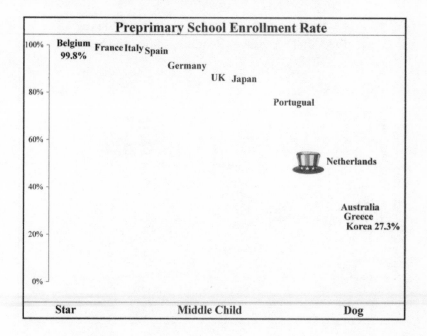

Preprimary School Enrollment Rate

since the parents' levels of education is one of the strongest predictors of their children's educational achievements.[35]

Given all this, it is pretty stunning that on this metric, preschool enrollment, we see the United States lagging far behind other countries. America's enrollment ratio for preprimary education[36] is far below that of the competition and is nearly one-half the enrollment level of leaders like France, Belgium, Italy, and Spain. One notable exception is the low ranking of Korea, which compensates through other mechanisms to achieve its performance. It is noteworthy that the enrollment in preprimary education in the United States has climbed from 27 percent in 1965 to about 60 percent by 1990 but has remained relatively stagnant ever since.[37]

LONGER SCHOOL YEARS: MORE TIME TO LEARN

In order to learn more, it seems that it would make sense to send children to school more. As it turns out, there is a correlation of about 90 percent between the number of days a child attends school and the PISA exam scores.[38] Although correlation doesn't mean causation, as every statistician knows, the

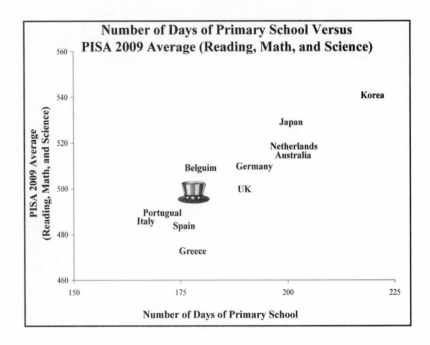

Number of Days of Primary School Versus PISA 2009 Average (Reading, Math, and Science)

strength of the relationship seen in the graph does seem to buttress the logic of more days in schools driving better performance, so it becomes hard to resist arguing that a longer school year would improve American academic performance. After all, the relationship is intuitive; as nearly every teacher will tell you, the long summer break sets children far behind in their learning.

In the American school system, there are no national standards for the length of the school year. Rather, this decision is left up to individual states. A majority of states require a minimum school year of 180 days; ten states require fewer than 180 days; and one state, Minnesota, has no minimum requirement for either the days of the school year or the hours of instruction.[39] The American minimums are in stark contrast to the 220 days averaged by top-performing South Korea and the 201 days in Japan, also a top performer.[40] It seems clear that 25 percent more days of school provide more exposure to educational materials. Almost as important, however, is the timing of school vacations.

The long summer vacation in the American school year is not beneficial for student education, although it may be highly beneficial for some industries—tourism, summer camps, airlines—which rely on the long summer vacation for much of their revenue. American students typically are given ten weeks off for the summer,[41] plenty of time to regress in their knowledge and study habits. Forgetting curves, developed in the late nineteenth century by German psychologist Hermann Ebbinghaus, demonstrate that memory retention declines exponentially over time, so the long American summer vacation takes a major toll on a student's ability to progress.[42]

In Korea, the school year is divided into two semesters separated by two vacation periods of about five weeks each: summer vacation (mid-July to late August) and winter vacation (late December to early February). Korea's students also have one week off in the fall. After winter break, students return to school for one week to take end-of-year exams; they then enjoy a short vacation from mid-February to early March. As of 2008, Korean students attend school from Monday through Friday, and, calendar permitting, also attend for a half day every first, third, and fifth Saturday of the month.

Japanese students also have shorter breaks than their American counterparts; their school year consists of three terms with brief holidays in spring and winter and a month-long summer break.

The recommendation of a longer school year for American students is not new. The US Department of Education made the recommendation in 1992,[43] and President Obama repeated the call for longer school days and school years in September 2010 during an interview on a television morning show. Some charter schools have implemented more classroom time. The Knowledge Is Power Program (KIPP) academies, typically established in inner-city school districts, mandate some 60 percent more classroom time than traditional programs.[44]

STANDARDS

The United States is unusual in lacking national education standards. The reason, of course, lies in the US Constitution, which separates federal and state responsibilities; education is the responsibility of state governments. Throughout the rest of the world, national curriculum is the norm. Korea funds the Korea Institute for Curriculum and Evaluation to regularly monitor and reassess its national curriculum. In Japan, the Ministry of Education, Science, and Culture establishes not only curriculum guidelines, but also standards for school administration, thereby helping to ensure a relatively consistent level of school conditions.

A Nation at Risk called for the creation of meaningful standards in all subjects, but course content became fodder for ideological battling and the idea fizzled. The National Education Goals 2000 program, established by Congress in the 1990s, provided federal money for states to write academic standards, but this also failed when the details could not be worked out.[45] Currently, no national standards exist due to constitutional restrictions on federal powers. The National Governors Association and the state education department heads, however, have developed the Common Core State Standards Initiative to establish clearer, more consistent, and higher expectations for schools across the country. The initiative involves forty-eight states, two territories, and the District of Columbia and is aimed at improving student outcomes through a robust national agreement on standards and a strong minimum curriculum. The draft standards have been internationally benchmarked and represent a positive step forward.[46] Lacking federal involvement, however, this effort, too, may fade away.

FUNDING

While the United States spends about 50–60 percent of its educational budget on the salaries and benefits of its teachers, other countries typically spend some 70–80 percent. This reflects the fact that only about one-half of the education employees in the United States are teachers, while in Asia and Europe about 70–80 percent of total educational staff are teachers. Some of this difference is due to the fact that the fragmented American system has far more administrative staff than other systems.[47] When we examine the distribution of expenditures of American public elementary and secondary education, we see that, besides the expense for teachers, some 10 percent goes to operations and maintenance, about 8 percent to administration, 10 percent to student and instructional support, and more than 11 percent for transportation, food, and logistical support.[48]

One key issue is that with education being a state rather than a federal responsibility, much of the funding for it must be drawn from local taxes. In fact, less than 10 percent of school revenue comes from the federal government; about 50 percent comes from the state, while local governments provide the remainder.[49] Funding across the country thus varies from state to state, and funding within a state also tends to be unequal.

Here's how the inequality works: since a substantial amount of the funding for public schools is local, students from the poorest areas, which are the most disadvantaged educationally, attend schools where the funding per student is the lowest, thus exacerbating the existing disadvantage. As of 2006, schools with the highest poverty rates receive on average nearly $1,000 less per student than schools with the lowest poverty rates,[50] and in some states, like New York and Illinois, this gap is more than $2,000 per student.

Further exacerbating this funding disparity is the formula under which the federal government awards its education funding to states; it is based on a state's per-pupil spending[51] rather than on equal distribution of the funding between poor and wealthy locations. Yet it has been shown that low-income students attending affluent schools tend to perform better than higher-income students attending poor schools.[52] Moreover, historically, when states have reduced the funding gap between rich and poor districts, they have experienced a corresponding decline in the performance gap.[53]

The concern about this inequity was clearly identified in Title 1 of the Elementary and Secondary Education Act of 1965, aimed at "improving the academic achievement of the disadvantaged," according to the wording of the law. In 1973, however, in a pivotal event for school funding, the US Supreme Court ruled five-to-four in *San Antonio Independent School District v. Rodriguez* that it was constitutional for states to fund public schools unequally. This narrow decision, along nearly partisan lines, concluded that education was neither explicitly nor implicitly protected in the US Constitution.[54] It meant that in order to push for more equal financing, the fight had to be taken to the state level, where the bulk of funding for public education was determined. In the 1970s and 1980s, courts in ten states found that the funding for public education was unconstitutional.[55] Corresponding court-ordered changes in state funding closed the achievement gap in states required to make changes; in states where no such order was forthcoming, the achievement gap persists.

The gap tends to be self-nurturing. For example, top teachers are more likely to gravitate toward the schools that pay the most, offer the best facilities, present the safest working environments, and provide the most advanced learning environments—unless lucrative incentives are provided to encourage these top teachers to work in poorer communities. As a result, poorer students are far more likely to encounter uncertified teachers, fewer resources, and substandard facilities, despite the recommendation that low-income students need on average 40 percent *more* funding for these things in order to achieve proficiency standards.[56]

By contrast, in most of our competitor countries, the national government wields a stronger direct influence on education, providing students more equitable support for their education. In Korea, for example, free after-school academic programs and lessons available over the Internet[57] are part of an effort to address disparities in wealth that may cause disparity in education. So it is not surprising that US educational outcomes are more unequal than in other wealthy countries.[58]

They Call It "Social Promotion"

In 2003, Joelis Polanco sued New York City on the grounds that at the age of fourteen, she was unable to read. Every year since entering school, this resident of one of the city's lower-income neighborhoods had been promoted by her teachers—passed on to be another teacher's problem. The practice, known as "social promotion," is theoretically banned in New York City, and the court awarded Ms. Polanco a $15,000 settlement to pay for private tutoring.[59]

But Joelis's story is not unique. Some 60 percent of students at two-year colleges and about 25 percent of students at four-year colleges need one or more years of remedial coursework.

Thanks to her private tutor, Joelis learned to read at the age of sixteen.

AFTER HIGH SCHOOL COMES . . .

Postsecondary education comes in many forms, from technical training programs to two-year community colleges to large-scale universities. An individual's particular choice will depend on career goals, academic qualifications, financial resources available, and/or financial support needed. This breadth of options, plus the dearth of high-quality comparable data for all the countries in our competitor list, makes comparisons of tertiary-level education more difficult than comparisons of primary and secondary education. The importance of tertiary education, however, cannot be overemphasized.

The United States currently has an average rate of performance in tertiary education for people aged twenty-five to thirty-four versus our competition, with about 42 percent of that American age group having attained a tertiary education; the top performers among our competitors are Korea, Canada, and Japan.[60] It is not surprising that these three countries excel in tertiary education since they also took the top-three rankings in secondary education as measured by the PISA scores for reading, math, and science. This result for America reflects a broader comparative decline: America's rate of college education has slipped from first to sixteenth in the world.[61] The decline corresponds to the aging of the highly educated workforce that fueled much of America's economic dominance in the twentieth century. It has been identified clearly by such organizations as the National Center for Public Policy and Higher Education, the independent nonprofit that tracks and analyzes issues in tertiary education. Since the United States has an above-average rate of secondary education, this means that American high school graduates are less likely to receive college degrees than leading countries like Canada and Korea.[62]

As with so many metrics in our analysis, tertiary education outcomes show huge differences depending on which state you examine. Top-performing states like Massachusetts, Connecticut, and Maryland produce and attract well-educated populations. In these leading states, more than one-third of the population has at least an undergraduate degree, and at least 15 percent have a

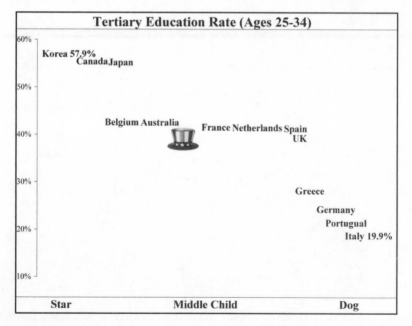

graduate or professional degree. Contrast this with Arkansas and West Virginia, where less than 20 percent of the population have undergraduate degrees and where the rate of those with a graduate or professional degree is less than one-half that of the leading states.[63]

College education in the United States is often a question of affordability, with lower-income students obviously most affected by rising college costs. Yet, as of this writing, it is becoming more and more difficult for families to afford to send their children to any college at all. The cost of attending college has been rising rapidly, increasing by 30 percent from 2000 to 2008. In fact, not adjusting for inflation, college tuition and fees rose 439 percent between 1982 and 2007, while the median family income increased only 147 percent over that time period.[64] During the years 1993 to 2007, the tuition and fees for attending in-state public universities rose an inflation-adjusted 79 percent, while those for private colleges and universities rose 57 percent.[65] In 2008, the cost of attending a public college was $14,000 a year, about one-half of the nation's median personal income, while for a private college or university, it was $30,000—more than the median income.[66]

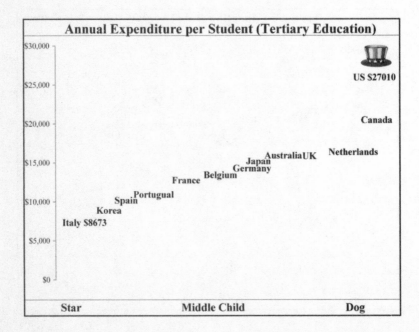

Lucky Manuel

Born in California and of Mexican origin, Manuel was the first person in his family to attend college. His working-class parents put in substantial overtime at their respective jobs to be able to cover the nearly $4,000 it cost in annual tuition for Manuel to attend UCLA, and they were there proudly watching when he graduated in 2002.

His younger sister, Maria, entered the same college only three years later and ran smack into a serious case of sticker shock. Annual tuition by then cost in excess of $6,000 at the famed university, and it was still climbing as of this writing. With federal grants covering less and less of the costs of college, it was unclear how the family would pay for Maria's education. Their situation begs the question: are more and more families being priced out of the American dream?

How does this rising cost affect enrollment? It has been estimated that the high cost of higher education prevents nearly one-half of college-qualified high school graduates from attending a four-year institution and keeps nearly one-fourth from attending any college at all.[67] These rising costs in American education have resulted in the United States spending a greater proportion of GDP on higher education than any other country, 3.1 percent versus 2.6 percent for the next highest competitor, Canada. Put another way, the United States spends about twice the average rate of the competition on higher education.[68]

We obtain a clearer demonstration of the growing unaffordability of tertiary education in the United States when we observe that the average annual expenditure per tertiary education student here is 33 percent higher than in our next closest competitor, Canada, and about three times higher than in the market Star, Korea.[69] These expenditures cover instructors, school buildings, teaching materials, books, and administration.[70]

From the point of view of the student, the more critical comparison is the tuition. Not surprisingly, the United States registers the highest average tuition for full-time students at public universities.[71] Public universities in some competitor countries—Japan, Korea, Canada, Australia, and the United Kingdom, for example—show a similar cost range, while public tertiary education institutions in Belgium, France, Italy, the Netherlands, Portugal, and Spain charge only minimal tuitions that are one-third or less that of the United States. In Greece, the public universities are tuition-free, as are many of the public universities in Germany.

There is another side to the affordability equation: however much it costs, how can students pay? We can see that the costs of tertiary education in America are much higher than in other countries, but what about financial support? While the data comparing financial support for tertiary education are sparse, we can generally say that the American students are at least as likely, if not more likely, to receive financial support via loans and scholarships than tertiary education students from most other countries.[72] But the issue isn't just the percentage of students who receive financial support, it is also how much support is provided. For example, if tuition rises from $5,000 to $7,000 a year, it means little if a very high percentage of students receive a $50 scholarship. What counts is the number of students receiving loans or scholarships that enable them to meet the increased financial need.

In this regard, while the costs of US tertiary education have been rising rapidly, public financial support has lagged far behind. In 1979, Pell Grants, the need-based grants by the federal government to lower-income college undergraduates, covered about 75 percent of the cost of a four-year college; thirty years later, this had dropped to 33 percent.[73] This lagging public support for postsecondary education can be seen in the ratio of public money to private money invested at this level of education: the American ratio is smaller than in every competitor country except Japan and South Korea.[74]

As a result of the rising costs of tertiary education in the United States, about two-thirds of four-year undergraduate students graduating in 2007 and 2008 did so burdened with some debt. The average student-loan debt of these graduating seniors was $23,186,[75] a sum that is nearly double the average amount graduating seniors owed in 1995.

So the costs of tertiary education in America are rising rapidly while the financial support is being drawn away, but what about quality? Certainly, it varies widely—from noncertified for-profit schools of questionable quality to the world-class universities that millions strive to attend. America is well known for having some of the top universities in the world, drawing talent from around the globe for undergraduate and graduate studies, as the rising number of foreign-born students at American undergraduate and graduate schools evidences.

A large number of criteria go into ranking colleges and universities, and because most are arbitrary, as are the weights given to each criterion, it is noto-riously difficult to obtain a truly objective measure of quality. Three sets of rankings prominently used to compare universities are: the Academic Ranking of World Universities, the QS World University Rankings, and the Times Higher Education World University Rankings. Because the ranking method-ologies of the three differ, and because none of the resulting rankings are truly objective measures, we averaged the three scores for each university, computed the number of schools in the top twenty, top one hundred, and top two hun-dred, and then divided the number by the population in each country to reflect the number of top schools per capita in each country. Such per capita normal-izing is necessary to account for differences in size of population. It's important to note also that all three sets of rankings focus on large universities and ignore other tertiary education options. They therefore reflect the elite of each country's academic world, not the broad ranks of institutions most students can expect to attend.

Given all those caveats, the United States gets an above-average rate for countries with the top two hundred universities; it is ranked fifth out of four-teen, with the Netherlands on top. Greece and Portugal failed to place any uni-versities in the top two hundred. For countries with the top one hundred universities, the United States ranks third, and for the top twenty universities,

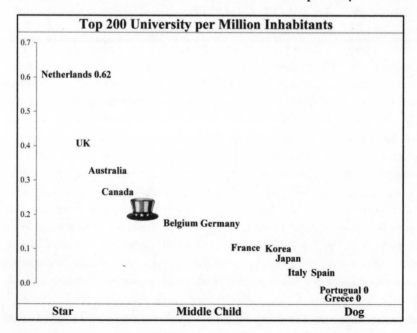

the United States ranks second. Regardless of which cutoff is used, the United States, the United Kingdom, Canada, and Australia all place in the top five, while Italy, Spain, Greece, and Portugal are always near the bottom. While the density of top universities in the United States is above average, the total number of top universities vastly exceeds other countries because of the comparatively larger US population.

THE FINAL MARKET ANALYSIS: THE UNITED STATES IS A MIDDLE CHILD IN EDUCATION

The American educational system used to lead the world in producing a strong educational foundation in primary and secondary education, and it contained some of the top colleges and universities in the world. But its advantage is now gone.

The issue resonates deeply in American public life. Nearly every president has presented himself as a champion of education while simultaneously acknowledging the disturbing trend of declining American performance. From Lyndon Johnson's educational focus in the Great Society to Ronald Reagan's boldly declared 1983 goals, from George H. W. Bush's America 2000 plan to Clinton's tax credits and embrace of charter schools, from George W. Bush's No Child Left Behind to Barack Obama's Race to the Top, presidents have talked a great deal about their commitment to education. The topic draws passionate attention and causes fierce arguments throughout the country. Yet the trend continues to be disappointing. The rapid rise in high school graduation rates that occurred during much of the twentieth century flattened out decades ago, while our college education rate has been surpassed by other countries.

Education is one of the rare areas in which public support, expressed as government expenditure, is much higher in the United States than in other countries. But as with many other aspects of American society, inequities damage the average performance of American students. Discrepancies in outcomes between states, racial groups, and income groups litter the educational landscape. "Separate and unequal," the racial segregation of schools swept away in law by *Brown v. Board of Education*, the landmark Supreme Court decision, is now the on-the-ground reality in education investment, quality, and performance outcomes for lower-income and many minority students. Indeed, looking at America's schools today, we see racial and income segregation at levels that mirror the pre–Civil Rights Era.[76] For example, in Chicago, 47 percent of public schools have student populations that are 90 percent or more African American.[77]

SILVER BULLETS?

"Fixing" education has certainly been a focus of attention by experts and the general public for decades. It is an ongoing challenge that has engaged some of our best minds and has stirred our most passionate advocates. But too often the "fix" has been a silver-bullet solution that has garnered mixed outcomes at best and occasionally drawn worse outcomes than if no bullet had been fired at all.

Many of these fixes triggered the "law of unintended consequences," a reference to the way a seemingly good idea may create unanticipated and possibly undesirable outcomes.[78] This is perhaps seen most dramatically in the massive testing requirements of the No Child Left Behind (NCLB) law. While regular testing seems a reasonable way to monitor student performance in order to track standards-based reform, NCLB's emphasis on monitoring has instead created a culture of testing; the result is that testing skills, rather than broad educational goals, has become the classroom focus. In practice, NCLB has been a boon to such test-preparation companies as Princeton Review and Kaplan Learning,[79] while it has inadvertently encouraged lower local standards that enable more students to be promoted on flimsy claims of proficiency. For example, in New York City, the percentage of correct answers in the reading test required for promotion was dropped from 41 percent in 2006 to 17.9 percent by 2009,[80] a score that might easily be achieved by random guessing!

Moreover, because each state defines its own standards, tests, and cutoffs for NCLB testing, it has become easy to game the system. A more objective measure is the National Assessment of Educational Progress (NAEP), a national exam given to a sample of students throughout the United States. On the NAEP test, fewer than 35 percent of students in Texas, Tennessee, and Nebraska qualified as proficient, yet all three states reported 85 percent proficiency rates in the results of their own, state-controlled exams for NCLB in 2007. The explanation for this disconnect is that states can simplify the tests used for NCLB, lower the proficiency standards, and spend as much classroom time as possible teaching to the test, but they don't have that control over the NAEP exam. Students may be learning test-taking proficiency, but they aren't being educated.

Charter schools have also failed as a magic bullet. Certainly, some charter schools have innovated effective strategies, yet only 17 percent of charter schools were shown to have higher student-performance gains than regular public schools, while 37 percent performed less well and the rest offered no significant change.[81] Attrition rates in charter schools tend to be high. In the KIPP charter schools in the San Francisco area, which start at fifth grade, 60 percent of initial enrollees had left by the eighth grade, according to a 2008 study.[82]

Nor do charter schools in any way "prove" that a free-market approach solves educational issues. Charters are free to select only the more motivated students, typically from homes committed to education, and they can dismiss students who don't work out (sending them back to the public schools). Given that they are thus able to skim the cream of students and dismiss the less promising, the overall performance records of charters schools are even less impressive, although they could ideally serve as laboratories for exploring teaching methods and learning environments.

Another so-called free-market solution that has failed is the voucher system. Where vouchers have been introduced, students using them to study in private schools have failed to show statistically significant improvement over those not receiving vouchers.[83]

Reducing classroom size is a solution beloved of the media and popular with teachers, parents, and such advocacy groups as the Educational Priorities Panel and Class Size Matters. The intuitive appeal of smaller classes is that they can ensure better focus and greater individual attention by the teacher. The data, however, do not support this argument. From 1980 to 2005, for example, the student/teacher ratio in the United States declined by 18 percent,[84] yet more than 90 percent of the 112 studies examining the impact of class size showed either no effect or a negative effect on learning. Those studies that do show an effect indicate that a massive decrease in student/teacher ratio would be necessary for the impact to be considered substantial.[85] In fact, efforts to reduce class size often result in lower teacher quality as hiring standards and salaries are reduced. When California implemented a small-classroom policy in 1996, the percentage of unprepared teachers increased sharply, with the lowest-income schools absorbing the largest increase in unprepared teachers while wealthier schools were only marginally affected.[86]

Moreover, top-performing countries like Japan and South Korea have the highest class sizes. The average primary-school class in both countries is greater than twenty-eight students; the United States averages about twenty-three, and other competitor countries have a mean and median of around twenty-one students. For secondary education, the average class size in Japan and Korea exceeds thirty-three students, much larger than the US average of twenty-three and a mean and median of twenty-three in the other competitor countries.

This certainly doesn't mean that larger class sizes improve education. In South Korea and Japan, however, the larger class size allows those school systems to pay teachers more competitive salaries while containing overall costs. The difference is in the approach: one invests in recruiting and retaining higher-quality teachers through incentives, higher salaries, training programs, and other career advancement opportunities; the other approach massively increases the number of teachers hired so as to reduce the student/teacher ratio but, along the way, suffers a decline in the quality of the teachers.

The Rise and Fall of Edison

Edison Schools, Inc., now known as EdisonLearning, Inc., was hired in 2002 to manage twenty schools in Philadelphia, which thus became the company's largest market. Soon after taking over, however, Edison defaulted on its contracts and saw its publicly traded shares drop in value by over 95 percent. In order to remain solvent, Edison sold most of the textbooks, computers, laboratory supplies, and musical instruments for cash, leaving most students with decades-old textbooks and no equipment. In 2008, the School District of Philadelphia announced plans to dismiss Edison; the long-term damage to students' education, however, may not be as easily dismissed. Philadelphia wasn't the only failed experiment for Edison; an analysis by the *New York Times* showed that the Cleveland public school system had better academic performance than the Edison schools in that city as well.

RECOMMENDATIONS

So, if these silver bullets didn't work, what should America do to regain its global leadership position in education? As always, the data point us to best practices of other countries and, in this case, to homegrown solutions as well.

The first recommendation of central importance to improving American students' educational performance is to **expand preprimary education nationally with quality controls in place**. As we have seen, preschool is nearly universal in our competitor countries and was included as one of the six education goals laid out by President George H. W. Bush in 1991.[87] It has been shown repeatedly to be an effective means of developing young children and increasing the likelihood of future productivity. Early education investments have a much higher rate of return than most other public projects carried out for economic development.[88]

To ensure that early-childhood interventions successfully boost "children's language, numeracy, socio-emotional, attention, and executive function skills,"[89] as research shows they can do, proper quality controls will be needed. Otherwise, programs risk devolving into public daycare. A recent evaluation of the Head Start program showed that limitations to its long-term impact may have been due to the uneven quality of the program across the country. Fewer than 5 percent of the centers studied were identified as "excellent," and only about one-half of the students were in centers with recommended pupil/staff ratios.[90] One result was that while short-term positive impacts on three- and four-year-olds were evident in nearly every measurement, longer-term impacts were less apparent.[91] These and other concerns raised about the impact of Head Start in particular should prompt research into improving these programs and actions for doing so, rather than attempts to defund them.

Affluent parents don't question the value of investing in their children's education, nor do they shy from jockeying for positions in the finest preprimary schools available. Why should the opportunity to enjoy a high-quality education be denied to those most in need?

Second, the United States must **invest in developing and maintaining better teachers**. As we have seen, a key best practice in the top-performing countries is the ability to attract superior college and university students to the teaching profession—and then to maintain their edge through ongoing professional development, a process that some of the more successful charter schools have emulated. Certainly, salaries will need to rise, and practices will need to change in order to "flip" the current ratio of American teachers spending far more time teaching and far less time preparing lessons or improving their craft than our competitor countries. For example, 80 percent of an American teacher's work time is spent teaching, compared with an average of about 60 percent in the OECD countries.[92] The National Education Commission on Time and Learning,[93] an independent advisory committee to Congress, cited this disparity in 1994 in recommending more professional development for US teachers to do their jobs better, yet little progress has been made.

Many techniques exist for teaching teachers, any of which can be adapted to good purpose here in the United States. In Japan, teachers work in teams to analyze and develop model lessons, while peer observation of classrooms enables teachers to learn the techniques used by colleagues. Boston's teachers in the high-performing Massachusetts school system do both as well: peer observation and joint teacher lesson planning facilitated by the principal or a coach.

Third, we need to *equalize funding* for education. While funding per primary and secondary student is comparatively high in the United States, the data show that it is also unequal, with the most disadvantaged students receiving the least funding. This creates a death spiral for low-income students: The schools they attend receive less funding, have worse facilities, and often pay teachers less, thus attracting less qualified teacher candidates. To some extent, this is due to the small role the federal government plays in education, providing less than 10 percent of the funding but leaving the primary role to the state and local governments. For that reason, the way to equalize funding is to ensure that state-level court orders on school financing are implemented. It took thirty years of litigation on this issue before real change occurred in New Jersey, while Ohio and New York courts have repeatedly—and futilely—ordered new systems of school financing to correct inequalities they deem unconstitutional.

One obvious and straightforward recommendation from the competitive intelligence is *having a longer school year.* While not a silver bullet for fixing the system, more days in school, as the data make clear, can certainly mitigate the student regression that a ten-week summer vacation inevitably causes. Longer seasons of instruction than in the United States are a best practice followed in the leading countries like South Korea and Japan and have been adopted by the more successful charter school programs. Since the publication of *A Nation at Risk* in 1983, a longer school year has been cited as a clear opportunity for the United States to catch up to the education leaders of the world.

In addition to overcoming the resistance of those who enjoy and prosper from the long summer, it will be necessary to create new teacher-union agreements, to find increased funding for facilities maintenance and staffing, and to achieve buy-in from parents. Moreover, extending the school year will require legislation at the state level. But given that the National Governors Association and the state education department heads have already collaborated on the

Common Core State Standards Initiative, there is precedent for state officials to act on school-year length.

Fifth, *federal involvement* in education could be used more effectively to drive positive change. Specifically, it is recommended that the federal government become more involved in three areas: providing financial support for the development of national curriculum standards through the Common Core State Standards Initiative; equalizing disparities in state school funding by identifying which states and localities have poorly funded schools despite spending a high percentage of their revenue on public education, then developing a judicious way of filling the gaps for those students most in need; and expanding NCLB to include measuring such opportunities for learning as well-qualified teachers, appropriate curriculum materials, technology, and supportive services. Tracking the opportunities for learning sheds light on disparities in educational opportunities and lets local, state, and federal entities target resources to those most in need.[94]

Finally, we must *make tertiary education more affordable*. The mix of private and public institutions and the range of two-year, four-year, and professional educational programs have produced a broad and varied landscape in tertiary education. To make this topography financially accessible, it is necessary to either control costs or provide more financial support for those in need. Private institutions are able to charge tuition costs that reflect what the market will bear. As US universities open themselves up to more and more international students, the tuition costs of top private US universities will likely continue to rise uninhibited due to the increasing demand.

For public institutions, however, it is possible to control tuition costs by increasing either their efficiency (so the operating costs don't rise so quickly) or the amount of public financial support. The former sounds nice on paper, but finding "wasteful spending" seems an elusive proposition. Instead, lawmakers could expand tax-advantaged 529 plans, which now help middle-class families save for their children's college educations, while for needy students, they would need to expand both the breadth of Pell Grants and the amount of funding allocated to them.

Chapter 4

WE THE PEOPLE: DEMOCRACY

It has been said that democracy is the worst form of
government—except all the others that have been tried.
—**Winston Churchill (1874–1965)**

In May 1787, a small group of wealthy, white, male landowners gathered in Philadelphia to fix their fatally flawed government. Armed with the philosophical writings of John Locke and Montesquieu, an appreciation of the Magna Carta, experience with the bicameral British legislature, observations on Native American democracies,[1] historical works glorifying the ancient Greek democracies, and a distrust of the masses, they set out to craft an effective government for a mostly uneducated population consisting of citizens who despised monarchies and passionately associated themselves with their newly created states. The Founding Fathers were the elite, not the common crowd, and the document they crafted was a balance of political philosophy and the practical desires of men of wealth to preserve their power and property as much as possible. Much of the structure of our present democracy still reflects the values of those Founding Fathers and is imbued with the strengths and biases they had at the time.

So many questions needed answers in order to create a government from scratch! How powerful should the federal government be? It had to be strong enough to avoid the challenges presented by the Articles of Confederation but not so strong as to threaten states' rights. America's first constitutional failure taught that the federal government needed to collect taxes, support an army, and establish a functional system for passing laws.[2] This federal power had to be balanced with state demands for a strong level of independence. How would this document ensure fair representation for citizens in small states? How could the people's voices be heard without creating the possibility of government-sanctioned mobs? Who should vote and who could be elected? After all, as an African American Congresswoman from Texas would say not quite two hundred years later, "when that document [the US Constitution] was completed on the seventeenth of September in 1787, I was not included." The founders had no thought to extend the vote to women, and as for African Americans of the time, they were, for the most part, slaves—property—and were looked upon as the basis of the Southern economy, not as citizens with a role to play in the new democracy.

The Founding Fathers had the foresight, however, to realize that they needed to establish both the rules of government and the instructions on how to change the rules. After four months of debate, argument, negotiation, and compromise, the delegates signed the final draft, and then waited another ten months for their draft constitution to be officially ratified.

With its separation of powers among three branches of government, its checks and balances, and its protection of minority rights and due process, the US Constitution inspired myriad other democracies. Some changes to the Constitution occurred over time, as rights and the definition of who could vote were expanded, but the general architecture of the system it laid out has remained relatively unchanged for more than two centuries. The history of the democracy it defined is also pockmarked with blemishes: slavery, internment camps, presidential assassinations, Watergate, impeachments, election fiascos, and the legacy of racial inequality.

Maybe that is why, as the data in this chapter demonstrate so vividly, new democracies may feel inspired by America's founding but have consistently emulated other models of how a democracy should function. Some of the basic principles of the US Constitution, like fundamental human rights, due process, and separation of powers, have been incorporated into just about every democracy that followed America's creation. But when it comes to the way representatives are elected, providing ways for all voices to be heard, and ensuring the fairness of elections, among other functions, most of the world's democracies have looked to other exemplars and chosen other models. If imitation is the sincerest form of flattery, then it is resoundingly clear that many of the mechanisms of the US democracy are getting the global equivalent of a thumbs-down.

Why? The US Constitution was a bold innovation for its time, but the arteries of America's democracy have hardened since then. Sure, we have seen some changes, like the end of slavery, women's suffrage, and the direct election of senators, but the bulk of the system has failed to change in the face of shifting realities; it lacks the greater flexibility and agility of newer democracies around the world. The comparative data laid out in this chapter make the results dramatically clear:

- The United States has one of the lowest voter turnout rates of any wealthy, democratic country.[3]
- Broader measures of democracy like those from the World Bank and the *Economist* magazine rank the United States as a Middle Child among our competitors on democracy "performance."
- The American system is dominated by two political parties and a winner-take-all voting system that drowns out other voices.
- Although the United States had the first modern design for democracy, the nation hasn't corrected such basic anomalies as the lack of congressional voting representation for Washington, DC, residents or addressed the undemocratic Electoral College system for presidential elections.

Moreover, how can the technological leaders of the world tolerate voting processes so ripe for fraud and manipulation? How is it that other countries have figured out how to allow smaller parties to have a political voice without letting the small, squeaky wheel get all the oil? How do other countries ensure that their elected representatives reflect the will of the people?

One distinguishing feature of American democracy is that it is rife with internal inconsistency, a consequence of the Tenth Amendment, which grants states control over any aspect of the government not identified as belonging to the federal government in the Constitution. Voting procedures vary from state to state. Some states use referendums; others do not. Some states allow voters to register online; others require a personal appearance and a signature on the dotted line. This diversity of state-level approaches to the democratic process offers us an opportunity not only to learn from other countries but also to identify best practices in certain states that other states can adopt.

WHAT DO WE MEAN BY "DEMOCRACY"?

The etymology from ancient Greek is clear: "democracy" means "people power," a form of government in which the power is vested in the people and exercised by the people either directly or through their freely elected agents. Closely associated with this definition is the principle that in a democracy, everyone is equal before the law.[4] For many Americans, the concept of democracy is encapsulated in the phrase from Lincoln's Gettysburg Address: "government of the people, by the people, for the people."

But that's about as far as agreement on the subject goes. From here on in, it's a highly subjective game. That may be why democracies take so many different forms, although most are variants on one of three basic forms—direct democracies, representative democracies, and consensus democracies.

Ancient Athenian democracy is the exemplar of a *direct democracy* in which all eligible citizens vote on legislation. The idea of so many people acting as lawmakers is not as unwieldy as it sounds because in ancient Athens, eligible citizens consisted of adult males who had completed military training and who owed no debts to the city—a minority of the population. Still, all of these men voted directly on everything. The impetus behind this is that it would have been prohibitively expensive to bribe or pay kickbacks to so many "legislators," thus mitigating the influence of money in Athenian politics.

Contemporary America's equivalent of direct democracy is the town meeting, found in New England and in some Midwestern states like Michigan and Minnesota, in which all residents can vote on local issues. Direct democracy is also seen in state or municipal referendums—also referred to as plebiscites, ballot questions, or propositions—and in recalls[5] and constitutional amendment initiatives[6] in which the electorate is asked to vote "yay" or "nay" on an issue, or, alternatively, to overturn enacted legislation or remove an elected official from office.

In *representative democracies*, eligible voters elect representatives to do the legislating.[7] This is perhaps the most common form of democracy, embraced by all the countries in our competitor group. In two competitor countries, Canada and the United Kingdom, both parliamentary systems, representatives are elected by a plurality of those who vote. A candidate has a plurality when he or she has won more votes than any other candidate in the race but not necessarily the majority— more than 50 percent—of the votes cast. Using a plurality system allows smaller political parties to have an impact on an election, often by siphoning votes from one of the larger parties and, hence, tipping an election one way or another. Some argue that third-party candidates Ross Perot in 1992 and Ralph Nader in 2000 played this role in the US presidential elections of those years, siphoning votes from one major-party candidate and tipping the election to the other.

France and some American states, such as Louisiana and Georgia, use a runoff voting system. If any candidate in the first round of voting gains a majority, then that candidate is declared the winner, and there is no second round. If no candidate receives a majority, a run-off election is held, either between the two candidates with the highest number of votes in the first round or among all candidates above a certain threshold number of votes in the first round.

Australia's representative democracy uses preferential voting, also known as instant runoff elections, for almost all elections involving the federal, state, and territorial legislatures. Australian voters rank the candidates in order of preference. If no candidate has an absolute majority of first preference votes, then the candidate with the fewest votes is eliminated from the count. The ballots of the eliminated candidate are reallocated among the remaining candidates according to the second preference votes, and this continues until a candidate has a majority. While about 95 percent of Australian voters cast votes along party lines in federal elections,[8] the preferential voting system allows people to vote for smaller parties without tipping an election.

In Belgium and parts of Canada, *consensus democracy* ensures that minority voters—whether the minority is of race, culture, language, or other feature—are not ignored in general elections.[9] For example, some of Belgium's senators are appointed by the three community parliaments that represent the official languages of French, Flemish, and German. Without the consensus democracy structure, there is a fear that the Dutch-speaking Flemish regions would dominate the democratic process because they represent a majority of the population.

But although the forms of democracy vary, all models seek the same goal—to create a government that represents the will of the people. How will we measure how well governments do that?

Unlike health, where quantitative measures were readily available—life expectancies, health expenditures, physician densities—democracy offers neither absolute definitions nor objective quantification. Everything about it tends to be subjective. As a result, competitive intelligence on democracy requires us to consider our measuring tools carefully and to recognize that some form of bias—cultural, gender-based, religious, ideological—has probably influenced the people who define the metrics.

Two key attributes of any democracy—competition and participation[10]—lend themselves to objective scrutiny and are widely accepted as indicators of the robustness of a democratic process. So that's where we'll begin. Later, we'll consider other measures more subjective in nature that add richness to the quantitative picture. It is interesting and instructive that the subjective democracy measurements often correlate with the objective measures.[11] For example, the Netherlands and Australia are consistently identified as top democracy performers while South Korea just as consistently is seen as struggling to realize true democratic functioning.

COMPETITION AND PARTICIPATION:
BEING COUNTED COUNTS

By "competition," we mean how easily and how freely citizens can organize themselves into competing blocs in order to press for the policies and outcomes they desire. What's a good measure of that? Some have suggested that having a large share of the votes being received by smaller parties is an indication of a competitive race. Why? Because it indicates that many parties are active and represented, and that makes for a highly competitive situation. Contrarily, in a country with no competition, all of the seats would be held by the largest party and smaller parties would have no voice.

By "participation," we mean who and how many people in the country are engaged in the democratic process. In the past, when women and some minorities were denied the right to vote, inclusion—rather than participation—was a powerful indicator of democracy. After all, if a large percentage of citizens are excluded from voting, then the participation rate is by definition low. In 1893, New Zealand became the first country in the world to grant all women the right to vote; South Australia followed in 1895, empowering women also to stand for parliament. Overall, Australia and Canada were the first two countries on our list to grant women suffrage in the early 1900s, while the last countries on our list to do so were Belgium and Korea in 1948 and Greece in 1952. American women received the right to vote in 1919, but inclusion in voting remained an issue, with poll taxes, literacy tests, and grandfather clauses still in place to block other minorities, most notably African Americans, from voting.

In our list of competing countries, inclusion is less of an issue now, but the extent to which people participate in their own representation is a major concern. Intuitively, we understand that a failing democracy is one in which only a small percentage of the eligible population votes or is otherwise engaged in the democratic process. The matrix that follows shows how we'll rank competitor countries in terms of participation versus competition.

When we apply these democracy criteria, we see that the United States rates poorly in both dimensions compared to other countries in its competitor group—most notably, Belgium, the Netherlands, and Australia.

The dataset defines competition as the percentage of seats won in national legislatures not from the largest party—with a maximum score of seventy—and defines participation as the percentage of the population that votes in national legislature elections.[12] The competition/participation measurement agrees with our intuition that if a large percentage of the population votes, it is

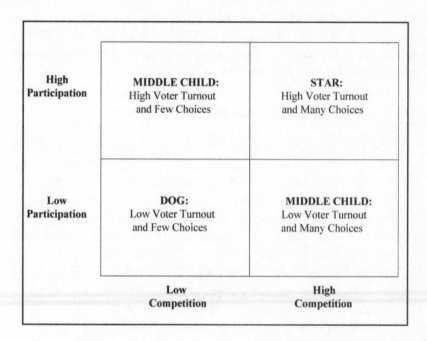

	Low Competition	High Competition
High Participation	**MIDDLE CHILD:** High Voter Turnout and Few Choices	**STAR:** High Voter Turnout and Many Choices
Low Participation	**DOG:** Low Voter Turnout and Few Choices	**MIDDLE CHILD:** Low Voter Turnout and Many Choices

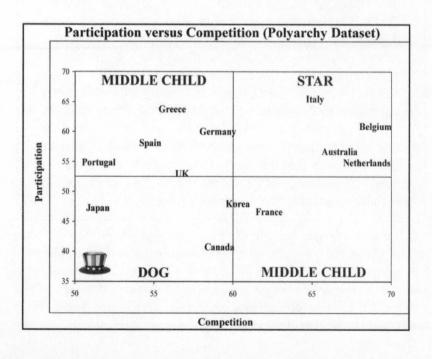

Participation versus Competition (Polyarchy Dataset)

good for democracy. But there are some caveats: this metric ignores the fact that some countries have younger populations or higher rates of immigrants who may not be eligible to vote, and it uses a snapshot in time—in this case the most recent data, which are from 2000.

Taxation without Representation

During America's Revolutionary War, colonists rallied around phrases like "no taxation without representation." This same phrase adorns the license plates of Washington, DC, residents. Why? When the Constitution was written, the founders didn't anticipate that people would live year-round in Washington, DC. As a result, they created a representative hole that has been left unfilled for more than two hundred years. In fact, it is only since 1964 that DC residents have had any say in presidential elections, but they still have no voting representative in Congress. District of Columbia residents and businesses paid $20.4 billion in federal taxes in 2007, more than the taxes collected from nineteen states. Residents of the district also pay local taxes, yet they currently have only a single, *nonvoting* representative in Congress. With a population that exceeds that of the state of Wyoming, Washington, DC, and its nonrepresentation constitute a major flaw in America's democracy. Why has this gap remained? While numerous bills have been submitted to Congress on this issue, most attempts have died in committee because of partisan politics. It is unlikely that a constitutional amendment will be passed to correct this issue, and that means that DC residents will probably have to continue suffering the ironic fate of "taxation without representation" in America's capital.

The most obvious measure of citizen participation in the democratic process is voter turnout—how many people vote, and who they are. The numbers can be measured in various ways: by the percentage of registered voters who actually voted,[13] by the percentage of those citizens old enough to vote who voted,[14] or by the percentage of eligible voters who voted. In the United States, about 92 percent of the residents of voting age are eligible to vote; ineligible residents are mostly noncitizens and prison inmates. That percentage of voting-age voters has declined over time. Also, the percentage of eligible voters differs from state to state, ranging from 82 percent in California to 99 percent in Vermont.[15] But regardless of which metric of eligibility you use, the United States has one of the lowest voter turnouts of any of the comparator countries while Australia and Belgium have the highest.

PARTICIPATION: VOTER TURNOUT

The high voter turnout in Australia is due to its strictly enforced compulsory voting laws; no-shows at the polls are fined.[16] Belgian law has a provision for disenfranchising voters who repeatedly fail to appear at the polling station. The Netherlands, Greece, Spain, France, and Italy all had some version of compulsory voting laws during the twentieth century, but these laws are no longer in effect.[17] Yet these countries still rank better than the United States for voter turnout.

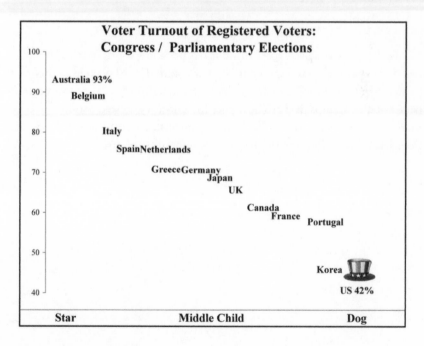

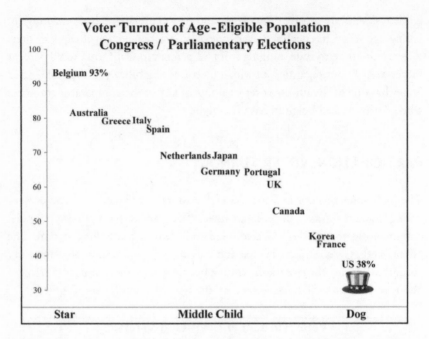

In the United States, voter turnout has been low for decades, although it rises for presidential races, when it is usually some 15–20 percent higher than in midterm elections. This reflects a basic characteristic of all voters in all countries: voter turnout is likely to be higher for a hotly contested national election than for an off-year election for local office. Still, voter turnout for US elections has been far lower than that of the competitor countries for decades.

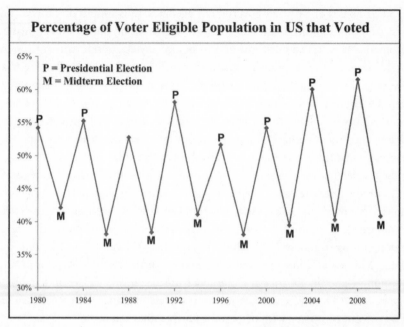

Percentage of Voter Eligible Population in US that Voted

P = Presidential Election
M = Midterm Election

American voter turnout also varies across the different states. For example, in the 2008 presidential election, the state with the highest turnout of eligible voters was Minnesota at 77.7 percent, while Hawaii had the lowest turnout at 50.5 percent.[18] This wide range of turnout is likely a result of local attitudes toward the electoral process as well as the state-defined institutional barriers to voting that we will discuss later.

Why don't people vote? There are countless explanations: the absence of trust in government, the degree of partisanship among the population, the lack of general interest in politics, and a failure of faith in the true effect of voting.[19]

Demographics also play a major role: older people are more likely to vote, which might explain some of the lower turnout for the two youngest countries on our list, the United States and South Korea. In the 2008 presidential election, the voter turnout for American citizens aged eighteen to twenty-four was more than 20 percent lower than the rate for citizens aged sixty-five and older.[20]

Convenience impacts voter turnout. In the United States, in all but one state, voters must go through a separate registration process before voting,[21] and the vast majority of states do not allow Election Day registration. This two-step process—register, then vote—is more complicated than the process in many other countries and discourages some Americans from voting. In Austria, Germany, France, and Belgium, voter lists are generated from larger population databases or by other government agencies, thus simplifying the voting process. For example, Germans who are eighteen or older on voting day automatically receive a notification card before any election in which they are eligible to vote. In Canada, the income tax returns are used for voter registration.[22] In the United Kingdom, every residence receives a notice of those registered within the household, and additional voters can be registered by mail.

Practices peripheral to the voter registration process itself also affect registration and, thus, voting—things like how late election offices are open in evenings and during weekends, the availability of absentee voting, and the length of the preelection-registration closing period. In the United States, the registration closing deadline has a major impact. A study of American voting data showed that residents of states with Election Day voter registration were 3–9 percent more likely to turn out to vote than residents of states with thirty-day registration closing deadlines.[23] In 2008, eleven states—Connecticut, Idaho, Iowa, Maine, Minnesota, Montana, New Hampshire, North Carolina, Wisconsin, and Wyoming—and the District of Columbia had some form of Election Day voter registration.[24] These Election Day registration states had an average voter turnout of 68 percent compared with 62 percent for the other states.[25]

Another critical factor is the convenience level for absentee voting. It has been shown that no-excuse absentee balloting increases turnout rates by some three percentage points.[26] Oregon's all-mail ballot, the most extreme example, increased voter turnout by 10 percent over the expected turnout in a traditional polling-place election.[27] Statewide policies concerning the voting rights of those with criminal records also affect voter turnout rates. Some states prohibit convicted felons from voting for a fixed period of time; other states impose a lifetime voting ban for ex-convicts. In the 2004 election, nearly five million Americans were prohibited from voting because of a felony conviction, and some 40 percent of those barred were African Americans.[28]

COMPETITION: HOW MANY PARTIES AT THE TABLE

While Americans are well aware of the fractious relationship between the Democratic and Republican parties, they may be less aware that the American two-party system is the exception, rather than the norm, for the world's democracies. Third parties have made sporadic attempts throughout the American past to gain power, from the Free Soilers to the Progressives, from the States' Rights Party to the Green Party, but our electoral system heavily favors a political structure with two parties. The competition index shown in the graph displaying the number of effective political parties confirms that,[29] while making clear how different we are from our competitors in having far fewer effective political parties.

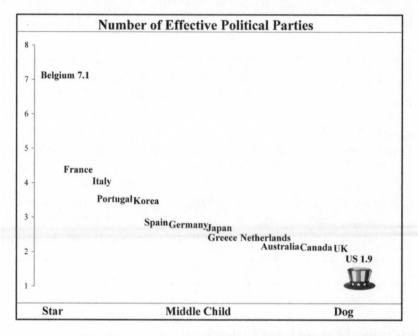

Having more political parties doesn't ensure a healthy democracy, but having only limited party options can undermine a democracy's health. Multi-party democracies often require coalitions in order to govern, so they tend to embrace broader political views. For example, Italy's former prime minister, Silvio Berlusconi, led a coalition of three major parties: the People of Freedom, the Northern League, and the Movement for Autonomy. In the United Kingdom, the election of 2010 resulted in a coalition government of the largest and third largest parties, the Conservatives and the Liberal Democrats, led by Conservative Party leader David Cameron.

The need to form coalitions drives some democratic countries to be more inclusive, although when coalitions break down, a new election must typically be held. One immediate downside to this process is that a high frequency of elections and new governments can lead to voter fatigue. Party fractionalization,[30] a measure of how representation is distributed among the different parties, has been identified as a good predictor of the strength of a democracy.[31] But sometimes it makes coalition forming difficult; in an extreme example,

Belgium went nearly two years without succeeding at forming a coalition government until finally establishing one in December 2011.

Voter Turnoff

Dan is a Republican living in Massachusetts's Eighth Congressional District. In 2010, Republican candidates received more than 30 percent of the vote in eight of the ten congressional districts in the state, yet all ten seats went to Democrats. Nine out of the ten Democrats who won were incumbents, showing that once in office, Massachusetts's politicians stay in office.

Dan used to vote in every election, but he stopped a few years ago. "What's the point?" he complained. "My vote doesn't count anyway." In 2010 he couldn't have been more correct. The Democratic incumbent from his district, Mike Capuano, ran unopposed.

WINNER-TAKE-ALL ELECTIONS LEAVE DEMOCRACY OUT

The winner-take-all elections or first-past-the-post elections that characterize American democracy weaken the democratic process. The candidate with the most votes is the winner in such elections, which therefore often fail to produce representation that reflects the will of the majority. In a winner-take-all election, if the Republican candidate wins 50.1 percent of the vote, that candidate goes on to represent 100 percent of the population, even though nearly one-half the voters do not support the Republican Party principles. Result: a large percentage of the population feel themselves to be representation orphans.

For example, Oregon has seven total representatives at the federal level in Washington, DC, two US Senators and five members of the House of Representatives. Of those seven, only one is a Republican. Does this reflect the overall state political preference? Absolutely not! Overall, in 2010, 46 percent of Oregonian votes for members of the House of Representatives went to

Republican candidates, yet only one out of five Republican candidates was elected and only 14 percent of the total representation (Senate and House combined) in Washington is Republican. In 2010 the Republican candidates in the five congressional districts received 42 percent, 74 percent, 25 percent, 45 percent, and 46 percent of the vote, respectively. Two of these districts were not competitive elections—that is, one of the candidates clearly didn't have a chance of victory. Of the six incumbents who ran for reelection in 2010, all six won, and in 2008 the Republicans didn't even field a candidate against Democrat Representative David Wu of the First Congressional District.

Uncompetitive elections, incumbent advantage, and unrepresentative outcomes: Oregon exemplifies these electoral phenomena, and the result is that a large percentage of the Oregonian population is poorly represented in Congress. Steven Hill, a political writer and policy analyst, has shown convincingly in *Fixing Elections: The Failure of America's Winner Take All Politics* that none of this is a coincidence.[32] Rather, these results are the product of single-seat, winner-take-all elections that have created and added gasoline to the fire of American political polarization. Those in uncompetitive districts are free to be as radical as they want, knowing that their reelections are virtually assured.

Proportional representation is one way to address this issue. Almost all other democracies use a proportional system in some form. Thirty-eight of the forty-one democracies with high ratings from Freedom House, an independent watchdog organization, and with populations of more than two million use some form of proportional or semiproportional representation in at least one of their national legislatures;[33] the United States is one of only three holdouts. That alone would seem to indicate that America's election mechanism—the more than two-hundred-year-old single-seat, winner-take-all contest—is past its prime and out of date, if not downright obsolete. Canada's House of Commons also uses the single seat, winner-take-all method of voting and has similarly unrepresentative results. For example, in the 2011 election, the Conservative Party won a majority of the electoral districts with only about 40 percent of the popular vote.

The Netherlands has solved this issue in a very straightforward manner. The entire country has only one electoral district, so its proportional representation elections produce an exact match in the parliament of the party preferences of the voters.

Some countries—for example, Germany, Japan, Italy, and New Zealand—have devised mixed systems that take advantage of the benefits of both geographic representation and proportional representation. Germany established such a system in 1949, and it is used on the federal and most state levels. Each voter gets two votes: one is a personal vote for a specific candidate; the other is for the voter's preferred political party. The second vote—the party vote—determines how many representatives will be sent from each party to the national parliament, the Bundestag. One-half of the seats in the Bundestag are allocated to the winners from the personal vote while the other half are allocated based on the party distribution. This voting method reflects both the individual's candidate choice as well as the party's share of the overall vote. Although the United Kingdom still uses single-seat, winner-take-all elections for the House of Commons, mixed systems are used in the Scottish parliament and in the National Assembly for Wales.

Think of it this way: if Oregon's US congressional representation were based on the proportions of the votes actually cast, then at least two of the state's five House members would be Republican. Maybe then Oregonian voters would feel less orphaned and political polarization would diminish. The Constitution doesn't prevent this type of election, but a federal law would need to be amended. In the meantime, state legislatures and city councils can implement this type of election immediately.

GEOGRAPHY: ANOTHER ISSUE UNDERMINING COMPETITION

Geographic over- and underrepresentation skews representation and thus undermines competition—and this, in turn, stalls participation in the democratic process. It all goes back to the Constitutional Convention and the Great Compromise that was forged in 1787 to balance the needs of larger states, favoring population as the basis of representation, and of smaller states, seeking equal representation for each state. The Great Compromise was a bicameral system: equal representation in the Senate, in which each state would have two representatives, and a number of representatives in the House proportional to the state's population. The Great Compromise passed by only one vote after eleven days of debate,[34] but its outcome is a massive distortion in the principle of one person/one vote. States with smaller populations have far more representatives per population than states with larger populations because of the requirement of equal representation in the Senate. For example, residents of the three least-populated states—Wyoming, Vermont, and North Dakota—have one congressional representative for every 200,000 people, while those in the three states with the highest population—California, Texas, and New

York—have only one congressional member for every 670,000 people. This representational inequality clearly gives citizens from small population states a stronger voice per person than citizens from large states.

The requirement of equal representation in the Senate isn't the only source of representational distortion. The House of Representatives doesn't perfectly reflect the population distribution among the different states. Indeed, the founders recognized that in order for the House of Representatives to continue being "representative," the number of members would need to increase as the nation's population grew.[35] For this reason, the first proposed amendment to the Constitution provided guidance on how to increase the size of representation as population increased, but this amendment failed to pass. Instead, the number of House members grew as territories became states by successive pieces of legislation, but the limit was capped at the 435-member count reached in 1910.[36] As a result, the House of Representatives has not come close to keeping pace with the population, which has tripled since 1910. The original ratio of representation has therefore gone from approximately one representative for every 30,000 people at the time the Constitution was enacted to about one for every 720,000 people as of this writing.

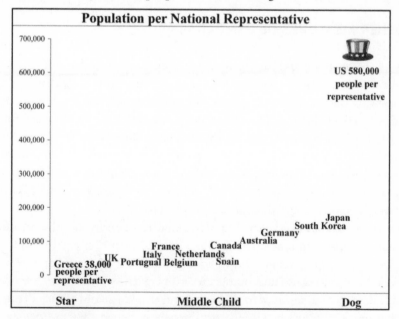

Moreover, the distortion gravely undermines the whole purpose of the House of Representatives, which was to represent the *national distribution* of the population. Today, even that is failing: Wyoming, with its population of 563,000 has the same number of representatives as Montana and Delaware with populations 60 percent and 75 percent larger, respectively. Rhode Island's population is only about 6 percent larger than Montana's, yet it has twice the number of representatives in the House. This issue is most acute for the less populous states that just reach or just miss the threshold for receiving an additional apportionment.

While it is somewhat impractical to grow the House of Representatives at the same rate as the nation's population, it is nevertheless the case that America's rate of national representation is on a completely different scale from that of its international competitors. Among our competitor nations, the average level of national representation (including both houses for bicameral systems and just the single house for the three unicameral systems of Greece, South Korea, and Portugal) is about one representative for every 85,000 people. The United States is thus nearly seven times *less* representative than the competition and more than three times less representative than the next closest competitor, Japan.[37]

OTHER MEASURES OF DEMOCRACY

While competition and participation are easily comprehensible and accessible measures of a country's democratic process, we sense intuitively that they are somewhat narrow. After all, to take just one example, Italy has high performance measures in both competition and participation, yet its multiparty divisiveness has given it more than sixty governments since World War II, and this instability has been exacerbated by massive corruption scandals. So, as metrics go, competition and participation, while providing important insight, do not tell the whole story. Consequently, we are going to explore some broader measures of democracy, and these are a bit more subjective.

A system known as Polity IV uses five inputs to measure the robustness of a country's democratic process: competitiveness of participation, regulation of participation, competitiveness of executive recruitment, openness of executive recruitment, and constraints on the executive branch.[38] This system was originally developed to test how long governments would last and so includes measurements for more than 160 countries through the period 1800 to 1999.[39]

Thanks to the breadth of this dataset, most of the countries on our competitor list currently receive the maximum score, ten out of ten. The only exceptions are

France, with a score of nine out of ten, and Belgium and South Korea, both of which receive a score of eight out of ten. Belgium and South Korea receive lower scores for competitiveness of participation because it was judged that nonelites are less able to gain significant access to political parties in those countries. Both also score lower on regulation of participation because their institutional structures for political expression are less well developed. France's lower score on executive constraints is due to the French president having less legal independence than heads of state of other countries.

The Will of the People

New York City, with its population of more than eight million people, has more residents than nearly forty of the fifty American states. In 1993 and 1996, New York City residents approved a ballot initiative—direct democracy—establishing term limits on their city officials: two terms and out. In 2008, Mayor Michael Bloomberg, one of the richest Americans, decided that he wanted to run for a third term. Bloomberg succeeded in persuading the city council to overturn the term-limit rule, allowing the mayor and several council members to run for reelection. Bloomberg then proceeded to spend $102 million of his own fortune and was barely reelected—at a cost of about $174 per vote. One year later, about 75 percent of New York City voters reaffirmed the two-term limit in a referendum that nevertheless exempted the elected officials at the time. The voice of the people keeps getting trampled in America's largest city.

THE WORLD BANK SCORES GOVERNANCE

The World Bank, comprising 187 member countries and committed to fighting poverty worldwide,[40] is a unique institution with a global perspective on governments. It amasses a tremendous amount of data about different countries and makes this information publicly available, offering in addition a number of tools to make the data digestible. Included in its data is an annual assessment of the quality of governance in each country in the world. The assessment uses six Governance Indicators, as the World Bank calls them: voice and accountability, political stability/no violence, government effectiveness, regulatory quality, rule of law, and control of corruption. These indicators are critical to the functioning of a vibrant democracy, and so they are examined here.

Where do the data for the assessment come from? The World Bank gathers perceptions of governance from thirty-one different sources provided by twenty-five separate organizations, then it analyzes the input in terms of the Governance Indicators. Admittedly, these are not purely objective measurements.[41] Nevertheless, since the World Bank Governance Indicators are widely cited in the scientific literature and are often used as inputs into other measures of governments, they are presented here—with the caveat that the World Bank offers little insight for why it gives a particular country its particular score. On the other hand, the number and diversity of the sources apply something of a brake on subjectivity, so the comparisons make sense even if they lack ideal objectivity. Because these metrics are designed to assess all countries, not just developed countries, the measurements for our competitive group tend to cluster at the higher end of the scale.

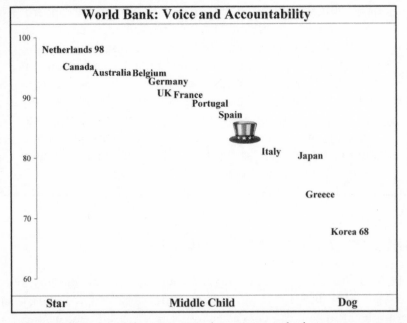

Voice and accountability measures the extent to which citizens can participate in selecting their government, and it rates freedom of expression, freedom of association, and free media.[42] Governments with low voice and accountability ratings do not reflect the will of the people. According to the World Bank ratings, the United States has an average measure, far below that of the Netherlands, Canada, and Australia, the leading countries on this indicator. This reflects issues with American applications of the First Amendment guarantees of freedom of speech, assembly, press, religion, and petitioning the government for redress of grievances, all of which have been eroded, in the view of many, by the American war on terror. The state-level variability in election procedures, problems counting overseas military voters,[43] and inconsistent policies on counting absentee ballots also raise issues on the voice and accountability front.

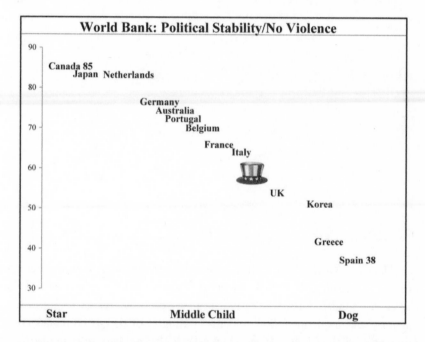

Political stability and absence of violence measures the perceived likelihood that the government will be destabilized or overthrown by unconstitutional or violent means, including domestic violence and terrorism.[44] The United States ranks below average on this measurement—a likely reflection of the high levels of violence in American society as well as the undermining of constitutional rights in the Patriot Act and other antiterrorist actions. In addition, of course, four US presidents have been assassinated while in office and two others have been hurt in assassination attempts—an amazingly high rate given that, at the time this book was written, there have been only forty-four presidents. No other competitor has this rate of violence against its head of state. Market Stars for political stability and absence of violence include Canada, Japan, and the Netherlands. Not surprisingly, homicide rates in the market Stars are less than one-half and incarceration rates less than one-fifth the rates in the United States.

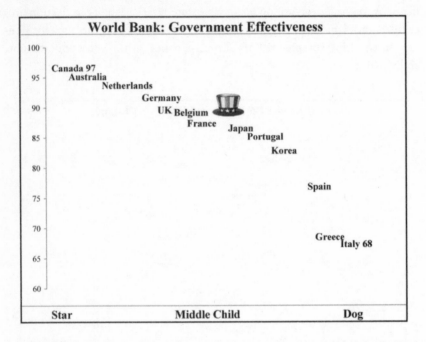

The third World Bank metric, government effectiveness, captures perceptions of the quality of public services, the quality of the civil service and the degree of its independence from political pressures, the quality of policy formulation and implementation, and the credibility of the government's commitment to such policies.[45] The United States has an average rating for government effectiveness, the market Stars for which are Canada, Australia, and the Netherlands. America's rating is likely affected by the influence of lobbyists over the legislative process; for example, more than 1,750 companies and organizations hired some 4,500 lobbyists to influence health reform bills in 2009.[46]

Regulatory quality addresses a government's ability to formulate and implement sound policies and regulations that permit and promote private sector development.[47] The United States again ranks average here, while Australia, the Netherlands, and Canada again garner the highest ratings. Underfunding of US regulatory agencies has been implicated in a number of major disasters, including the British Petroleum oil spill of 2010, the Bernard Madoff investment scandal, the subprime mortgage crisis, and, on the drug safety front, the Vioxx recall. Examples of former industry executives taking on the role of lead regulator are also cited as undermining regulatory quality by essentially putting the foxes in charge of the henhouse. Some recent examples include the following: Wall Street powerhouses Henry Paulson (formerly of Goldman Sachs) and Robert Rubin (also formerly of Goldman Sachs) running the Treasury Department; the Mine Safety and Health Administration under the leadership of Richard Stickler, executive of a mining company, Massey Energy, often cited for safety violations; and anti-safety-regulations lawyer Edwin Foulke running the Occupational Safety and Health Administration.

The rule-of-law metric captures the perceived extent to which enforcement agents have confidence in and abide by the rules of society in contract enforcement, property rights, police activities, and the courts. It also addresses

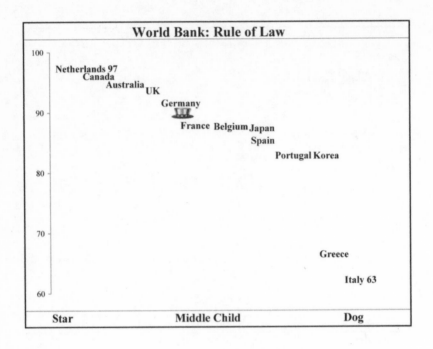

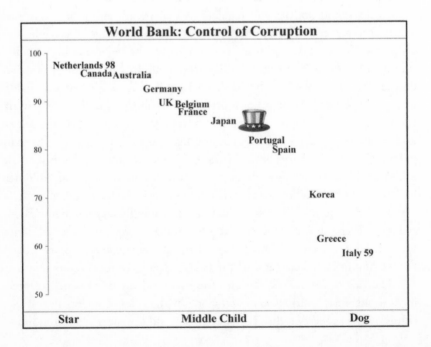

the likelihood of crime and violence.[48] With the Netherlands, Canada, and Australia again the Stars of the World Bank's assessment, and with Greece and Italy far below other competitors, the United States again draws an average rating for rule of law.

Control of corruption assesses the extent to which public power is exercised for private gain, including both petty and grand forms of corruption, as well as "capture" of the state by elites and private interests.[49] This metric is strongly correlated with rule of law, so it is not surprising that the United States again garners an average rating while the Netherlands, Canada, and Australia have top ratings. Italy and Greece are significantly lower than the other countries. The corruption issue has been a factor in Italy for decades and, most recently, has continued with now former prime minister Silvio Berlusconi's attempts to seek immunity from prosecution while he is in office. The US ranking likely reflects such overt corruption as the no-bid contracts awarded to Halliburton in the Iraq and Afghanistan Wars, as well as the insinuating influence on public policy of the financial industry during the 2007–2008 financial crisis. The revolving career door that finds elected politicians becoming paid lobbyists is another likely factor in the corruption assessment.

It's important to note again that, unlike the measurements for competition and participation, these World Bank assessments are based on perceptions of governance and are therefore inherently subjective. Yet the breadth of stakeholders represented gives value to the comparisons drawn. The fact that Australia and the Netherlands consistently rise to the top in nearly all of the measures is a positive sign for those democracies, while the consistently low ratings for South Korea, Greece, and Italy offer a strong negative warning.

THE *ECONOMIST*'S SPIN ON DEMOCRACY

The *Economist* magazine publishes an Index of Democracy that judges nations on five factors: electoral process and pluralism, functioning of government, political participation, political culture, and civil liberties. The judgments are based on what the *Economist* editors describe as expert opinion, although the experts are not identified. Nor has the index passed through external peer review. Although its Index of Democracy is scientifically limited and its measurements opaque, the results are of interest, especially when looked at along with the other assessments presented.

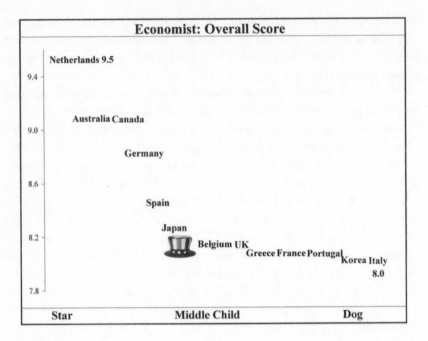

The index gives the United States an average total ranking, with relatively low scores for electoral process and pluralism as well as for functioning of government. The Netherlands, Australia, and Canada are the Stars, and Italy and South Korea are the market Dogs.[50] These overall results align almost exactly with the World Bank Governance Indicators.

Another subjective assessment of governments, Transparency International's Corruptions Perceptions Index,[51] also identified Canada, Australia, and the Netherlands as the best performing countries while Greece and Italy performed the worst. Transparency International's conclusions cannot be considered an independent assessment since two of their ten data sources are the World Bank and the Economist Intelligence Unit.

FREEDOM IS NOT FREE

Freedom House, the nongovernmental organization that monitors the expansion of freedom and advocates for democracy and human rights,[52] has developed a freedom metric for democracy. Freedom House rates a country's political rights and civil liberties and then combines these scores to determine if a country is "free," "partly free," or "not free." Like all ratings systems, this one is imperfect, with most of the criticism targeting the fact that the cutoff points between the three categories are arbitrary; another objection is that the rules for combining the weights for each indicator of political rights and civil liberties are not scientifically grounded but are also arbitrary.[53] But since freedom is a necessary attribute of a thriving democracy, we'll include this measurement in our democracy discussion, accepting it as a somewhat subjective take, but one that can add color to the portrait we're painting.

By Freedom House's freedom measure, all of the countries on our competitor list receive the free rating, although Greece, Italy, Japan, and South Korea get lower ratings on civil liberties.

THE FINAL MARKET ANALYSIS: UNITED STATES IS A MIDDLE CHILD IN DEMOCRACY RANKING

The United States has a low Middle Child rating in the democracy market. It has some of the lowest levels of participation among its competitors based on multiple measurements of voter turnout. It also registers some of the lowest levels of competition due to its two-party system. Idiosyncrasies like the Electoral College and the lack of congressional voting representation for the residents of the nation's capital also undermine our democracy standing. While America is generally a free country, the World Bank and the *Economist* rank it only average versus the competition.

Here as elsewhere, it seems America the corporation has grown tired and lost its vitality. In 1787, we the people created a bold and significant constitution in order to form a more perfect union. Our founders did an admirable job in setting up a democratic country from scratch, and later generations provided such midcourse corrections as abolishing slavery and extending suffrage to women, but then the arteries began to harden and the pulse began to slow, as the data make clear. No wonder our competitor democracies looked elsewhere for models of the mechanisms that enable a democracy to function at peak performance and fulfill its promise of representing all the people.

There is, therefore, much we can learn from the rest of the world, especially from the democracy market Stars like Australia and the Netherlands. But on this issue of democracy, there is also much we can learn in our own backyard. Many American states have already adopted innovations from other countries or developed their own experiments in making democracy more vibrant, more participatory, and more competitive. The nation as a whole can learn much from these efforts.

RECOMMENDATIONS

The data direct us to six recommendations that can improve US democracy. These recommendations do not exist in a vacuum; they are interlocking and interdependent. Implement one, and others may fall into place without the need for legislative or constitutional change.

The first step is basic: ***get more people out to vote.*** One of the most glaring issues with the state of American democracy is that about one-half of eligible Americans choose not to vote. Whatever the reason—lack of trust in government, too much partisanship among the population, low levels of interest in politics, disbelief in the true effect of voting, institutional barriers—it is sad to realize that one-half of us discard a right for which millions have fought and died.

Mandatory voting with a penalty for those who don't vote is a solution that would not work in the United States. It goes against the cultural grain. After all, as the saying goes, "not voting is a vote," and making it mandatory would strike most Americans as removing a right. Moreover, people driven to the polls out of fear of a fine will vote with an indifference that in no way advances meaningful participation in the democratic process.

There are simple legislative steps, however, that can help increase voter turnout without driving the apathetic to vote blindly. Perhaps the most important and effective would be eliminating the two-step process of first registering and then voting. Not a common practice in other countries, the register-first process is found in nearly all states in the United States. The simplest solution is Election Day registration; voter turnout in 2000 was about 15 percent higher in states that had Election Day registration than in those that did not.[54]

The voting process can be further simplified by generating voter lists based on such preexisting government information as driver's licenses, income tax returns, and juror registration information. Using government-run population databases to develop voter lists has succeeded in Austria, Germany, France, Belgium, and Canada.

With "inconvenience" often cited as a reason for not voting, it's time to move to electronic voting, enhanced absentee voting, or voting by mail to enhance the convenience factor. Oregon has embraced convenience in two major ways: first, by offering many ways for voters to register, including online, and second, by passing a 1998 ballot initiative requiring that all elections be conducted by mail. Oregon's voter turnout rate is in the top 20 percent of all states, and its election costs have been greatly reduced.

Electronic voting is also likely to increase participation by younger voters. Across most nations, younger citizens are less likely to vote than older voters. With the United States being one of the youngest countries among its competitors, it seems reasonable that electronic voting could have a significant impact on the younger, more tech-savvy American voters.

Yes, electronic voting raises the potential for voter fraud since it makes it possible to commit the fraud faster and on a more widespread basis. But there is nothing new about voter fraud. Witness "voting the dead" in Chicago in 1960 or Texas counties delivering 100 percent of the vote for Landslide Lyndon Johnson in 1948. Imagine that on a much bigger scale and done in nanoseconds.

The key to fighting fraud in electronic voting is made clear by what happened in Florida in 2000 when the voter rolls were "cleaned" of some one hundred thousand legitimate voters—the vast majority Democrats—by Database Technologies. This error was augmented by a poorly designed and insufficiently secure system from Global Election Systems that was incapable of explaining why or how more than sixteen thousand votes for presidential candidate Al Gore disappeared.[55] While the television reporters gathered to watch the spectacle of chad inspection, the real fraud had occurred long before and had been far more widespread than a few isolated counties. There is no simple solution to minimizing the risk of fraud, but these experiences make it crystal clear that private companies should never be allowed to perform this work without government-mandated and government-supervised quality checks. One good example is in India, the world's largest democracy, with a larger population—much of it illiterate—than the United States. Yet India has succeeded in holding national elections using computer technology that was developed, is owned, and is operated by the Indian government. Surely the US government can aspire to do as well as that.

Second, we must open the door to a *more accurate representation of the people's will, including enabling more political parties*. One of the most effective ways to get more people out to vote is to guarantee that their voices will be heard. Many Americans are frustrated by the limitations of a system of two parties that too often fail to represent their beliefs.

One market Star, Australia, uses preferential voting to enable more voices to be heard. Again, here's how it works: you, the voter, rank the candidates on the ballot. If no candidate receives a majority, the candidate with the lowest vote total is eliminated. The ballots of the eliminated candidate are reallocated among the remaining candidates according to the second-preference votes; that is, if you voted for the eliminated candidate as your first choice, your ballot goes to your second choice. This continues until a candidate has a majority.

This system can be simplified to a single vote through above-the-line voting for the preferred party, or the voter can exercise his or her right to specify whatever order of candidates he or she chooses. In the American system, preferential voting would allow voters to consider third-party candidates without fearing that their votes will be discarded. The existence of preferential voting would dramatically impact the voting and political landscape by empowering more voices to participate in the political process. It would also force the two major parties to recognize the interests of those whose first vote is for a third party since, for those candidates, the Democrats and Republicans will be battling to be their second choice. This preferential voting system is not unique to Australia; it is also used in London's mayoral election, Canada's major political party leadership contests, and in several cities in America, including Burlington, Vermont; Minneapolis, Minnesota; San Francisco, California; and Takoma Park, Maryland.

To make preferential voting viable, there must be a meaningful way to allow third parties to become engaged in the public discourse. That will require revising or eliminating the Commission on Presidential Debates, which effectively prevents third parties from participating by requiring a 15 percent polling rate before a candidate may join the debates. Before the commission began moderating the elections in 1988, the League of Women Voters was in charge; the league resigned as debate moderator, claiming that "the demands of the two campaign organizations would perpetrate a fraud on the American voter." This is a deliberate repression of third parties by the two-party power structure that all Americans should find unfair and unacceptable.

Third, we must end gerrymandering and must instead *draw political lines based on geography, not politics*, as originally intended. Gerrymandering congressional borders based on party affiliations, race, or some other criterion in order to maximize your support and minimize your opponent's creates congressional district maps that look like a combination of computer-drawn algorithms and children's crayon art. The idea is to pack the other party's voters into fewer districts, thus limiting the number of districts they can win, or to scatter your opponent's voters among a bunch of districts to deny them a sufficiently large voting bloc in any single district. The phrase was first created to describe the salamander-like shape of a district border drawn by Massachusetts governor Elbridge Gerry in 1812 to give his political party an advantage. Gerrymandering is often found in elections where there is a single winner, as opposed to elections where there is proportional representation, and is usually initiated by incumbents tightening their grips on power. The issue is so extreme in the United States that in 2004, election observers from the Office for Democratic Institutions and Human Rights, a part of the Organisation for Security and Cooperation in Europe (OSCE), criticized the congressional redistricting process and the resulting lack of competitiveness in congressional election contests.[56]

Among its undemocratic consequences, gerrymandering gives an extraordinary advantage to incumbents. It also has the side effect of increasing political partisanship since once a politician is assured of reelection (through redistricting), that politician now has less need for compromising with dissenting views or even campaigning in any meaningful way.

Gerrymandering has led to legislative standoffs. In 2003, the Republican majority in the Texas legislature redistricted the state. This redistricting resulted in diluting the voting power of the heavily Democratic counties by distributing their residents out to more Republican districts. Democratic legislators famously "hid" in neighboring states in an attempt to stall the vote. In 2006, the Supreme Court, in a shockingly antidemocratic ruling, upheld the right of states to redistrict for political purposes as often as they like, provided race is not used as a consideration.[57]

Some competitor countries address gerrymandering by tasking nonpartisan organizations or cross-party bodies with defining constituency borders, thus taking the responsibility out of the hands of politicians who have obvious self-interest in the results. Examples include the United Kingdom's Boundary Commission and Australia's Electoral Commission. The Netherlands circumvents the issue of gerrymandering by using an electoral system with only one nationwide voting district for the election of national representatives. In Iowa, the nonpartisan Legislative Services Bureau determines boundaries of electoral districts. The bureau forbids considerations of incumbent impact, previous boundary locations, and political party proportions while satisfying federally mandated contiguity and population equality criteria. Iowa's resulting districts are generally regular polygons—not strangely shaped, politically motivated lines.

Similarly, the states of Washington,[58] Arizona,[59] and California[60] have created standing committees comprised of nonpoliticians for the redistricting following the 2010 census. California's Citizens Redistricting Commission, for example, issued its maps in June 2011; the maps indicated clear and profound changes in the state's voting picture.

In addition to putting nonpartisan commissions in charge of redistricting, it's time to take legislative action to place regularity constraints on the shapes of districts; this would work better to combat gerrymandering than the current requirements for contiguity and population balance. The contiguity requirement is extremely weak, often resulting in districts with very thin threads of land connecting entirely different parts of a state. Similarly, constraining the shapes of districts would limit the ability of politicians and skilled computer programmers to determine the political representation.

One more point about gerrymandering: if proportional representation and some of the other recommendations of this chapter were to be implemented, the gerrymandering problem would lose much of its punch. For example, if the number of representatives from each political party for each state were to reflect the overall distribution of the votes, then how you draw the districts within the state would no longer be such an important consideration.

Fourth, we must aim for a more accurate representation of how our population is distributed by *expanding the House of Representatives*. If we don't, low-population states will continue to have a disproportionate amount of political power, thus exacerbating the inequality of citizens being treated differently based on which state they live in. While there will never be a perfect number of representatives, the current limit of 435 was established when America had one-third the number of people it has today. Residents of less populated states that are just below the threshold for apportionment, like Montana and Delaware, receive far less representation in the House than states that just exceed the threshold, like Rhode Island.

While most competitor countries have one national representative for every 40,000 to 100,000 citizens, the US representation rate is more than three times lower than that of the next closest country, Japan, and about fifteen times lower than that of Greece. It isn't realistic for the House to move to the representation rates that were originally indicated in the Constitution, but a rate that approaches the level of the closest competitor would be a good step, provided that other corrections to our democracy also take place.

Fifth, we should *make proportional representation the norm*. While proportional representation and mixed proportional representation models have grown over the last century, the United States still clings to the winner-take-all election structure developed more than two centuries ago. To elect members of the House of Representatives by proportional representation rather than by winner-take-all congressional districts would not take a constitutional amendment. All it would take is a modification of a single federal law that requires single-seat districts to elect members of the House. The result of using proportional representation would be that the number of representatives from each party would reflect the popular vote in each state. Remember the Oregon example? There, even though 46 percent of Oregon's votes for members of the House of Representatives went to Republican candidates, only one out of five Republican candidates was elected to the House. If the election had been held by proportional representation, two of the five Representatives would be Republican and the door would be opened more widely to third-party candidates.

Here's how it would work in the voting booth: instead of the ballot Oregonians now have, on which they vote for a representative from the congressional district in which they live (and into which they may have been gerrymandered), Oregonians would vote for their preferred party. The five Oregon representatives would then be distributed based on the percentage of the vote for each party, and the specific representatives themselves would be drawn from the party lists. In a five-seat district, it would take approximately one-sixth of the votes to win a seat, while one-third of the votes would win two seats.[61]

Proportional representation would also make room for third-party voices to be heard while dampening the disproportionate influence over national politics of small-population states. In proportional representation elections, fewer voters would feel "orphaned." Voter turnout would likely rise because the number of electable options would increase and, as a result of having more electable options, voters would feel more confident that they could elect representatives who reflect their values. It is also likely that partisanship would diminish —since more political parties would be represented and coalitions would probably need to be formed—which should also spur turnout.

Proportional representation has worked effectively throughout the world, including in our market Stars, the Netherlands and Australia. It enjoyed an American vogue in the middle years of the twentieth century, working successfully in more than twenty municipalities including New York City, Cincinnati, Cleveland, and West Hartford. It still operates in Cambridge, Massachusetts, and in some other local elections. A concerted effort by those benefiting most from the two-party system managed to put an end to proportional representation in most of these cities, unfortunately by rolling out scare tactics about racial groups and Communists seizing control of local governments.[62]

Still, proportional representation can be implemented in state and municipal legislatures at any time under existing law; it will require a federal law to change the national representation. It will also require the will to stand up to the two-party machine.

Finally, it's time—it's past time—to *correct constitutional errors* and to fill some persistent gaps in the Constitution. To fill the gaps, we should ask and answer two simple questions: (1) If we were designing our system of government today, knowing what we now know about democracy, what would we do differently? (2) How do other nations that formed democracies more recently deal with the issues we've identified as needing correction in our own Constitution?

To most of the world, it seems both bizarre and backward that residents of this nation's capital do not have a voting representative in Congress. There seems no justification for this profound gap, which is such an embarrassment to America's claims of being a shining example of democracy. It happens in no other functioning democracy, and clearly, if we were designing a system from scratch, we would not build this representational denial into the rulebook. It would take a constitutional amendment to correct this error; the amendment would require a two-thirds majority in both houses of Congress as well as in three-fourths of the states. Amendments have been proposed again and again to correct this error of omission, but they have not been passed—for one simple reason. Washington, DC, is overwhelmingly Democratic, and Republicans are not keen to let more Democratic votes into Congress. It took about 175 years for residents of Washington, DC, to get the right to vote in presidential elections, and it may take 175 more before they have a voting representative in Congress. Taxation without representation goes on.

Another needed correction is to the Electoral College. The Founding Fathers did not trust an uneducated and often illiterate populace, so they established the college as a filter through which popular choice could be transformed into what they assumed would be wiser Elector choices, if needed. The founders didn't anticipate the rise of the two-party system or the increasing rates of literacy and education. More than two hundred years later, America plods along with this archaic, antidemocratic system that routinely undermines the voice of the people. The Electoral College has not been reproduced by any new democracies, despite their admiration for our Constitution, and few Americans would contend today that if we were designing from scratch a way to elect a president, the Electoral College would be the way to go. They know that if you live in a state that is heavily of one party and you are of the other, you basically have no say in your state's vote for president, while voters in swing states have a disproportionate amount of power. In practice, the Electoral College is a huge step away from the principle of one person/one vote. The disproportionate power of those living in swing states is readily apparent during a national election campaign, when candidates rarely visit or invest campaign funds in states that aren't "in play"—that is, states whose electoral votes are considered to be already won or lost based on large margins of victory in previous elections and on current polling. For example, in the 2008 presidential election, the campaign of then candidate Barack Obama spent nearly $40 million on advertising in Pennsylvania, a swing state with twenty-one electoral votes, and about $25,000 in Illinois, with an equivalent number of electors.[63] The Obama strategists knew that there was no reason to spend any time courting voters in his home state, Illinois, since he would clearly win the majority of Illinois's popular votes and all twenty-one of its electoral votes. Republican and third-party supporters in Illinois had no chance of having their voices heard.

The odds of an amendment to eliminate the Electoral College and use the popular vote instead are virtually nil, but Maine and Nebraska have found a simple way around the structural issues of the Electoral College. All states should mirror their practice of allocating their electoral votes based on proportional representation. This would help correct for the current all-or-nothing system used in forty-eight of the fifty states and its resulting over- or underweighting of votes based on whether or not you live in a swing state. More importantly, it will force candidates to take the votes of every American seriously, not just that small percentage living in swing states. It's unlikely, given what we know about the power of the two-party structure, that many other states will follow Maine and Nebraska in this; after all, it's a mechanism that threatens the majority party in the state.

We must also find ways to ensure that election officials really are impartial and that they act impartially, one of the most basic principles in free and fair elections. Nowhere was this violated more egregiously than in the 2000 presidential election in Florida, in which the secretary of state overseeing the election, Katherine Harris, was also the cochair of George W. Bush's election committee. She should have recused herself, but a federal law is needed to ensure such impartiality.

While reforming our democracy seems like a daunting task, there's a shortcut. If two-thirds of the states submitted applications, then Congress would be compelled to call for an amendment-proposing convention, called an Article V Convention.[64] During one of these conventions, Congress cannot restrict the scope of the amendments that are proposed. After amendments are proposed, they would then have to be ratified by three-quarters of the states. Imagine the changes that could take place in our government if the American people, not Congress, drafted amendments in a convention with our accumulated knowledge of what works and doesn't work in a modern democracy.

Chapter 5

A BALANCING ACT: EQUALITY

We can have democracy in this country, or we can have great
wealth concentrated in the hands of a few, but we can't have
both.

**—US Supreme Court Justice Louis Brandeis
(1856–1941)**

I f we are going to compare our competitor countries in terms of how equal
each is, we must first know how to measure equality, and if we are going to
measure equality, we must first define it. Neither the definition nor the measuring of equality is easy, making this a challenging subject to discuss.

Certainly equality is one of the values that Americans hold most dear, and
it may be the one we take most for granted. After all, it was America's Declaration of Independence that articulated the phrase that has resonated down the
centuries and around the globe—that "all men are created equal, that they are
endowed by their Creator with certain inalienable rights," including, of course,
"life, liberty, and the pursuit of happiness."

But what exactly do we mean by equality? There are many different lenses
through which to view this question. Focused through a legal lens, equality
means that all people have the same rights and protections, but this isn't very
helpful for drawing quantitative cross-country comparisons. If we look at
equality through an economic lens, it might mean that everyone earns the same
wages or salary or possesses the same wealth. This runs counter to human
nature and to most people's perception of fairness. Few believe that a ham-
burger flipper at a local fast food joint should earn the same as a neurosurgeon
who has trained for years to acquire the specialized skills she uses in performing
hours-long, life-saving operations.

Rather, the interpretation of equality that resonates with most of us derives from our belief that we live in a meritocracy, a society in which an individual's success is determined by his talent and effort and not by inherited wealth, where he came from, or whom he knows. In a true meritocracy, everyone, regardless of race, creed, economic background, or parents' education, has an equally fair shot at achieving his or her own greatness, whether the achievement is social, economic, or intellectual. America proudly points to example after example of this American dream—from presidents who rose from humble beginnings to the self-made techno-billionaires who started their businesses in the garage.

This belief in American meritocracy—in every individual's boundless potential—has created the long-held perception of the United States as a "land of opportunity," the desired destination of countless immigrants for hundreds of years, many with dreams of political freedom, religious freedom, and economic opportunity. While it didn't take long for these immigrants to discover that the streets were not paved with gold, their children and grandchildren, and the many others who continue to come here, still tend to believe that the US meritocracy offers a greater opportunity to fulfill aspirations than other countries.

In the real world, however, there are no true meritocracies. In all societies, those born to parents of greater wealth, more connections, higher education, and other pluses are more likely to be successful than those born into families without such advantages. They inherit not just genetically transmitted intelligence but also their parents' focus on education or achievement, not to mention the contacts, connections, and other "helping hands" that parental wealth may offer. All these factors make it easier to succeed.

Knowing that there is no perfect meritocracy, we are left to ask which societies have the highest levels of equality. Since our focus is on how the United States stands compared to other competitor wealthy countries, we need to select measures of equality that compare countries both quantitatively and fairly.

Economics is the obvious place to look. Income (the money an individual earns) and wealth (an individual's total assets) are two areas in which we can measure equality. Vast differences between the wealthiest and poorest will indicate a society in which equality of opportunity is strained at best. Related to these economic measurements is the concept of socioeconomic mobility—that is, the ability to cross from one social and economic class or status to another. If it is relatively easy for a talented, ambitious, diligent person to jump from poverty to wealth, then large gaps between the rich and poor may be more acceptable. So, socioeconomic mobility is a critically important metric for equality. Gender equality, in which we compare the relative performance of women and men in each country, is also important. Here we will want to measure political representation as well as wage and income equality.

The problem with all of these metrics is that so many are simply not comparable country to country. It wouldn't make sense, for example, to try to compare equality among racial groups in the United States or in the United Kingdom with like data for Japan or Korea, which have substantively more homogeneous populations. Such a comparison would even be highly questionable between the United States and Great Britain, since these two competitor countries demonstrate different racial distributions in their populations. Data limitations as well as major differences in immigration policy make cross-country comparisons between citizens and immigrants impossible. Analyses of income inequality within different parts of countries—US states versus Canadian provinces, for example—come up against very different levels of disaggregation. The result may be computationally accurate, but due to the wide range in the number of groupings in different countries (fifty US states versus thirteen Canadian provinces and territories), it is generally not a fair cross-country comparison, and so we will avoid such data.

Instead, the measurements we'll use in exploring equality are income, wealth, socioeconomic mobility, and gender. But if these are the tools of measurement, what is the optimal value against which each country is being ranked? For the other values measured in this book, optimal performances were easy to determine: longest life expectancy for health, lowest homicide rate for safety, and highest test scores for education. But what is the "best performance" for income equality? Everybody earning the same income seems neither possible nor ideal. History and human nature have made it abundantly clear that a system like this, one that fails to reward people for different levels of talent and effort, is not likely to succeed. It is equally impossible and undesirable to have perfect inequality of income or wealth, in which one individual owns all the wealth of a nation. So for income and wealth equality, the optimal value is somewhere between these two extremes, and we don't know exactly what that value is. Since we are examining only wealthy countries in this analysis, we will identify the Stars as the countries with the highest levels of wealth and income equality and the Dogs as those with the lowest. For socioeconomic mobility and gender equality, there is no ambiguity: the country with the highest measure of mobility is the mobility Star, and the country with the highest level of balance between men and women in terms of achievement is the gender equality Star.

One other question is important to answer: Why should we care? That is, why does equality or inequality matter? Why does it matter that some people become fabulously wealthy while others can barely afford a place to live? Shouldn't we encourage the accumulation of wealth? Aren't large income disparities a natural occurrence in every wealthy country?

There are important reasons of self-interest for worrying about equality—or rather, about the erosion of equality. Extreme inequality—of income, wealth, or anything else, for that matter—undermines democracy. The concentration of a large portion of assets into the hands of a few has historically been associated with oppression and has typically become the eventual trigger of revolution. The problem was summarized with great eloquence in a quote attributed to Abraham Lincoln in 1864: "I see in the near future a crisis approaching that unnerves me and causes me to tremble for the safety of my country. . . . Corporations have been enthroned and an era of corruption in high places will follow, and the money power of the country will endeavor to prolong its reign by working upon the prejudices of the people until all wealth is aggregated in a few hands and the Republic is destroyed."[1]

When wealth is thus aggregated, the wealthy tend to have overwhelming influence on the design of laws that then tilt the balance more and more in their favor. Thus favored, the moneyed classes are even more advantaged when it comes to amassing still more wealth and power, while opportunities for mobility become rarer. In time, democracy shaped by high income and wealth inequality becomes transformed into governments that seem more like aristocracies. In that scenario, the rich, empowered to direct policy from their gated communities, and the poor, struggling to pay rent with their minimum-wage, service-sector McJobs, never meet across the vast disparity of wealth, power, and opportunity.

Inequality breeds instability. Two thousand years ago, Plutarch wrote that "an imbalance between rich and poor is the oldest and most fatal ailment of all republics,"[2] a statement proven time and again in history. If a highly unequal society is to be stable, the deprived majority needs to accept that the distribution of income, wealth, rights, and status is fair—or that it is unchangeable. (Physical intimidation has often been used to "encourage" such acceptance and enforce stability.) If the deprived majority does not accept this, then political change is likely to ensue—maybe through a democratic process, maybe through violence. That is why nearly all political experts agree that the existence of extremely large centers of private power and wealth is a threat to the long-term viability of a democracy. The intermittent influence of our own populist movements has shown how organized people can become an effective counterforce to organized wealth, shaking up the democracy and restoring it to a new level of stability.

So let's take a look at where America stands when it comes to equality—and see whether American democracy is threatened.

INCOME

It's important to draw a clear distinction between two separate kinds of income. One, which we'll call unadjusted, is an individual's income before taxes have been deducted and before any income transfers—in the form of Social Security, housing grants, or food stamps, for example—have been disbursed to the individual. Adjusted income, therefore, is income after taxes have been taken out and after any other income has been transferred in.

Looking at the distribution of income, we see first that wealthy Americans have a far higher share of the total unadjusted income than the wealthy in other countries, a trend that has been increasing rapidly since the 1980s.

Second, inequality in adjusted income—posttax and after transfers—is also far higher in the United States than in other countries and has increased more rapidly than nearly all of the competition.

Third, at the same time, the earnings of the American working poor are comparatively lower than those of other countries.

We'll use three separate metrics to look at income, and we'll first explain each—the Gini index, the 90/10 interdecile ratio, and percentile ownerships.

Probably the most common metric used to measure income equality/inequality is the Gini index. Developed in 1912 by the Italian statistician Corrado Gini,[3] the index measures the shape of distributions—in this case, of income. It ranges from zero to one, with zero representing perfect equality, where everyone earns the same amount, and with one representing perfect inequality, where all available income belongs to one person and the rest of the country earns nothing. Countries with strong social support systems like Sweden, Norway, and Denmark register Gini indexes of around 0.25,[4] while the highest reported Gini indexes, which tend to be from developing countries, reach about 0.60. There is a notable absence of data from many of the natural resource–rich economies in the Middle East, where Gini indexes are expected to be very high.[5]

The 90/10 interdecile ratio is the ratio of two quantities: the income level above which the 10 percent of households with the highest incomes are found is then divided by the income level below which the 10 percent of households with the lowest incomes are found. The closer this ratio is to one, the greater the equality; the larger the ratio, the more unequal the society. Among Organisation for Economic Co-operation and Development (OECD) countries, the interdecile ratios range from below three for Sweden and Denmark to nearly nine for Mexico.[6] Like all ratios, the interdecile ratio has the strength of being highly intuitive; its key weakness is that it contains less information than the Gini index.

A third way to measure income equality/inequality is to examine percentiles. For example, we could measure how much of the total income of a nation is earned by the highest-earning 1 percent of the population.

All three measures can be used to assess both adjusted and unadjusted income, and all three confirm the stark inequality of income in the United States.

Adjusted Income

Both the Gini index and the interdecile ratio measurements confirm that the United States has a high posttax, after-transfer income inequality compared to

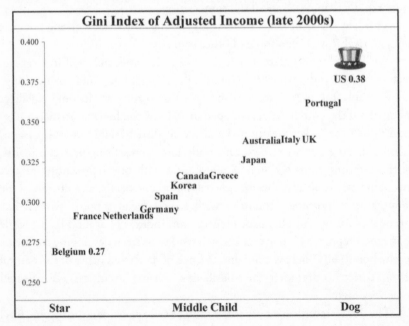

its competitor nations. Let's start with the Gini index from 2007 to 2008, the latest period for which figures are available, which predates the effects of the US financial crisis of 2008. As seen in the Gini Index of Adjusted Income chart, the United States is clearly the Dog of the field when it comes to adjusted-income inequality,[7] a fact accepted by all points along the political spectrum.[8] At the same time, Belgium, France, and the Netherlands, with the lowest Gini indexes, have the highest levels of equality.

The interdecile ratio confirms this conclusion, again showing that the United States has one of the highest levels of inequality, exceeded only by Portugal, while the most equal countries are, again, Belgium, France, and the Netherlands.[9]

Race is a factor in income inequality in the United States, as it is in virtually all of the measurements explored in this book. For example, the median earnings for Caucasians are about 45 percent higher than for Hispanics and nearly 30 percent higher than for African Americans.[10] This disparity persists when we examine men and women separately. Caucasian men earn over 50 percent more than Hispanic and African American men, while Caucasian women earn about 40 percent more than Hispanic women and roughly 12 percent more than African American women.[11] We will discuss the role of gender more

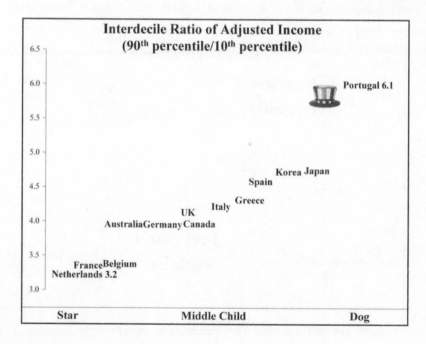

thoroughly later in this chapter. While the racial distribution of the competitor countries is different from that of the United States, it is important to note that racial disparities in income have also been reported in Canada.[12]

Some of the disparity can be traced to differences in educational outcomes, but racially based income differences persist regardless of educational level. For example, African Americans with masters degrees earn incomes some 25 percent lower than those of masters-degreed Caucasians; undergraduate-educated African Americans earn 30 percent less than undergraduate-educated Caucasians; and high school–educated African Americans earn some 25 percent less than high school–educated Caucasians.[13] The consistency of salary gap across all education levels indicates that education alone will not result in income equality due to persistent racial disparities.

While the current level of income inequality in the United States reflects changes over time both in earnings patterns and in policies affecting income redistribution through taxation and transfers, it is also the case that America's higher level of adjusted-income inequality compared to other wealthy countries has been observed for more than a century.[14] During the mid-1980s, the United States had the third-highest income inequality in its competitor group, topped at the time only by Spain and Portugal. In the decades since, its adjusted-income inequality has increased at a rate higher than in nearly every

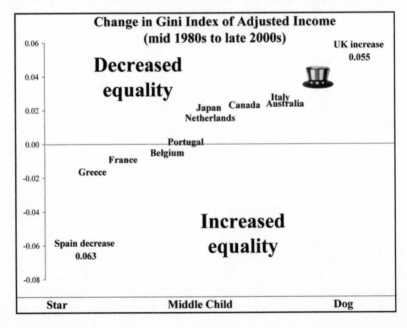

other competitor country—that is, the gap between the highest and lowest incomes has increased more in the United States than in other competing countries. More generally, during the last decade of the twentieth century and the first decade of the twenty-first, rising inequality in wealthy countries was not a foregone conclusion: while most of our competitors saw adjusted-income inequality increase, four countries—Belgium, France, Greece, and Spain—experienced increasing equality rather than increasing inequality.[15] Germany is not included in this graph since it saw the merging of poorer East Germany with wealthier West Germany during this time period.

It is inescapable that social policy has played a role in this growing American income inequality. One key study that examined the differences between the Gini indexes for unadjusted and adjusted income focused on how countries responded to changes in the unadjusted-income inequality.[16] While Australia, Canada, Germany, the United Kingdom, and the United States experienced an increase in the unadjusted-income Gini index, the United States was the only one of these countries that did not increase its rate of redistribution. The fact that the income disparity between higher- and lower-income Americans increased sharply, and that there was no increase in the relative support to lower-income Americans, reflects on America's cultural attitudes toward inequality and, perhaps, the lack of responsiveness of the legislative process.

In theory, redistribution should increase as market inequality increases since the typical voter, who is not seeing his or her income rise rapidly with the increasing inequality, will benefit more from redistribution policies.[17] In practice, this isn't always true; the theory presumes that most voters support redistribution laws and that the legislature is responsive to the needs of the majority of the voters—and that may not be the case.

In spite of the United States having high levels of unadjusted-income inequality, its rate of social spending is less than in nearly every other competitor country except Korea, which spends one-half of what the United States spends, and Australia, where social expenditures are marginally lower.[18] Confirming this, a thirteen-country study involving eight of our competitors and using data up to the early 2000s showed that the lower rate of redistribution in the United States is due mostly to its having the lowest rate of social transfers (such as welfare payments), far below the rates in the other seven of our competitors, Australia, Belgium, Canada, France, Germany, the Netherlands, and the United Kingdom.[19] Nor is this low level of social protection a new trend; as far back as the 1920s, the United States lagged the United Kingdom, France, and Germany in its rate of such public aid programs as vouchers and subsidies for lower-income families.[20] This tendency toward low levels of social spending is yet another reflection of the American belief in a small central government, of the presumed meritocracy of its economic system, and of pervasive race issues.

The low level of social protection also corresponds to the low overall level of taxation as a percentage of GDP in the United States. In fact, the United States has the lowest level of tax collection of any of the competitor countries, collecting only 25 percent of GDP, compared to countries like France, Italy, and Belgium, all of which collect more than 40 percent.[21] This lower level of tax collection is a reflection of policy decisions in the United States to have lower tax rates.

The data lead us to conclude that US cultural attitudes, including the belief in American meritocracy, do not support major redistributions of wealth to adjust for inequality. Some findings in the World Values Survey confirm this conclusion.[22] The survey found that Americans were more likely than respondents from other competitor countries to agree that "hard work brings success"; correspondingly, Americans were more tolerant of higher income inequalities than citizens of all other countries except Korea. Yet Americans were the second least satisfied with their financial situations; only Koreans were more dissatisfied. Americans were less likely to feel that work is a duty to society, compared to those in the other seven countries who responded to this question. More specific to the subject of inequality, 60 percent of Americans believed that the poor could become rich if they tried hard enough, a percentage that is more than double that of Europeans. Given how American perceptions on these subjects differ from those in other countries, it's appropriate to ask: Does a country's income-inequality rate reflect its national perceptions of what is fair, or does the perception of what is fair drive the country's inequality rate?

Another survey shows a stunning gap between Americans' perception of equality in their country and the reality of it. This survey asked Americans to estimate the current distribution of wealth in the United States and to state their notion of an ideal level of wealth equality. Respondents overestimated the current level of equality and described an ideal wealth distribution model that was even more equal than their overestimation.[23] The perception gap held across all demographic groups in the United States; everyone, including the wealthy and the politically conservative, supported a more equal distribution of wealth than the reality and seemed unaware that the reality is as unequal as it is. So, while we haven't defined an optimal level of equality, Americans intu-itively believe that their society should be more equal.

Unadjusted Income

For unadjusted income—before taxes and before the payout of any transfers—we'll use a percentile metric to look at the income share of the very highest-earning people in the United States. Here we once again see that America's level of income inequality is much higher than that of our competitors. The top 0.1 percent of income earners earned 7.7 percent of the total income, a rate that vastly exceeds that of the competitor countries; the competitor country with the next-closest rate is Canada. This unadjusted-income share shows an Anglophone bias; four of the five most unequal countries are English-speaking.

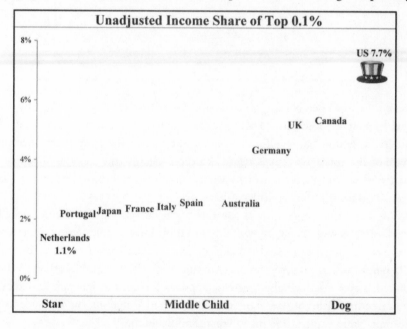

While the United States always had a comparatively higher rate of income inequality, the unadjusted inequality rate has exploded in the last few decades. In the 1970s, the unadjusted-income share of the top 1 percent of American earners was less than 10 percent; as of this writing, it is nearly 25 percent. This rise in unadjusted-income share has not occurred broadly. You'll note in the graph on unadjusted-income share in the United States that the income-share

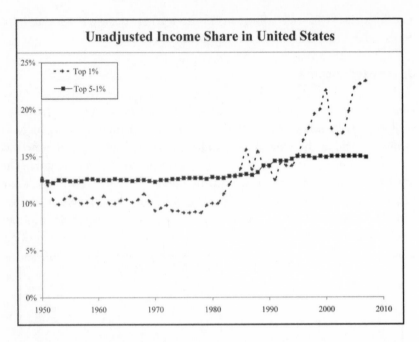

rise for the top 1 percent was much sharper than the rise in income share by the next highest income earners, the people comprising the top 1–5 percent of America's income earners. Since roughly one-half of the gain in the income share of the top 1 percent is related to capital gains (the income on investments),[24] we can understand why the reduction in the capital gains tax has been a top priority for wealthier Americans.

A consistent conclusion about the comparatively rapid increase in US unadjusted-income inequality was supported by another study using the interdecile ratio. The study looked at unadjusted income in different countries during different time periods across an era spanning from 1979 to 2000. It showed the United States with the highest increase in pretax-income inequality, followed by, in descending order of size of increase, the United Kingdom, the Netherlands, Australia, Italy, Canada, Germany, Japan, and Belgium.[25]

"A rising tide lifts all boats,"[26] President John F. Kennedy famously said, but the reality is that some boats in the United States have been lifted far higher than others. One study measuring income by quintiles—the population divided into fifths by household income from lowest to highest income—makes it clear that in Kennedy's generation, cumulative adjusted income growth had remained fairly even among the different income quintiles between 1947 and 1974. From 1974 to 2005, however, the growth was dominated by the wealthier quintiles.[27] Unadjusted-income shares for the top 1 percent were relatively flat from 1950 to the late 1970s as productivity and median household income generally rose together in the decades following World War II.[28] That is to say, for a few decades, the top earners did not capture a larger share of the total income pie; it was a time of comparative income equality. But that time has long since passed in the United States.

Where are the top income earners getting their income? About 20 percent of the top 0.1 percent of American income earners work in the finance industry, about 40 percent are executives and managers in nonfinance industries, while doctors and lawyers make up roughly 10 percent.[29] Given the highly reported Wall Street bonuses that exploded following the dismantling of the Glass-Steagall Act (the law that separated commercial banking from investment activities), it is not surprising to see financial speculators on the list of the superrich. Nor is it a shock to see corporate executives make the grade: it is no secret that the ratio of pay between chief executives and the workers in their companies has gone from about forty in 1980—that is, the CEO was paid forty times what the average worker on the line received in wages—to more than two hundred times that amount by the mid-2000s.[30] Put another way, in the mid-1990s, the five highest-earning executives in the typical US corporation were paid about 5 percent of their company's total earnings. This figure had doubled by the early 2000s to 10 percent of total earnings, and even further increases were reported as of 2006.[31]

Wage Earners

While America's wealthiest have benefited greatly since the 1970s and 1980s, how did the rest of the population do? Not only has the wealth not trickled down, but also the income of those at the lowest end of the scale has grown comparatively less than in other countries. We can readily compare the US minimum wage—the legally determined lowest remuneration employers may pay workers—to that of other countries by computing the expected annual salary of a minimum-wage earner and comparing it to the country's GDP per capita. The computation shows that a US minimum-wage worker earns about 33 percent of the GDP per capita. That is lower than all the other competitor countries with a reported minimum wage (Australia, Belgium, Canada, France, Greece, Japan, Korea, the Netherlands, Portugal, Spain, and the United Kingdom).[32] Minimum-wage laws in the United States have not incorporated cost-of-living adjustments (COLAs), so over time, even though new legislation has raised the wage, it has tended to drift downward in real terms.

A simple way to track this declining drift is to compare the minimum wage to the living wage, which is the theoretical wage level that would allow the earner to afford adequate shelter, food, and other necessities. A high ratio of minimum wage to living wage would indicate that the minimum wage is sufficient to allow the worker to afford basic standards of living, while a low ratio means that the worker is not earning enough to pay the bills. As it turns out, the ratio of minimum wage to living wage in the United States dropped from 94 percent in 1968 to 57 percent in 2003.[33] Conclusion? Those earning the minimum wage were paid far less than was necessary for a decent standard of living.

Connecting the data about America's comparatively high income inequality and its low minimum wage, we see that where income is concerned, America's rich have grown much richer and the American poor struggle to make ends meet to an extent that is not seen elsewhere in the competitor countries and, to an extent, hasn't been seen in US history for generations. This gap in America between the top of the scale and the bottom is disturbingly stark.

Many Americans readily perceive what the data on rising inequality clearly show. In 1988, for example, according to one survey, only 26 percent of Americans thought the United States was divided by class; by 2007, that figure had nearly doubled to 48 percent.[34] In 1988, only 26 percent of those surveyed judged the United States to be a haves-versus-have-nots society; by 2001, the rate was 44 percent.[35] The disparity entered the political debate in the unsuccessful 2004 campaign of Democratic vice-presidential candidate John Edwards, who delivered a stirring convention speech about the dangers of living in "Two Americas" and made that his campaign rallying cry.

Generation to Generation: Can Hope Survive?

Tom, a forty-two-year-old widower, has twin daughters, Britney and Brianna. The twins are in their freshman year of high school and, with their solid grades, dream of being the first in their family to go to college. But due to the financial crisis and ensuing recession, Tom lost his job at the plant. The only job he was able to find was as a stock boy at a discount department store, where he earns the minimum wage of $7.25 an hour with no health benefits. He supplements his $15,000-a-year salary with odd jobs, but his total earnings barely cover rent, utilities, and food, leaving him far short of buying health insurance for his family. Tom encourages the girls to study, but in his heart he knows that his minimum-wage salary cannot cover the costs of sending two children to college and that tuition aid will fall far short. The last thing he wants is to see the dreams of his daughters crushed. Will one have to forgo a college education to help pay for the other's tuition? Will the cycle of being trapped in the lower rungs of America's wealth continue for his daughters? Tom buys a lottery ticket every week and hopes for a better life for the next generation.

WEALTH

By wealth, we mean an individual's total financial assets—both physical assets like real estate and financial assets like stocks, bonds, and cash—minus liabilities like consumer debt or mortgages. Wealth is cumulative. It is amassed over a lifetime and often passed down from generation to generation. It has been estimated that 50–70 percent of all wealth in the United States is inherited rather than generated by the individual.[36] It is this cumulative nature of wealth over time that results in wealth-inequality measures that in general are even higher than income-inequality measures.

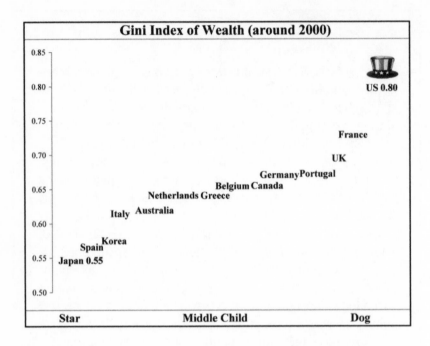

The Gini index for wealth once again finds the United States with the highest inequality, vastly exceeding that of other countries, while Japan and Spain register the highest wealth equality. But it is interesting to note that some of the countries with the lowest income inequality—France, the Netherlands, Germany, and Belgium—exhibit average or even worse than average wealth inequalities,[37] although this may be an artifact of what does and does not get reported.

As with income inequality in the United States, race plays a large role in wealth inequality: African Americans have, on average, about 10 percent of the wealth per capita of Caucasians, while Hispanics fare only slightly better at 12 percent.[38] Here, too, the cumulative effect of wealth inheritance from generation to generation and the cumulative effect of income differences over a lifetime, which enables those receiving higher incomes to have greater savings and investment options, make the wealth gap between races greater than the income gap.

The ability of Americans to accumulate wealth is reflected in the number of billionaires, expressed as the rate of billionaires per one million inhabitants; on this metric, the United States is the undisputed market Star.[39] Nor is it surprising that there is a strong correlation between the rate of billionaires and wealth inequality, as both are measures of wealth accumulation. Since the

wealth accumulates with the few billionaires and isn't spread around the population, a country with a high rate of billionaires will tend to have more unequal
wealth distribution than a country of similar wealth but with a lower rate of
billionaires.

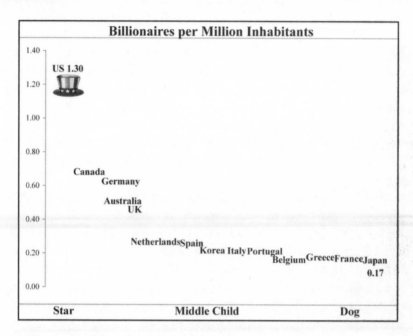

Warren Buffett, one of the richest men in the world, famously said of
wealth accumulation in the United States that "if there was a class war, my class
won."[40] The data bear him out. Between 1983 and 2007, household wealth of
the least-wealthy 40 percent declined from $5,600 in total assets to $2,200,
while the household wealth of the top 1 percent of households roughly doubled from $9.2 million to $18.5 million.[41] The sharp rise in wealth inequality
in the United States over the last couple of decades makes us wonder whether
President Kennedy's "rising tide" isn't really just the wake from the billionaires'
yachts drowning the poor folks paddling in leaky rowboats.

The sharp rise in wealth is easily attributable to increases in compensation,
housing prices, and stock prices, coupled with a decreasing tax burden. Perhaps
the most extreme example of wealth inequality is this: in 2005, the net worth of
two individual Americans, Warren Buffett and Bill Gates, was about the same as
the total combined net worth of the bottom 40 percent of the US population.[42]

SOCIOECONOMIC MOBILITY:
MOVING UP, SIDEWAYS, OR DOWN?

While we all recognize that people will earn different amounts of money and accumulate different amounts of wealth, Americans cling to a belief in a meritocracy in which talent and hard work enable anyone to succeed. Regardless of political philosophy, few in America would argue that a society with little social mobility is a good thing. Societies in which there is little opportunity for social mobility will lack incentives for people to strive. Those born in lower socioeconomic classes will be resigned to their station in life, a self-destructive pattern that all countries seek to avoid. Countries that can generate opportunities for all of their citizens to succeed will maximize the talent pools of their populations, while countries that fail to do so will fall behind, relying on the talents of only the privileged few.

Americans intuitively believe that their country is a meritocracy. A 1999 study found that 61 percent of US respondents agreed or strongly agreed with the statement that "people get rewarded for their effort." This was a higher percentage than in Australia (58 percent), Canada (49 percent), Japan (41 percent), the United Kingdom (33 percent), and France (23 percent); in fact, it was a higher percentage than in every one of the twenty-six countries in the survey except the Philippines.[43] A different survey asking people how much freedom and control they feel they have over the way their lives turn out showed that Americans are tied with Australians and Canadians for the highest self-belief in their freedom and control.[44]

It is particularly difficult to capture income mobility quantitatively. Governments do not generally measure mobility, so special research projects are needed to fill in the gaps where national data are lacking. Those sources cover some but not all of the countries in our competitor groups.

One method of measurement looks at the relationship between the income of one generation and that of the following generation. We expect there to be some correlation between the incomes of the two generations; after all, it is reasonable to assume that wealthier parents provide not only material assets to the next generation but also attributes that may aid their wealth generation. Wealthier parents are typically more educated, are able to invest in their children's development, and tend to entertain higher expectations that their children will gain success.

Your receipt

The Westport Library...

www.westportlibrary.org

Customer Name: DALY, MICHAEL
Customer ID: **********1502
Messages
Patron status is ok.
Patron status is ok.

Items that you checked out

Title:
 The measure of a nation : how to regain
 America's competitive edge and boost
 our global standing
ID: 34015071200420
Due: Saturday, August 06, 2016

Total items: 1
Account balance: $0.45
7/16/2016 1:10 PM
Checked out: 1
Overdue: 0
Hold requests: 0
Ready for pickup: 0
Messages:
Patron status is ok.

Circulation Desk
203.291.4805

A Tale of One City, Two Worlds

In 1987, Dr. Benjamin Carson, a physician on the staff of the prestigious Johns Hopkins Hospital, succeeded in separating a pair of craniopagus twins, Siamese or conjoined twins joined at the cranium. Following this landmark event in neurosurgery, Dr. Carson became an international celebrity, bestselling author, and winner of the Presidential Medal of Freedom. Dr. Carson, who rose from poverty to achieve greatness, credits his mother, who completed only the third grade and was married at the age of thirteen, with encouraging him to succeed.

The hospital's East Baltimore location may be a reminder of the doctor's humble origins. The neighborhood, distinguished for its rampant violence, was made famous—or infamous—through depictions on television's *Homicide* and *The Wire*. Within a few blocks of the surgical ward where Dr. Carson performs his medical miracles, African American youths are growing up in a dangerous urban setting with homicide rates and life expectancies comparable to that of a developing country rather than what we should expect from the richest country in the world. The differences between the haves at this world-famous hospital and the have-nots living blocks away are painfully apparent. Will any of the young men growing up in East Baltimore have a chance to accomplish what a great role model like Dr. Carson has achieved?

The quantitative expression of this mobility measures how much the variability of a son's income can be explained by the father's. If the father's income can be used effectively to predict the son's income, then that would suggest there is little mobility. Richer fathers would have richer sons, and poorer fathers would have poorer sons. Alternatively, if there is no relationship between the father's income and the son's income, this would suggest perfect mobility—that is, the chances of a son having a high income would be independent of the father's income.[46]

Income Mobility Elasticity (1=no mobility; 0=perfect mobility)

Income-mobility elasticity is expressed as the percentage of increase in a son's income associated with a 1 percent increase in the father's income; the higher the elasticity measure, the more a son's income is explained by his father's and the lower the income mobility. The findings show conclusively that the United States has far less income mobility than other countries, as measured not just in the ranking but in the magnitude of the elasticity as well.[47] A man in the United States is nearly twice as reliant on his father's background (an income-elasticity rating of 0.41) than a man in Canada (income elasticity, 0.23), despite the two countries having relatively similar cultures, income levels, and racial diversity.

Another set of data measures the correlation between the incomes of fathers and sons in four Scandinavian countries (Norway, Sweden, Denmark, and Finland) as well as in Canada, Germany, the United Kingdom, and the United States.[48] Of these eight countries, the United States shows the lowest social mobility; that is, the amount of a son's income that is explained by his father's income is the greatest in the United States. Although the Scandinavian countries are not on our list of comparison countries, Canada and Germany clearly outperform the United States, with the United Kingdom performing marginally better than the United States.

Still a third study examines the probability that a son will remain in his father's income quintile, a quintile representing one-fifth of the population ranked from lowest to highest income. Six countries were included in the study: Denmark, Sweden, Finland, Norway, the United Kingdom, and the United States.[49] While only two of these countries are part of our competition, the results are still instructive. The data demonstrate that 42 percent of the American sons of fathers born in the poorest quintile landed in the poorest quintile themselves. This rate of the persistence of poverty was far higher than the 30 percent found in the United Kingdom and well above the 25 percent to 28 percent range found in Denmark, Sweden, Finland, and Norway.

This same study on income quintiles examined what might be called the rags-to-riches version of mobility, looking at the percentage of sons born to fathers in the poorest quintile who ended up in the wealthiest quintile. The US rate was 7.9 percent, far lower than that of the United Kingdom (12.4 percent) and of the Scandinavian countries, where rates ranged from 10.9 percent to 14.4 percent. Some of this measured immobility may derive from America's striking income inequality, meaning that an American born into the poorest quintile has farther to travel to reach the highest quintile than those in countries with greater income equality.

More telling is the fact that this comparatively low rate of going from rags to riches is declining rapidly. A separate study looked at the movement in socioeconomic scale (a combination of income, education, and occupation) for different quartiles, a quartile representing one-fourth of the population ranked from lowest to highest on the scale. The researchers observed that in 1973, sons of American fathers in the bottom quartile of the population had a 23 percent chance to move to the top quartile, compared with a 10 percent chance in 1998.[50]

Overall, these statistics are very depressing for those who subscribe to the notion that America is a meritocracy and a land of opportunity. We see that there is far less social mobility in the United States than in other countries *and* that this mobility is declining.

Many cite education as the key to socioeconomic mobility, and here the inequalities in the American educational system (see chapter 3) clearly play a role. For example, the US Department of Education has shown that the highest-performing eighth graders from low socioeconomic backgrounds have about the same chance of completing a bachelors degree as the lowest-performing eighth graders from high socioeconomic backgrounds. The latter were also about ten times more likely to complete a college degree than low-performing eighth graders from low socioeconomic backgrounds.[51] Translation: when it comes to higher education, the amount of money your parents have is much more critical than academic potential, and higher education is a key to socioeconomic mobility.

What role does race play in mobility? African American children born in the bottom quartile are nearly twice as likely to remain there as compared to their Caucasian counterparts. Moreover, these bottom-quartile African American children are some four times less likely than Caucasian children to rise to the highest quartile.[52]

Clearly, these data fly in the face of the American dream—the idea that you can be anything you want to be if you just work at it. Rather, they point to a rigid and entrenched structure of wealth at odds with our own sense of the mobility and elasticity of American opportunity, especially when we note the influence of race.

"ALL MEN ARE CREATED EQUAL"; WHAT ABOUT THE WOMEN?

There are many aspects of gender equality on which differences among the competitor class can be charted and findings compared: income, wealth, education, career advancement, and political leadership, among others. The problem is that different countries often measure these things in different ways. For example, the data on wage differences between men and women often fail to adjust for the number of years of work experience—a key factor in income that tends to be lower in women who take time off for maternity leave during child-bearing years. Similarly, wage-difference data typically won't control for differences in the education of the employed populations. The failure to take such critical factors into account leaves researchers running the risk of drawing inaccurate conclusions.

Life expectancy is one difference between men and women that is not really an issue of equality. Women live longer. Period. That is a phenomenon found throughout the world. Life expectancy measures how long those who are born are expected to live, but what about the unborn? One metric, the ratio of baby boys to baby girls, yields a particularly interesting data point about one of the competitor countries. The naturally occurring ratio is usually around 1.05 boys born for every one girl, and this ratio is seen throughout the world. In Korea, the ratio had reached 1.14 boys born for every one girl in 1988[53]—a result of gender-selective abortion deriving from a culture that historically has seen boys as more valuable than girls. The ratio has since approached more typical values, but the historically high ratio speaks to the thousands of female fetuses that were selectively aborted. Our other competitor countries show ratios more in line with the natural ratio.

Given the variability in metrics country to country, we'll begin our measurement of gender equality with a widely cited aggregate metric from the United Nations—the Gender Inequality Index (GII).[54] The GII is composed of measures of reproductive health (maternal mortality and adolescent fertility), empowerment (parliamentary representation and educational achievement), and labor market (labor force participation). These three measures are meant to parallel the health, education, and wealth measures of the United Nations Human Development Report and make the GII an interesting metric, albeit one that is suspect in its design.

First of all, the maternal mortality ratio and adolescent fertility rate are not actual measures of gender health *equality*—since only females become pregnant. Second, the developers of the GII have stated that the reproductive health component dominates the metric;[55] this means that not all the components that comprise the GII have equal impact on the overall score.

Nevertheless, the GII shows the United States with the worst rating for gender equality, while Belgium and the Netherlands score the best. Much of

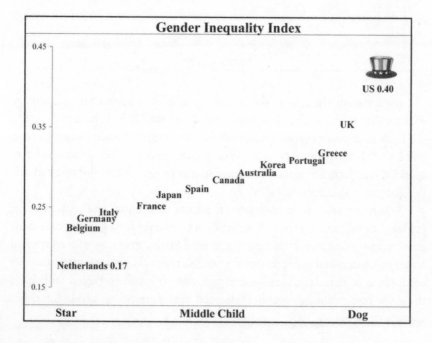

the poor performance by the United States is due to our lower scores on reproductive health, including America's comparatively high maternal mortality rate
and adolescent fertility rate discussed in chapter 1, the measure that admittedly
dominates the metric.

It makes sense, therefore, to move beyond this aggregate metric to look at
the nonhealth components of gender equality.

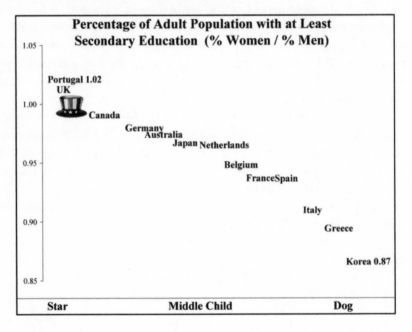

In education, the ratio of the percentage of adult women to the percentage
of adult men with a high school education shows the United States with one of
the highest levels of equality. Laggards on this metric include Korea, Greece,
and Italy.[56] Since this metric is based on the adult population aged twenty-five
or older, it reflects not just current educational prospects but also those of earlier generations that are still alive.

When we turn to a measure of current education, the difference in
expected number of years of schooling for a boy versus for a girl, the data show
that in most countries, including the United States, girls now exceed boys in
terms of educational expectations. In fact, Korea and Germany were the only
countries in which the educational expectations for women lagged far behind
those for men, although sex-disaggregated data were not available for either
Canada or Japan.

Another metric related to gender equality is participation in political institutions. Certainly the United States has shown progress in this regard. Women hold elective office at every level of government and have risen to positions of considerable power in both elected posts (for example, former Speaker of the House Nancy Pelosi) and in critical appointed posts. Perhaps the most notable example of the latter is that the sixty-fourth, sixty-sixth, and sixty-seventh US secretaries of state have all been women (Madeleine Albright, Condoleeza Rice, and Hillary Rodham Clinton, respectively). Yet apart from these celebrated and important leaders, the data on women's participation in political institutions do not paint a particularly rosy picture of rising political power for women in the United States.

A common metric for female political participation is the percentage of seats women hold in national legislature. Women occupying a percentage of legislative seats that matches their percentage of the population would constitute perfect equality on this metric, but no competing country on our list comes close to that. The Dogs are Greece, Korea, and Japan, while the Stars in this are the Netherlands and Belgium.[57] Some of the gap is due to different national perceptions of women in politics. A World Values Survey found that Americans have more negative views of women's abilities in politics than do citizens of Australia, Spain, and Germany. Korea and Japan show even more neg-

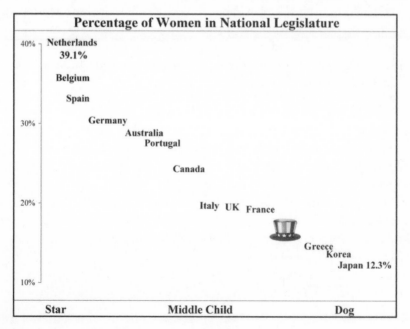

ative views, which correlates strongly with women's representation in those nations' legislatures—a likely reason why researchers conclude that gender attitudes are a primary factor in determining the level of female representation.[58]

The United States is not only a low performer in terms of the percentage of women representatives but also an outlier when it comes to the use of gender quotas as a means for driving greater female political representation. Of our competing countries, four (Belgium, Korea, Portugal, and Spain) have legislative quotas; eight (Australia, Canada, France, Germany, Greece, Italy, the Netherlands, and the United Kingdom) have voluntary party quotas. Only the United States and Japan lack any form of quota.

The final metric for gender equality is economics. A large number of factors affect earnings—number of years employed (universally lower on average for women due to maternity leave), educational background, job experience, and qualifications, to name just a few. We know of no broad, cross-country study that accounts for these differences and covers most of our competing countries. Instead, the most commonly cited metric, the ratio of male to female earned income, combines two measurements: the rate of participation in the labor market (among members of the working-age population aged fifteen to sixty-four) and how well those employees are paid. Because the two factors are combined in this metric, it's difficult to see which factor is driving the results. To better assess the gender gap in our competitor countries, we'll separate the two factors—labor force participation and median earnings of full-time employees—with the understanding that both may be influenced by differences in education, years of work experience, and individual career choices. Here's how we'll plot the results:

Small Gender Gap in Earnings of Full-time Workers	**MIDDLE CHILD:** Few women work but those that do are paid similar rates to men	**STAR:** Many women work and those that do are paid similar rates to men
Large Gender Gap in Earnings of Full-time Workers	**DOG:** Few women work and those that do are paid much lower rates than men	**MIDDLE CHILD:** Many women work, but those that do are paid much lower rates than men
	Low Level of Female Labor Force Participation	**High Level of Female Labor Force Participation**

And here's what the results look like:

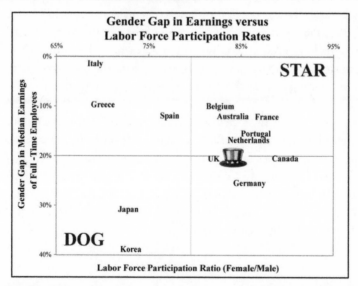

The data show that all of our competitor countries struggle to achieve gender equality in the workforce.[59] It is not surprising that all have lower rates of female labor participation than male labor participation, due mostly to maternity leaves as well as to some admitted cultural attitudes toward gender roles. What is perhaps surprising is that all of our competitor countries show a gender gap in earnings for full-time workers, with the varying sizes of the gaps reflecting differences in career choices, educational attainment, and compensation within careers. In the United States, for example, about one-third of the gender gap in workforce participation has been shown to be related to the time women withdraw from the labor market to either raise children or care for elderly relatives.[60]

While there is no outstanding performer in labor gender equality, the best-performing countries are France, Belgium, Australia, Portugal, and the Netherlands, with the United States not far off the lead, while the Dogs are clearly Korea and Japan. The major lagging component for the United States is the large gender gap it shows in median earnings, which is noticeably larger than among the gender leaders. This gender earnings gap persists across all races, with Asian American women achieving median earnings that are only 71 percent of the earnings of Asian American men, and with corresponding ratios of 64 percent, 86 percent, and 73 percent for Caucasians, African Americans, and Hispanics respectively.[61]

Japan and Korea are the worst performing countries regarding women and economic status; these countries' low levels of female participation in the labor market and large salary gaps are a reflection of the fact that these societies still rest in the shadow of a long-standing sexism inherent to the culture. One interesting case is Italy, where there is a low level of female labor participation but virtually no earnings gap. In short, Italian women who do work earn on average the same as Italian men.

But overall, unlike the other issues explored in this book, the competitive intelligence on gender equality finds no Stars, only relatively better and worse performers. All countries fall well below true gender equality as it relates to political participation and economic status. The bright story regarding improvements in girls' and women's education over the past few decades leads one to be optimistic that the long-term trend will be toward greater equality in the economic and political arenas.

> ## Woman Power: Sidelined or Flatlined?
>
> Although women comprise one-half the US workforce and are the responsible decision makers for the majority of consumer purchasing decisions, their median annual earnings are only around $24,000.[62] Hillary Clinton mounted a powerful campaign for the presidency in 2010 yet in the end fell short of gaining the nomination, while the Republican ticket, with Sarah Palin as the vice presidential candidate, lost. The 2010 elections saw the number of women in the US Congress slip and the percentage of women in statewide executive positions decline to 22.4 percent from a high of 27.6 percent at the turn of the twenty-first century.[63] It took more than 130 years for American women to gain the right to vote, and it wasn't until 1933 that the United States saw its first female cabinet secretary. Competitors like the United Kingdom and Germany have been led by women, yet the United States still hasn't seen a female vice president, let alone a president. As female representation in the United States slips even lower, one has to ask whether women will ever experience the political strength found in some of the competing nations.

EQUALITY PERFORMANCE:
NO STAR, BUT THE UNITED STATES IS THE MARKET DOG

Overall, the data show that there is a major disconnect between Americans' self-perception of living in a land of equality and the reality demonstrated through competitive intelligence. As the facts make clear, the United States has higher degrees of inequality for income and wealth, along with lower socioeconomic mobility than other countries in our competitor class, while its performance on gender equality is fair-to-middling in a nonstellar field. In particular, the trend in the United States toward decreasing income equality raises concerns for the nation's long-term growth potential and stability.

While Americans show comparatively greater faith in the meritocracy of their economy than do citizens of other countries—and therefore tend to be more accepting of income and wealth inequality—the data show that this faith is misplaced and the acceptance of inequality is misguided. As shown clearly, Americans vastly overestimate the equality of their system. The survey asking them to estimate the current distribution of wealth in the United States and present their ideal level of equality showed a populace that stubbornly overestimates how equal its society is and yearns for a level of wealth distribution even more equal than the level of equality it mistakenly perceives.[64] This suggests something more like a religious belief in mobility than a willingness to look at the facts—a belief that permeates all demographic groups in the United States and crosses the political and ideological spectrum.

The revelation that the United States has less intergenerational income mobility than other countries is a blow that strikes at the heart of the American dream. Many Americans accept a high degree of income inequality in the belief that if you work hard enough you have a fair chance of achieving success. But the data are clear that the path to socioeconomic success in the United States is tilted more toward those born with a silver spoon in their mouths than it is in our competitor countries. For the moment, too, many Americans seem content to accept that this increasing inequality is caused by trends in globalization and the market economy and, thus, is something outside their control. Yet the data reveal that government policies play a significant role in shaping the socioeconomic environment, not unseen forces. While the American public can become angry about the inequality situation—it showed enormous anger over the bank bailouts prescribed in 2008 to deal with the financial crisis, but this anger soon dissipated—it does not seem able to target its anger and take back control over the policies that are keeping it stuck in a comparatively rigid class structure.

What is driving this rise in American inequality?

Race or gender differences are not the cause of the rising inequality. The gap in median family income between African Americans and Caucasians in the United States is slightly smaller now than it was in 1979, while the median annual income for women is closer today to that of the median annual income of men. The rise in single parenthood is also not a driving factor; it occurred before the sharp rise in inequality.

Trade liberalization and technological change are generally not to blame for the rise of inequality. These factors have affected nearly all developed countries to the same extent. However, few of those countries have experienced the kind of inequality increase that the United States has suffered; some, in fact, have seen declines in inequality.

Arguments that the inequality increase derives from a skills gap also don't hold merit. The sharp spike in American inequality has reserved its benefits for the top 1 percent of income earners, but those in the top 1–5 percent are also educated and skilled; if the skills argument were sound, those in the top 1–5 percent should have also benefited significantly, but they did not. Also, an entry-level worker with a bachelors degree earned only $1,000 more in 2006 than in 1980,[65] adjusted for inflation, while the median real income for a college-educated male rose only 17 percent from 1973 to 2007.[66]

Rather, a key factor in the rise of American income inequality has been the change in institutions and norms, including the declining role of unions in America and the changing pay structure of corporate executives and of the finance industry. Unions have historically served as an organizing mechanism to encourage more equitable pay; through collective bargaining agreement, unions help control the ratio of executive-to-worker compensation. Unions sought and achieved higher wages and better benefits from companies and constituted a strong political influence on such government policies as the minimum wage, Social Security, and Medicare.

Another key contributor to America's rising inequality is the pay structure that has become pervasive in the corporate world and in finance in particular. The scandals of Enron, Tyco, and the like were a shocking wake-up call to those unfamiliar with such pay structures; the scandals showed the extent to which boards of directors, which are charged with overseeing the entire workings of a company, are staffed by friends of the CEO. These friends then work with a compensation specialist, usually hired by the CEO or his friends on the board, to determine the pay of the CEO. So it is often quite an insular process that leads to the oversized compensation packages of corporate CEOs.

Americans got another glimpse into the process when they saw that the failing institutions bailed out by TARP (the Troubled Asset Relief Program that was enacted in 2008 to address the subprime mortgage crisis) continued to pay out billions in bonuses, just as they had before—only this time, with tax-payer money.[67] This was a graphic peek into the disconnect between Wall Street compensation and that of the average American worker.

One other conclusion to emerge from the data on equality—and it's a sobering one—is the lack of a single Star in *all* the equality metrics: income, wealth, socioeconomic mobility, and gender. While Belgium, France, the Netherlands, and Germany are the Stars in income equality, when the issue is wealth equality, they yield the title to Japan, Spain, Korea, and Italy. When the issue is economic mobility, even incomplete data make clear that Canada and Germany vastly outperform the United States. On gender equality, Belgium and the Netherlands consistently receive positive ratings, while Korea and Japan are the clear Dogs. This lack of a clear, single leader, a real equality Star, means we must draw lessons on best equality practices for the United States from the different countries excelling in each aspect of equality rather than look to a single country as was possible for some of the other values examined in this book.

RECOMMENDATIONS

It was noted at the outset of this chapter that equality is a difficult subject to deal with. It's also difficult to narrow down recommendations that address the inequality we've found in the United States and that can create a more equal society here. We'll start, therefore, with a set of practical, implementable recommendations that could begin to reduce America's inequality today. We'll then discuss a number of practices from the various Stars of the field, though they are practices that have less of a chance, if any, of finding fertile ground in the American culture or in America's political environment.

Implementable Recommendations

Let's start with the issue most threatening to our democracy, *income and wealth inequality*. In theory, the fix for income inequality is simple: either control unadjusted-income inequality or increase the redistributive actions like taxation and social spending. Unadjusted-income inequality can be controlled on the lower end of the income scale through higher minimum wages; it can be controlled on the upper end of the income scale through limits on earnings, either through corporate oversight mechanisms, public scrutiny of compensation, or other transparent means. Adjusted-income inequality after taxes and transfers can be reduced through aggressively progressive tax rates, tough enforcement of tax laws, and strong social safety-net policies.

All these measures will similarly reduce the level of wealth inequality, as will aggressive taxation of the components of wealth itself—physical properties, financial assets, and inheritances.

So how do we translate these broad suggestions into practical, implementable recommendations? Let's divide the answers into three categories: (1) tax policy, (2) minimum wage, and (3) corporate governance; and let's start with tax policy.

1. Tax Policy

Increase progressive taxes, reduce regressive taxes. In America's past, when there was a large increase in tax collection from the wealthy, there was a correspondingly large increase in government support for the poor, and income inequality shrank dramatically. Perhaps the most aggressive such tax increase occurred in the period from 1929 to 1939, when the highest marginal tax rate more than tripled.[68] Tax policy to promote greater equality is therefore a part of the American past and is a legitimate, indeed, an essential place to begin to correct today's inequality and bring greater stability to US democracy.

Certainly, it's well known that the Republican Party in the United States regards tax cuts as a core plank of its political platform. As of April 2012, there are four major candidates in the Republican presidential primary: Mitt Romney, Newt Gingrich, Rick Santorum, and Ron Paul. The first three profess support for tax reduction while Ron Paul wants to abolish the income tax entirely, along with the IRS.[69] Indeed, the Republican Party sees tax reduction as a cure-all for whatever ails American society—a way to return money to those who deserve it during surplus times, a way to stimulate the economy during a recession, and a way to control government spending at all times. Reducing taxes has thus become a primary subject of America's political debate, with little distinction made between progressive taxes, in which the rate rises with the payer's income, and regressive taxes like sales taxes, which tax everyone, rich and poor, at exactly the same rate, such that poorer purchasers pay a higher percentage of their income in taxes than do richer buyers. Yet if we are going to reduce income and wealth inequality in the United States, increasing progressive taxes and reducing regressive taxes are essential and constitute a key recommendation of this book. Importantly, competitive intelligence makes it crystal clear that countries that have greater levels of income equality than the United States have more aggressive tax policies. Among those policies are progressive taxes like the broad-based wealth taxes that tax net assets, as in France, and national sales or value-added taxes, as in all the competitor countries, although the implementation of any form of national sales or value-added tax would need to be done in a way that does not excessively burden those least able to pay.

One practical way to begin addressing tax policy changes is to close the loophole that defines hedge fund managers' incomes as capital gains rather than as earned income. This income is taxed at the rate of 15 percent as of this writing; were the managers' incomes defined as earned income, hedge fund managers would pay the same marginal tax rates the rest of us pay. Granted, there is a relatively minuscule number of people profiting from this loophole, yet the loophole is estimated to be costing the US taxpayer about $6 billion a year, with almost $2 billion of it attributed to only twenty-five individuals.[70] Unfortunately, this small-but-well-heeled group of hedge fund managers contributes substantively to politicians of both parties, so there continues to be resistance to closing this blatant loophole.

More broadly, long-term capital gains tax rates in the United States are levied at only 15 percent for those with ordinary income tax rates of 25 percent or higher and at 0 percent for those with lower tax rates. The lower tax rates for capital gains were again in the news in early 2012 when it was disclosed that candidate Mitt Romney paid only a 13.9 percent federal tax rate on the $21.7 million he earned in 2010.[71] In 1978, Congress voted a deep cut in the capital gains tax and touted this as a major policy shift aimed at helping those with lower incomes. The reality, however, is that the shift barely affected the tax bill of those in the lower brackets while costing the government billions in revenue from those in the higher brackets. The impact of the succeeding shift in policy, the 2013 increase in the capital gains tax to 20 percent for those in the 25-percent-or-higher tax bracket, remains to be seen as of this writing.

Even more basically, adjusting income tax rates at both the top and the bottom of the scale is recommended. The top federal marginal tax rate in the United States stands at 35 percent as of this writing—versus highs of more than 90 percent in the post–World War II period of great overall prosperity and of 70 percent in the 1970s, a period of recession.[72] While we do not recommend returning to the stratospheric levels of the top federal marginal tax rates of the mid-twentieth century, raising the top federal marginal tax rate back to the levels found in the late 1990s (e.g., 39.6 percent in 1998 and 1999) would go a long way toward improving equality. It's a suggestion echoed by one of the country's wealthiest and most successful investors, Warren Buffett, who in 2011 called on Congress to increase taxes on millionaires, arguing that it would hurt neither investment nor job growth.[73]

At the other end of the scale, today's payroll taxes are highly regressive in that they are assessed at a fixed rate up to an annual wage maximum ($106,800 as of 2010) and are not assessed beyond that salary. As a result, an individual earning $50,000 pays a far higher effective tax rate than one earning $500,000. A simple measure to resolve this glaring inequality is to eliminate the annual wage maximum.

2. Minimum Wage

Increase the minimum wage. In addition to changing tax policies, increasing the minimum wage provides a direct, positive impact on the income of the working poor and reduces income inequality. Despite enormous popular support in all segments of the population for increasing the minimum wage, it remained unchanged in nominal terms from 1997 to 2006 while the value in real terms declined. This is typically a partisan issue: between 1949 and 2004, the Democrats held the White House for twenty-five years, and the real value of the minimum wage increased by sixteen cents per year; in the thirty-one years in which Republicans had the White House, the real value declined by six cents per year.[74]

In terms of purchase power, the minimum wage, as of this writing, is lower than in the 1970s, and, as noted earlier, the ratio of minimum wage to living wage dropped from 94 percent in 1968 to 57 percent in 2003.[75] Some state governments have made up for part of the lag in federal minimum wage laws by passing their own minimum wage laws, and even some local governments have passed higher-level "living wage" laws.

The argument against increasing the minimum wage typically comes from business interests and claims that large increases in minimum wages will result in inflationary pressures and potentially higher unemployment as companies struggle to absorb the higher costs. It has been demonstrated, however, that gradual increases in the minimum wage do no such thing.[76]

Some also argue that expanding the Earned Income Tax Credit (EITC) is preferable to increasing the minimum wage. It is argued here that the opposite is true: an increase in the minimum wage provides direct benefits to those in need and, as a 2007 analysis by the Congressional Budget Office confirmed,[77] provides more money to poor families. (One reason is that receiving the direct transfer of the wage eliminates the often inconvenient or difficult need to file for benefits as well as the possibility of administrative errors.) Moreover, the EITC tends to lack transparency and, perhaps most importantly, may actually encourage or even promote a downward spiral of low-wage jobs.

3. Corporate Governance

Organize for transparent corporate governance. Finally, competitive intelligence shows that in the countries with lower rates of unadjusted-income inequality, there tends to be a stronger union presence and often more transparent corporate governance than in the United States. For example, in Germany, executive compensation is reviewed by what is known as codetermined boards—that is, corporate boards on which workers have a seat at the table and can thus control the ratio of executive-to-worker pay. Such a structural change would be difficult to legislate in the United States, where union membership and, therefore, union power are on the wane. Rather, shareholder activism can be a potent tool in the United States for reining in corporate excesses—for example, huge salary packages and the golden parachutes given to poor-performing executives. Large institutional stockholders like CalPERS, the California Public Employees' Retirement System, have shown such activism on a number of issues in companies in which they hold shares. After all, it is the shareholders' money that boards spend on executive salaries and golden parachutes. Therefore we recommend that shareholders in publicly held companies organize for action to ensure the good of the shareholders and not just the executives and the board.

When it comes to recommendations for improving America's **socioeconomic mobility**, both public opinion[78] and the experts agree that education is key.[79] We noted in chapter 3 the key challenges the United States faces in terms of ensuring educational equality; the recommendations in that chapter will go a long way toward lubricating the rungs of the socioeconomic ladder as well. After all, this is a country in which no individual should be doomed to a certain socioeconomic class by birth; the very idea is anathema to our perception of America, yet it is increasingly the reality.

Education makes a difference, as the facts make clear. Of the adults who grew up in low-income families but earned college degrees, only 16 percent stayed in the lowest income quintile. Of the adults who started in the lowest income quintile and failed to earn a college degree, 46 percent stayed there.[80] End inequality in education and we strike a blow for social mobility—although persistent disparities in income by race and gender still need to be addressed.

In **gender equality**, as noted, the United States does reasonably well regarding both education and economic achievement. All countries show gaps in the median earnings and labor force participation rates of men and women; the United States is not far off the rates of the market Stars in this regard.

Political representation is one immediate area of opportunity for improving gender equality in the United States, and one key solution is in the electoral process itself. Shifting to proportional representation models rather than our winner-take-all system could help elect more women representatives[81]—and it might encourage more women to enter politics.[82] In proportional representation models, voters would cast ballots for the party of choice, and gender issues would have to be addressed within the parties. This situation would make gender bias less anonymous and therefore easier to confront directly. Moreover, women candidates, who typically face greater challenges raising financial support, could rely more on party money.

Probably Not Implementable Recommendations

Some of the best practices of other countries with far less disparity of income and wealth, practices that might be instructive for reducing inequality in the United States, simply won't work here. In some cases, the cultural disconnect may be too great; in other cases, the political reality simply won't allow it; and there are some best practices of other countries that would not pass muster constitutionally. Because political views can sometimes change rapidly, we are listing these competitor best practices here even though they are not applicable in the United States today.

1. Revamp Worker Power

The dramatic decline in the US union movement has been more pronounced than in most of the competitor countries. For example, in the EU nations, union density fell from about 38 percent to 26 percent between 1970 and 2003, while in the United States it was halved from 24 percent to about 12 percent. At the same time, Canada, Korea, Belgium, and Italy have experienced little or no decline, and in Belgium a majority of workers are unionized.[83] The rate of unionization in the United States, by contrast, is noticeably lower than in all other competitor countries except France and Korea.

The decline of union membership and influence in the United States has been driven in part by government policy—for example, the Taft-Hartley Act of 1947, which restricted union activities and prohibited certain kinds of strikes. Exacerbating this weakening of unions was the decline of the US economy's manufacturing sector with a corresponding impact on the power of collective bargaining and on how companies function.

The current strength of the unions in some competitor countries is evidence that the US decline in union participation and in worker power is not necessarily a function of globalization. Yet despite the government policies and the decline of our manufacturing sector in favor of a service-and-knowledge economy—factors that have eroded union strength—the US labor movement is by no means dead. The movement could, however, take a page from the book of competitor countries like Germany. The world's second largest exporter, Germany has been able to maintain a major manufacturing industry in spite of globalization pressures for lower wages and outsourcing. It absorbed the much poorer East Germany in 1990, yet it maintains a comparatively low adjusted-income inequality. It achieves this by supporting skilled labor both in its educational system, with five types of secondary schools—including vocational education—and in its corporate structure.

The latter includes work councils, codetermined boards, and regional wage-setting institutions.[84] Work councils are elected by the workforce and serve to tailor national labor standards agreements to the local circumstances at the company. (Five other competitor countries—the United Kingdom, the Netherlands, Belgium, France, and Spain—also have work councils, which operate in companies that have a significant presence in the European Union.[85]) Codetermination reserves a significant percentage of a corporate board as seats for workers' representatives. One result is that Germany has not seen the astronomical CEO-to-worker pay ratios experienced in the United States.

While it seems unlikely that codetermination could work broadly in the United States, this kind of large-scale rethinking about the role of the worker in US society is important for the long-term sustainability of manufacturing in America and for the stability of American democracy.

2. Enact Major Tax Increases

As noted earlier, while there are some areas where progressive taxes may be increased, in general, taxes are an incredibly sensitive topic in the United States. Many Americans are devoutly committed to the principle of tax cuts— to the point of being willing to let senior citizens do without Social Security checks and to allow the federal government to shut down in order to reduce their tax liability or taxes in general. In addition, Americans suffer from what might be called some cognitive dissonance about tax increases. For example, while most Americans believe that the rich don't pay enough in taxes, they have generally supported tax cuts targeted to benefit the wealthiest—that is, the so-called Bush tax cuts of 2001 and 2003. Even those who would benefit least from tax cuts seem to prefer the small, short-term benefit of a cut rather than looking down the road to the larger, long-term impact on prosperity.

One case in point is estate or inheritance taxes. Even though estate taxes in the United States affect very few families—in 1999, only the top 2 percent of estates paid any tax at all, and one-half the estate tax was paid by only 3,300 estates[86]—a broad-based disdain for estate taxes makes it highly unlikely that increases in the estate tax will be enacted.

3. Provide Birth Grants

Wealth inequality is partially addressed in other countries through birth grants to the mother or lump-sum payments directly to the child provided for every birth. These grants are given in nearly every European country as well as in Australia, Canada, and New Zealand.[87] The impact of this wealth transfer is straightforward, but in America's current political climate, still laced with the mythology of "welfare queens" and its corresponding racial overtones, this practice is not likely be adopted.

4. Set Gender Goals

Political quotas for women are a common tactic used in our competitor countries. In the United States, legislating such quotas would be unconstitutional and is therefore not a potential tool for improving equality. While many of the competitor countries have voluntary quotas for women candidates within the political parties, quotas are generally unpopular in the United States and are not likely to be implemented (although "silent quotas" certainly exist in numerous realms of American public life).

The United Nations Development Fund for Women (UNIFEM,[88] now subsumed by UN Women) also supports the idea of gender quotas and makes this one of the three actions it recommends for increasing women's political representation:

- fair and balanced media coverage of men and women so that the candidate's gender doesn't receive or generate undue attention,
- campaign finance controls that compensate for the fact that women

candidates generally have a more difficult time raising funds than male candidates (voting for party lists rather than for single candidates eliminates this need), and

- either mandated or voluntary gender quotas.

As to increasing women's participation in the corporate hierarchy, two of our competitor nations, Spain and France, have followed the lead of Norway in requiring that 40 percent of a publicly held corporation's board members must be women. As this book goes to press, the Netherlands and the German governments are considering it, and the European Parliament has called for a European Union–wide law by 2020.

Chapter 6

WHAT THE DATA
HAVE SHOWN US

W e have offered a systematic approach to comparing the United
States to a small set of developed countries on five fundamental
aspects of society—health, safety, education, democracy, and equality. The goal
has been to identify objectively how the United States compares and, in areas
where America is lagging, what can be learned from those countries that perform better. The countries used for the comparison span a broad range of populations, geographic size, ethnic diversity, and even wealth. All meet a minimum level of wealth and population size, but still the countries are not and
never will be perfectly similar to one another.

Some readers will argue that the differences between these competitor
countries and the United States render comparisons meaningless. My view is
that while we acknowledge the differences, avoiding or dismissing cross-
country comparisons seems to be no more than an avoidance or dismissal of
reality, one that may derive from a nagging fear that the United States won't do
well in such comparisons. That's a self-defense mechanism that smacks of a
rather mindless "American exceptionalism"; it's anathema to critical thinking
and to the scientific mind, and it provides little benefit to future improvement.

The fact is that the United States walks into this competition with a distinct
advantage. America's GDP per capita is at the very upper end of our competition,
topped only by Australia or the Netherlands, depending on which source you
choose.[1] We can take it a step farther and look at an alternative measure of GDP
per capita that adjusts for different levels of purchasing power within countries,
the price-purchase-parity adjustment. It reflects the fact that even if two people
earn the same amount of money in two different countries, measured according
to the currency exchange rate, one may nevertheless be able to buy more equivalent goods. That person is said to have a higher price-purchase-parity adjusted

income, despite earning the equivalent nominal amount. Measuring GDP adjusted for price purchase parity, the United States comes out farther ahead, with the highest GDP per capita in our competition.[2] Either way, therefore, the United States is one of the wealthiest countries in our comparison, and for that reason, we might expect it to have advantages in the areas measured. As our analysis shows, however, the results are quite the opposite.

Instead of being the dominating Star, the data demonstrate that the United States is the Dog in most of the markets covered. In the health comparison, it has the lowest life expectancy for both men and women, in spite of spending more on health-related goods and services than any of the other countries. Similarly, in primary and secondary education, the United States shows only average performance in spite of vastly outspending the competition. While one might think its wealth would make the United States immune to safety concerns, the reality is that our country is much more dangerous than other countries; our rates of both incarceration and homicide are multiples higher than even our closest competitor. The functioning of our democracy is less vigorous than that of the other democracies, with low voter turnout and limited choice. Lastly, and perhaps most shockingly, America, the self-proclaimed "land of opportunity," has less equality and socioeconomic mobility than the competition.

Clearly, America's strong average economic numbers, as measured by GDP per capita, are masking fundamental weaknesses in many aspects of our society. This masking occurs on a daily basis. Every day we hear endless news reports about stock market movements and the global economy, yet we rarely hear about how these aggregate measures of wealth hide major cracks in the armor of America's strength.

While the cross-country comparisons have clearly identified areas in which the United States is faltering versus the competition, the data also show that America was not always a poor performer. In many areas of comparison, we were near the top throughout the latter part of the twentieth century. History has witnessed our leadership decline; as the competition invested and improved, our growth slowed down, stagnated, or receded altogether in some areas. In health, for example, the United States had the twelfth-lowest rate of infant mortality in 1960 but has fallen out of the top thirty as of this writing. In education, America once enjoyed the highest rate of college education in the world but has become a Middle Child today. In democracy, we introduced the world to modern representative democracy, with landmark documents including the Declaration of Independence and the Constitution with its Bill of Rights, but now we struggle with an inefficient and archaic voting system and we rank poorly in levels of voter participation. In equality, the United States has been extolled since the days soon after its founding as a land of opportunity and a destination for millions of immigrants striving for a better life, yet our social mobility is worse than in many other countries, while income inequality has been exploding since the late 1970s.

The declining performance of America over time and our overall poor *comparative* performance versus the other countries in this analysis point to a major disconnect between American self-perception and the reality of the data. For example, during the debates over healthcare reform leading up to passage of the Patient Protection and Affordable Care Act of 2010, few politicians were willing to acknowledge the fact that the American health system was rated thirty-seventh in the world by the World Health Organization. Rather, we heard sound bite after sound bite about America having the best healthcare in the world. Most Americans would intuitively say that while they think American democracy is not working well, "it is probably better than anywhere else," yet the data show that this statement is not true, that other countries demonstrate democracies with greater political representation. Many Americans are confident that their educational system is one of the best in the world, but again, the data indicate that this perception is not supported by objective fact. Perhaps the most surprising disconnect for most Americans is that the American dream of socioeconomic mobility is a myth; such mobility is comparatively lower here than elsewhere, not higher.

Where do these disconnects between perception and data reality come from? Most of us draw our opinions from our knowledge, personal experiences, and local surroundings. An overwhelming majority of Americans have never traveled abroad and do not own passports. Their perceptions, therefore, derive from the education they receive, the information they are exposed to, and the lives they live within our vast borders. Since culture, experience, and education are all somewhat local, the perspectives of Americans living near the Canadian border differ greatly from the perceptions of those near the Mexican border; the experiences of those living in small towns in the Midwest differ from the experiences of people living in the major cities along the coasts. In order for Americans to better understand the reality of how America performs in fundamental areas of society, they need to be exposed to information like the data compiled in this book or they need to experience firsthand the differences in how other countries approach health, safety, education, democracy, and equality. Broadened experience and deeper knowledge also expand perspective and can shift perception. This in turn equips people to judge whether there are areas in American society that are not optimal and that can be improved.

Traveling abroad is a privilege that many Americans cannot afford, but the Internet, books, and movies can be sources of information and vehicles of at least second-hand exposure to other cultures.

I will always remember my first trip abroad—not all that far, just north to neighboring Canada. I was amazed at the different perspectives I found there on politics and America's role in the world. Though I may not have agreed with everything I saw and heard, the experience was eye-opening. I returned to the United States with a greater appreciation of my own country and of the cultural differences between the two countries. By stepping outside my local environment, I was able to view with a better perspective the culture in which I grew up. I could see more clearly the aspects of America that I valued; I could also see that America struggled with challenges to which our neighbors to the north seemed to have found successful solutions. It's been a long time since that first trip abroad, yet I continue to view my times outside the United States as an opportunity to find some aspects of a new culture that I would like to adopt, modify, or somehow transport back with me when I return home.

It's this greater exposure to other cultures, letting us see how those cultures respond to challenges in society, that enables us better to judge our own culture's response. Sometimes, the broadening effects of travel or of other forms of cross-cultural exposure—books, newspapers, magazines, for example—show us that what seems normal in our hometown is unheard of elsewhere and, vice versa, that what's unheard of at home is the norm somewhere else. Take the case of gun laws. Americans have grown up in a "gun culture"; the right to ownership is in our Constitution, and gun use is pervasive. This leads many Americans to the false assumption that the rest of the world shares a similar culture. It doesn't. But when people draw general conclusions from their personal experiences without looking at what occurs outside their local environments, false assumptions are bound to occur.

One of the primary purposes of this book is to remove the national blinders that many of us wear in order to expose readers to a broader, more global perspective that embraces other ways of approaching fundamental aspects of society.

In fact, I hope this book serves as something of an inexpensive trip abroad, showing readers what works well in other countries so they can decide what they might like to adopt locally. As we Americans do a better job of accurately identifying how our country performs, we can proceed to productive discussions about how to improve, devising rational plans based on our national strengths and opportunities and on best practices from other countries.

Certainly not all of the global best practices can or should be adopted here in America. Cultural differences, different histories, local perspectives, and even popular biases may render some best practices of another country simply not applicable or not implementable in America. The forces of capitalism alone can be barriers to implementation. Just recall the long fight with the tobacco industry as it did its best to obfuscate the science tying smoking to cancer. Or consider how the pharmaceutical industry defends the direct-to-consumer marketing of drugs while trying to block consumers from purchasing cheaper identical drugs outside US borders. Self-interest makes for powerful resistance to change, and it permeates everything we have looked at in this book.

In chapter 1, for example, we saw how for-profit health insurance companies, malpractice lawyers, and some healthcare workers generate far more profit and income in the American system than they would if we moved toward implementing some of the competitive best practices. Those players represent a high hurdle to jump for implementing major changes in US healthcare. In chapter 2 on safety, we noted that the massive military industry has continued its explosive growth in the post–Cold War period. Domestically, entities like private prisons have actively tried to implement legislation to expand our comparatively astronomical incarceration rates. In education, as we saw in chapter 3, the for-profit education companies and test-preparation organizations benefit from the current system. In democracy, as chapter 4 made clear, insiders in the two-party system benefit from a system that blocks the voices of third-party candidates and will be hesitant to open the door to more voices. Chapter 5 showed that the privileged class in the United States benefits from the high level of income and wealth inequality and low level of socioeconomic mobility, meanwhile large parts of the population suffer. This does not mean that these powerful pockets of self-interest are necessarily to blame for America's comparatively poor performance. Rather, it means that they have profited handsomely while US performance has declined, and we can therefore anticipate that they will seek to defend their current and future profits.

APPLYING COMPETITIVE INTELLIGENCE

From the start, the premise of this book has been based on three fundamental, fact-based, logically connected points: first, that the United States is very different from other countries in its approach to many aspects of its society; second, that the United States is not always the best performer in carrying out its approach; and third, that when we are not the best, we should be willing to learn from other countries.

This last point speaks to the heart of competitive intelligence—the chance to apply the results of these cross-country comparisons to improve US performance. Competitive intelligence is only useful if those involved in the study take the time to understand the data, review the analysis for themselves, select the recommendations that are most clearly valid and implementable, and then focus on applying these improvements based on the intelligence.

Imagine if in the early 1990s IBM had reviewed the competitive intelligence data it so carefully gathered and then decided simply to ignore everything the data made clear. No modification to its business approach, no shift in strategy, no changes at all. Had the company continued operating merrily along the same declining trajectory, IBM would now most likely be a small company struggling for survival, a subsidiary of a larger company, or out of business. As we know, of course, it did just the opposite—it paid close attention to the data and followed the lessons it learned—and today it is once again a powerhouse.

The point is that competitive intelligence is not meant to be an academic exercise that interests only a small set of scholars or that sits unread on a bookshelf. Rather, the aim is to drive informed change. After all, the best practices discussed here are not theoretical exercises but are examples drawn from reality. They have already been shown to be implementable and effective in the real world. Implementing them will not provide a magical cure that will instantly restore the United States to world leadership in all the areas studied. Rather, implementing them can constitute powerful steps along the right road to restoring our leadership.

For competitive intelligence to work, those who look at the data must also be willing to drop many of their preconceived notions and concede that others may do things better. The defensive reflex has no place in the competitive intelligence exercise; people must be willing to learn from others, adapt what they learn, and possibly improve on what they learn. Certainly, there are those who will simply choose to deny the evidence presented in this book—most likely because of intrinsic biases. Competitive intelligence cannot dent those biases. Others may accept the data but ignore the recommendations as being too difficult to implement in America. This argument against implementing the lessons learned from competitive intelligence is weak. The fact that other countries have already successfully implemented these solutions means they are, by definition, implementable. Some may even argue that the best practices are simply not applicable to American society. But isn't achieving excellence always relevant to all societies? And isn't inertia a poor defense against real-world-tested solutions?

Defense of the status quo is always easier, and it is human nature to see one's own self-interest as equivalent to the good of society. But without change, there is no improvement, and the drive for constant self-improvement has always been part of the American aspiration. It is this drive that helped propel a weak, sparsely populated group of colonies to eventually become the strongest and wealthiest nation on earth.

It's important not only to use the lessons learned from this competitive intelligence but also to repeat the exercise. The gathering and examining of competitive intelligence should not be a one-time event. Rather, the process of assessing how America performs versus other countries and identifying where it can improve needs to be an ongoing process, one repeated on a regular basis.

INEQUALITY IN AMERICA

Unfortunately, inequality is a theme that runs through much of the data in this book. One whole chapter has been devoted to it (see chapter 5), and it tells us that the United States has substantively higher levels of income and wealth inequality than our competition. In America, the rich rise higher and the poor sink lower with less social support than in other high-income countries. At the same time, in America the slice of the pie taken by the wealthiest is far bigger than in other countries, and this slice has been growing rapidly over the decades. This trend in inequality has been observed not just by politicians and economists, but by all Americans, as they sense it in their daily lives.

Americans are more generally accepting of these higher degrees of inequality because of their staunch faith that America is more of a meritocracy than other countries. This faith is woefully undermined by the data, which show that in America, who your parents were is far more important to your success than it is in other countries. Americans' acceptance of inequality is based on this misconception of meritocracy—on the false belief that America rewards those of sufficient ability and diligence more readily than other nations.

There's a second false belief driving the acceptance of inequality in American society—the notion that the inequality is a function of market forces such as globalization or technology changes that cannot be controlled. But the data expose this as another instance of American perception contradicted by real-world facts. The main factors associated with the rising American income inequality, as the data make clear, are institutional and political—changes in pay structure and tax policies. These are factors well within the control of citizens, shareholders, and the government, if they choose to exert their influence. The proof that inequality can be controlled comes from the competitive intelligence. Again, as the data make clear, a number of our competitors have seen declining rather than rising inequality, a direct consequence of direct action. Perhaps these nations have done so because they don't have the same faith in meritocracy that we have; as a result, their governments provide greater social support mechanisms to enable those at the lower income levels to access the playing field. The bottom line is that there's no question that we, as a society, can shape our inequality rather than passively blaming market forces and absolving ourselves of responsibility.

The implications of America's inequality can be seen in how our average performance is suppressed by the existence of poorer families and by the unfortunate reality that income and disparities of race or ethnic origin too often go hand in hand. These inequalities suppress performance in every aspect of society examined in this book. They also produce a mirroring effect; that is, the best-performing segments in the United States do very well versus the competitor countries while the worst-performing segments are vastly worse than the comparison. Some of this is due to the distortion of comparing the best-performing segments of one country to the average-performing segments of another, but it further reminds us of the vast differences between the top and bottom of American society.

Unfortunately, the inequalities run deep. For example, African Americans and Hispanics have only about 10 percent and 12 percent of the wealth of Caucasians, respectively. The median earnings of Caucasians are nearly 50 percent higher than those of African Americans and about 30 percent higher than those of Hispanics, while Asian Americans earn the most—about 10 percent more than Caucasians.[3] Earnings disparities cut across educational levels as well. As noted in chapter 5, African Americans with masters degrees make about 25 percent less than graduate-degreed Caucasians; undergraduate-educated African Americans make about 30 percent less than undergraduate-educated Caucasians; and high school–educated African Americans make about 25 percent less than high school–educated Caucasians.[4]

As with other aspects of American society, race plays a role in mobility. African American children born in the bottom quintile are nearly twice as likely to remain there as adults than are Caucasian children of parents from the bottom quintile. As for the long socioeconomic leap from being born into the bottom quintile but landing at the top, that is an even worse story: African American children are about four times less likely to make that jump than Caucasian children.[5]

That the influences of race are tightly linked to inequalities is evident in just about every aspect of American society. African Americans live about four fewer years than Caucasians and about thirteen fewer years than Asian Americans.[6] An even starker comparison is that the infant mortality rate of African American children is about twice the national rate.[7] It is difficult not to marvel at the ethnic disparities in American health when the data show us that Asian Americans, the wealthiest of the American population, have longer life expectancies than the population of Japan, the overall Star in health, while the average life expectancy for the United States overall is lower than all the rest of the competing countries.

In education, wealth and racial inequalities rear their heads in a very transparent manner. Starting from the earliest days, income plays a role: US preprimary-school enrollment rates are about 20 percent higher for children of middle-class parents than for kids of parents at the lowest income levels. This initial advantage passes through to later years of schooling as poorer children attend less well-funded public schools and are taught by less well-qualified teachers than in the public schools attended by wealthier children. As a result, it is not surprising that the average reading score for Americans from higher-income schools exceeded that of all the competitor countries, while the average reading scores for lower-income American schools was far lower than in any of our comparison countries. More pertinent to our discussion of equality is the fact that socioeconomic class had a greater influence on test scores in the United States than in any other country.

At the same time, the relationship between wealth and race is also evidenced in education. Asian American students averaged higher test scores than students in any other country, and white, non-Hispanic Americans scored the equivalent of second in the overall rankings. At the same time, the average scores for Hispanics and African Americans were significantly lower than in the lowest country on our competition list. The role of wealth inequality and education can further be seen in the fact that the top-performing eighth graders from low socioeconomic backgrounds have about the same chance of completing a bachelors degree as the worst performing eighth graders from high socioeconomic backgrounds. This evidence of wealth trumping talent in America represents further proof that the US educational system is no meritocracy.

The income and racial inequality links are transparent in safety and are often closely tied to the educational inequalities. Simply put, growing up poor and/or a minority in America means being destined to a much more dangerous life than being wealthy and/or Caucasian. While poorer children show lower rates of preprimary education, when they do attend preprimary school, they are less likely to become chronic criminal offenders. But since young African American and Hispanic children, who are statistically more likely to be poor, have less access to educational opportunities, the crime statistics soon stack up against these groups, exacerbated by policing and sentencing biases. America's explosive rise in incarcerations, due to the so-called War on Drugs and the resulting overall incarceration rate that dwarfs that of other countries, clearly shows an overrepresentation of minorities. This overrepresentation reflects differences in underlying crime rates as well as differences in arrest and sentencing rates. The data show that African American men have nearly seven times the incarceration rate of Caucasian men and more than twice the rate for Hispanics; African American women have nearly four times the incarceration rate of Caucasian women and more than twice that of Hispanics. Meanwhile, there is also marked racial inequality among crime victims: homicide is the sixth-most-common cause of mortality for African Americans and the eighth-most-common for Hispanics; it is not among the top fifteen causes of death among Caucasians.[8]

Much of this inequality is tied to our democratic system itself. Our set of rules for government was established by a small group of educated, wealthy white men during a time of slavery and when most of the population was denied basic rights, including the right to vote. While other countries saw radical revisions in their rules of government, the United States has basically stuck to its original structure. This tenacious clinging to an antique rulebook for government has left America mired in a system of winner-take-all, two-party elections that largely ignore the desires of much of the citizenry.

In recent times, moreover, in a dramatic shift, the American democratic process has become dangerously dependent on large political contributions to pay for increasingly expensive election campaigns. The Supreme Court's 2010 *Citizens United* ruling has added further gasoline to the fiery mixture of money and politics by igniting the growth and flexibility of super PACs to influence American elections.[9] As a result of this dependence on large donors, the wheels of American democracy are now greased even more heavily in favor of the wealthy. This tightening link between money and politics has produced a democracy in which the views of constituents in the upper one-third of the income distribution received about 50 percent more weight than those in the middle one-third, while the views of constituents in the bottom one-third of the income distribution appear to have no impact at all—at least, according to one study, no impact on members of the US Senate.[10] Meanwhile, the traditional exclusion of women from politics is still widely felt: the United States has one of the lowest rates of female representation in its national legislature.

The inequality thread that runs through all of the data is clearly a fundamental weakness in American society. The data show that our meritocracy is a myth and that our highly touted social mobility is a delusion. The unhappy truth is that Americans born with the least find fewer opportunities for mobility than their counterparts in other countries. As things now stand, these people are more likely resigned to a life of less safety, worse education, and less responsive government, and they often live shorter lives than those in other countries.

WHY SHOULD WE CARE?

Why is America on a declining performance trajectory in the areas of health, safety, education, democracy, and equality—and why should we care? Is the decline a natural result of losing the initial advantage as our competitors developed? Or are there fundamental holes in our society that need to be filled? What's in store if we don't address these concerns? Will our society head farther and farther down the road of mediocrity?

I believe the data point to two major underlying factors for our declining performance, two major holes to fill. One is constitutional and points to some major changes with the form of our democracy; the other is the pervasive inequality in our society, the fact that our misplaced faith in American meritocracy has created an increasingly fragmented society with far fewer social supports than other countries. If we address these issues, we can make major improvements in US performance on the fundamental aspects of its society. If we do not make such shifts, the trajectory is depressingly predictable: further comparative declines that will eventually drive economic decline.

Let's look first at changes with our democracy.

The original set of rules for our government was designed by individuals who did not trust the masses and who were afraid of a strong central government. Yet we tend to cling to the Constitution as though it were of divine inspiration, and that has driven us to dismiss or avoid making a number of societal changes developed over the last few centuries. We have ignored the fact that every competitor country has developed universal healthcare while we debate endlessly the value of a universally pilloried free market for healthcare. We have ignored many of the improvements in how people vote by steadfastly holding onto a voting system that is outdated and incomplete. We have ignored the fact that our previous advantages in education, driven by support for basic universal public education and by government grants for higher education, have been surpassed by countries that support preprimary education, longer school years, and systems for developing world-class teachers. We have ignored the fact that in nearly all other countries, guns are not pervasive and these countries achieve homicide and incarceration rates that are far, far lower than ours. In summary, we have ignored much of the advancements that other societies have developed as we use an old rulebook that, while outstanding for its time, reflects a great first effort at developing a society and not a final product to be idolized for all eternity.

The second hole to be filled is inequality, for it burdens every aspect of our society, as the data in this book make dramatically clear.

Let's start with education. As globalization has made it easier to gain knowledge and thus add value, education will play an increasingly critical role in determining which economies dominate in the future. The data show that we are leveraging only some of the nation's intellectual capital—from those at the top of our society—while we squander talent from those less fortunate. This is unsustainable. At the same time, our competitors have devised more efficient and effective educational systems. While our world-renowned universities and graduate schools will certainly continue to draw top talent from abroad, our domestic production of talent is not keeping up with the rest of the world, and our ability to retain the top talent that arrives here from abroad is diminishing. There is no doubt that losing the educational race will result in depressing America's long-term economic prospects, making us more of a tourist destination than a site of innovation.

At the same time, the exploding health costs of our for-profit health system will continue to swallow massive amounts of the American economy, far more than in competitor countries. As of this writing, the costs of American healthcare are roughly one-fifth of the US GDP and are growing annually at rates that far exceed GDP growth or rates of inflation.[11] This drain on our economy will further suppress our long-term growth prospects. Clearly, we need to make major changes even to approach the rest of the world—changes that better preserve the quality and length of American lives while improving the cost-effectiveness of American healthcare.

This double-whammy burden on our economy—the declining production of top talent by our educational system and the exploding healthcare costs—is exacerbated by the disturbing trend of our democracy. Without major shifts in how we elect our officials, we will increasingly move toward an aristocracy in which the majority of people have no say in their government's operations while the wealthy class purchases more and more favorable legislation. The shifting sands will accelerate the rising inequality and further depress any likelihood of social mobility. America will become an increasingly fragmented society, the kind more commonly found in developing countries than in wealthy countries. Picture it: in their gated communities cluster the elites who daily capture more of the wealth and political power; they send their children to private schools and concierge physicians take care of their health. They have no need at all to mingle with other classes. Below these elites are educated working couples, putting in longer hours to cover the rising costs of healthcare and college tuitions while striving to maintain a voice in their government. Finally, there are "all the rest"—the disappearing middle class, the working poor, the unemployed, and the voiceless minorities. They confront limited opportunities for advancement, jobs that are diminishing in number and in pay, abundant safety risks, poor educational opportunities, little more than emergency care for their failing health, and often a jail cell or parole officer waiting for them on the horizon.

It is not an entirely far-fetched picture. In fact, this scenario is playing out already in American society, and as it builds momentum, it propels us toward the kind of feudal system that the forebears of many Americans sought to escape centuries ago. For any and all inequalities tear at the fabric of society. Abraham Lincoln said it best in 1858: "A house divided against itself cannot stand."[12] Yet right now, America is a house sharply divided by class, race, and power.

Americans are acutely aware of this trend in rising inequality, as evidenced by survey responses. It isn't clear, however, that most Americans sense how this rising inequality threatens not only the long-term growth of America but also its long-term stability. Societies in which there is little opportunity for social mobility will lack incentives for most people to strive. Those born in lower classes will be resigned to their station in life or will violently oppose the structures of their society; either response is self-destructive and eventually destructive of the society at large.

The media is filled with warnings that this may be the first American generation that won't live as long as their parents. At the same time, median-adjusted income for college-educated men has been virtually unchanged for about thirty-five years while middle-class families are working on average ten weeks a year longer than they did one generation ago.

Again, it's a trajectory that is simply not sustainable.

WHERE DO WE GO FROM HERE?

You know the illustrative parable about boiling a frog? As the story goes, if a frog were dropped into boiling water, it would sense it immediately and jump out. On the other hand, if the frog were placed in cold water that is then heated slowly, the frog wouldn't notice the temperature change and would eventually be boiled alive.[13]

Imagine if we were to announce tomorrow that we are going to establish one of the wealthiest countries in the world. This country would offer a few special features: the rich can get richer than in other countries, but the poor will be comparatively poorer and will have less chance of breaking free of poverty. Those who can afford healthcare can purchase it, and the rest must rely on emergency care only. Education will be slanted heavily to favor the rich, while the jails will be filled with people mostly from lower-income families. The voting system will be designed so that the voices of the less-affluent majority will be ignored. In this scenario, you would sense at once this is boiling water and, like the frog, you would instinctively jump away. But the comparative decline in America's performance in health, safety, education, democracy, and equality has been so gradual that we have not noticed how hot the water is getting—how poorly we perform and how well our competitor countries perform.

The truth is that we're in danger of boiling to death. America is slowly creeping toward a critical point in its history. It's not entirely surprising; all great nations have a period of growth during which their stature increases in the world economically, politically, culturally, and militarily. They reach a peak and maintain it for some time before other countries catch up, or they are attacked from outside, or they self-destruct because of internal weaknesses. All nations have control over their destiny only up to a point. For example, America's comparative dominance in the economic sphere is bound to decline as the economies of countries like China, India, Brazil, and others grow and take a more prominent role. But our former leadership in education, health, democracy, and equality did not have to disappear. While other countries improved themselves, the United States could have invested in the future of its entire population rather than in just a privileged segment, and it thus would have remained best in class. We can recapture our leadership in those areas but, in order to do so, we need to reset the course of increasing inequality and declining comparative excellence that the country has been on for the last several decades.

The United States is still the preferred destination for millions of people around the world. It is still viewed as a great place for innovation, for higher education, and for unlimited potential, yet the reality is that other countries are also competing for the same top talent and for investment money. America is still admired for its entrepreneurial spirit, its cutting-edge technology, and its resourcefulness. We are praised for our research facilities, universities, hospitals, innovations, and world-leading companies. We can use these positions of strength as a starting point for improving many of the deteriorating aspects of our society.

When thinking about our nation, we need to take a long-term view and not merely look from election cycle to election cycle. After all, the changes we have documented in this book didn't happen overnight; the water warmed up gradually. The changes occurred over a span of decades, so to develop significant, fundamental improvements in American society, it is necessary to take a similarly long-term viewpoint. By asking ourselves where we want to be fifty or one hundred years from now, rather than trying to achieve fundamental change in the next year or two, we allow ourselves greater opportunities to challenge the status quo and make more significant change. It will take some time to recapture America's leadership position, but resurgence is certainly possible given sufficient determination, commitment, and long-term vision. After all, the best practices identified in our competitive intelligence comparisons specifically focused on shorter-term solutions. If the suggested next steps in each chapter were implemented over the next few years, then this alone would lead to substantial long-term improvements.

American history has seen deep, fundamental social changes before. It took a Civil War to end slavery while mass popular movements drove advances in women's suffrage and civil rights. I don't recommend or anticipate violence as a means of change in America, but people's empowerment can certainly bring fundamental change.

For example, the gross inequalities that occurred during the Gilded Age of the late nineteenth century and the Roaring Twenties of the early twentieth century provoked a populist backlash that spurred the Progressive Era, the trust-busting activities of Teddy Roosevelt, and later the implementation of Franklin Roosevelt's New Deal.[14] One might have expected a similar backlash in 2007–2008, when the financial crisis affected families in all demographic segments and sparked rising unemployment, sunk mortgages under water, and tightened credit even as bailed-out investment banks paid their employees billions in bonuses. Economic inequality could not have been more prominently displayed than in this disparity between the plight of most American taxpayers and the further enrichment, at their expense, of the elites who had helped create the crisis. Populist anger raged; politicians grandstanded in response. But nothing happened. Soon the populist anger dissipated, and the public focused on other issues. Why was the anger not sustained? Perhaps because we didn't see people starving to death in the streets. Or maybe because, as a wealthy nation, even our comparatively modest social supports were sufficient to placate the working and middle classes. No one wishes us to revert to times of greater desperation that might ignite stronger passions, but one wonders if the nation must be pushed to the brink of self-destruction before it will implement change.

Nearly all political experts agree that the existence of extremely large centers of private power and wealth is a threat to the long-term viability of democracy, and the main effective counterforce to organized money is organized people. Passion is not enough. A movement would need to be organized, financially stable, and broad-based, for it would not be fighting the typical American battle of small government versus big government. Rather, it would have to wage a deeper battle—a fight over what role the government should play in shaping a society and who should drive these decisions, the majority of the people or the privileged elites.

We saw this kind of movement—with support ranging from the bottom of American society to the top of the executive branch—during the New Deal. The upheaval of World War I and the Great Depression had created this widespread popular support for a major reshaping of society, and that is precisely what happened. During the late 1930s and early 1940s, income inequality shrank dramatically.[15] Not coincidentally, the highest marginal tax rates more than tripled from the early 1930s to the end of the decade. The popular support continued through to the presidency of Lyndon Johnson, whose Great Society legislation provided even more support for the bottom of American society.

Today, however, such support seems elusive. As in the example of the recent economic crisis, our two-party system lends itself to political inertia, and proposals for change—especially substantive change—easily become trapped in the legislative process. One case in point was the 2011 debt-ceiling standoff between the president and Congress. Because of the current limited influence that the poorest Americans have on the legislative process, an effective movement will require significant momentum to override not only those who oppose change but also the natural inertia in our current system. We may have seen the beginning of this momentum in the two populist protest movements of recent years, the Tea Party and Occupy Wall Street. Although the aims of the two movements are at opposite ends of the political spectrum, both rise from a deep discontent with what adherents see as destructive forces beyond their control; hence, they have taken to the streets.

Still, the trajectory of current American society is clear and depressing. Further delays in implementing changes will only speed our declining competitiveness and turn our nation into a land of mediocrity. This is a trajectory we cannot and should not accept.

OUR COUNTRY, OUR FUTURE

America is responsible for many of the greatest human accomplishments of the last several hundred years. From the Declaration of Independence and US Constitution to the first airplanes, to landing on the moon, to inventions— from lasers to the Internet—that have changed the world, our nation has left its mark. The United States has reached a level of military power and economic size never before seen in the history of the world. Yet right now, many jaded Americans seem resigned to living in a country whose greatest moments were in the past.

It is neither fair nor appropriate to future Americans for this generation to accept lowered expectations and rising malaise for our nation. Those who do accept this declining trajectory are defeatists. Defeatists point to the challenges in American society and throw up their hands in disgust. They look at the kind of competitive intelligence we've provided in this book and see more evidence that America's decline is inevitable. They claim that lessons from our competitors cannot and will not be implemented here. But our nation was not founded on defeatist thinking or on the acceptance of mediocrity. And it most certainly would never have achieved greatness with that kind of mind-set.

I am not willing to accept the fate defeatists seem ready to receive. I am not willing to accept the notion that America's relative performance in health, safety, education, democracy, and equality must decline. My vision is long term. I am less focused on what my country will be in the next year or two than on what America can be in the next fifty and one hundred years. I see a country of tremendous wealth and human capacity that is locked in an internal struggle and right now is slowly self-destructing. But this self-destruction is not inevitable. It is a choice. I see a country with enormous advantages that is underachieving by wasting the talents and skills of many of its citizens. But this underachievement is not inevitable. It is a choice.

In fact, it is a choice we make on a daily basis. We can choose to ignore the competitive intelligence. We can allow those elements of American society that are benefiting from the US decline to continue unimpeded. If we do, then we are complicit in America's declining stature. Or, we can choose to break out of our comfort zone and implement changes that help us catch up to the world's leaders in all these essential aspects of society—health, safety, education, democracy, and equality. For me, this seems more our responsibility than a choice—a responsibility to improve America for future generations rather than to allow the further loss of our leadership role.

It's our country. It's our choice. Let's change direction—away from a future in which a small percentage of us thrive while the nation as a whole declines— toward a path that secures a greater future for all Americans. We can tell stories of past greatness that has faded, or we can choose to achieve a new greatness for America.

ACKNOWLEDGMENTS

Developing this book has been a goal of mine for years. This book is a reflection of my love of data analysis and concern for the trajectory of the United States.

I wish to acknowledge those who helped directly in creating the book as well as those who helped me to reach this point in my career.

I would like to first thank Gordon Warnock, an incredible person who has helped move this project from the first stages of a book query all the way to a final product with enthusiasm, perseverance, and vision. By Gordon's side has been Andrea Hurst's watchful eye and guidance. Susanna Margolis was invaluable for her advice, support, and guidance in writing and editing. Steven L. Mitchell and Mariel Bard were most helpful in editing the book.

A number of people provided critical reviews of the content, including Sameer Sampat, Alan Friedman, Jerrold Friedman, Eva Weissman, Stan Bernstein, Steven Hill, Brett DiResta, Martin Leshner, Scott Walsh, Michael Friedman, Kin Chung, Paul Thurman, Anna Yusim, Mengjia Liang, and Christos Constantinidis. I would specifically like to mention Phil Bastian for his support in developing the equality selection as well as Peggy Cleveland and Christopher Snowden for their detailed reviews of the entire book.

This book represents a merging of research, analysis, business skills, teaching, and writing. As such, I wish to recognize some of the people who helped me develop in those different areas.

There are a number of teachers who helped me develop my critical thinking skills that I wish to recognize, including Muriel Cohen, Phil Pignatelli, Howard Bender, Louise MacCallum, Julia Yanoshefski, Daniel Weiss, Noel Yeh, Robert Pompi, Eric Cotts, Robert Silverstein, Tania Eicoff, and Yong Ho.

There are some excellent researchers who also helped me in developing my scientific skills and motivating my interest in science, including Charles Nelson, James Dix, Craig Tepley, Carey Priebe, Rudiger von der Heydt, Vernon Mountcastle, Eric Young, Hong Zhou, Tessa Tan Torres, Prakash Navaratnam, Lynne Curry, Karin Stenberg, Michael Steinmetz, Eva Weissman, Stan Bernstein, Netsanet Workie, Carlos Carrera, Bidia Deperthes, Garry Conille, John Stover, Brian Lutz, Tom O'Connell, Gonzalo Pizarro, Jacqui Darroch, and Sharif Egal.

Some of the managers I have had the pleasure to work for have also been most important in my development, including Paul Collins, Mac Purrington, Charissa Lin, Peter Schnall, Werner Haug, Laura Laski, and Hedia Belhaj. I specifically would like to single out Jacqueline Mahon for her tremendous leadership, support, and friendship.

Additionally, I would like to recognize Columbia University, especially Dean Dan McIntyre and Professor Paul Thurman for providing a wonderful environment for teaching and learning, as well as the university's tremendous students.

I would also like to thank my family members for their support (and forgiveness for missing so many family events as I worked to finish the manuscript): Ann Friedman, Alan Friedman, Joshua Krulewitz, Tammy Krulewitz, Jerrold Friedman, and Marizabel Baez Friedman. Though it has been many years since we last spoke, I fondly recall my grandfather's passionate interest in politics, flavoring nearly every piece of news with a healthy dose of skepticism.

Lastly, I would like to thank Shui Chen not only for helping me with finishing the graphs but, much more importantly, for believing in my dreams.

NOTES

INTRODUCTION: COMPETITIVE INTELLIGENCE FOR AMERICA

1. I wish to acknowledge that the analogy between the United States and IBM was developed independently from the use of this same analogy by Thomas L. Friedman and Michael Mandelbaum in their book, *That Used to Be Us: How America Fell behind in the World It Invented and How We Can Come Back.*

2. Louis V. Gerstner Jr., *Who Says Elephants Can't Dance* (New York: Harper Business, 2002), p. 63. This book is recommended for those interested in reading about the process of turning around a struggling former industry leader.

3. "Fortune 500: Our Annual Ranking of America's Largest Corporations," CNN Money, May 3, 2010, http://www.money.cnn.com/magazines/fortune/fortune500/2010/snapshots/225.html (accessed May 7, 2011).

4. There is a large class of books about the topic of American Exceptionalism. These books often take a historical perspective on the psychology of the American approach toward international politics. Examples include John W. Kingdon, *America the Unusual* (New York: St. Martin's/Worth, 1999); Godfrey Hodgson, *The Myth of American Exceptionalism* (New Haven, CT: Yale University Press, 2010); and Seymour Martin Lipset, *American Exceptionalism: A Double-Edged Sword* (New York: W. W. Norton, 1997).

5. We selected the nominal GDP per capita as reported by the International Monetary Fund (IMF) for 2010 in the World Economic Outlook Database, April 2011, http://www.imf.org/external/pubs/ft/weo/2011/01/weodata/index.aspx (accessed April 3, 2011). Nominal GDP refers to the GDP evaluated at current market exchange rates. An alternative is the Purchase Price Parity (PPP), which is a theoretical construct that seeks to represent the exchange rate that would allow for a basket of goods to cost the same in different countries. The PPP can vary based on the basket of goods sold and has sometimes undergone major adjustments, such as in 2005, when China's PPP was adjusted by 40 percent.

6. "Population: Current Population Estimates," New York City Department of City Planning, 2009, http://www.nyc.gov/html/dcp/html/census/popcur.shtml (accessed August 19, 2011).

7. Central Intelligence Agency (CIA), *Central Intelligence Agency World Factbook*, https://www.cia.gov/library/publications/the-world-factbook/ (accessed August 1, 2011).

8. It is important to note that data for Taiwan, which might have otherwise been included, is not generally available.

9. "Counting Immigrants and Expatriates in OECD [OECD] Countries: A New Perspective," *Trends in International Migration: Sopemi*, 2004 ed. (Paris: OECD, 2005). Also available at http://www.oecd.org/dataoecd/46/33/37965376.pdf (accessed July 30, 2011).

10. For his hierarchy of needs, see Abraham H. Maslow, "A Theory of Human Motivation," *Psychological Review* 50, no. 4 (1943): 370–96, http://www.altruists.org/f62 (accessed August 20, 2011).

11. World Bank, "Data," World Bank, http://data.worldbank.org/ (accessed August 1, 2011).

12. World Health Organization (WHO), "Data and Statistics," http://www.who.int/research/en/ (accessed August 1, 2011).

13. OECD, "Stat Extracts," http://stats.oecd.org/Index.aspx (accessed August 1, 2011).

14. "Indices and Data," Human Development Reports, http://hdr.undp.org/en/statistics/hdi/ (accessed August 1, 2011).

15. CIA, *Central Intelligence Agency World Factbook*.

16. CIA, "European Union," *Central Intelligence Agency World Factbook*, February 10, 2012, https://www.cia.gov/library/publications/the-world-factbook/geos/ee.html (accessed May 8, 2011).

17. Books include T. R. Reid, *The United States of Europe: The New Superpower and the End of American Supremacy* (New York: Penguin, 2005); Steven Hill, *Europe's Promise: Why the European Way Is the Best Hope in an Insecure Age* (Berkley: University of California Press, 2010); Thomas Geoghegan, *Were You Born on the Wrong Continent? How the European Model Can Help You Get a Life* (New York: New Press, 2010).

18. "Data: Indicators," The World Bank, http://data.worldbank.org/indicator (accessed April 3, 2011).

19. Human Development Report criteria, background information on the indicators, as well as the data itself are available online from the United Nations Development Program (UNDP) website, http://hdr.undp.org/en/statistics/hdi/ (accessed May 8, 2011).

CHAPTER 1. THE NATION'S HEARTBEAT: HEALTH

1. Organisation for Economic Co-operation and Development (OECD), "Health: Key Tables from OECD," http://dx.doi.org/10.1787/lifexpy-total-table-2011-1-en (accessed June 1, 2011), table titled "Life Expectancy at Birth, Total Population 2011."

2. OECD, "Health: Key Tables from OECD," http://dx.doi.org/10.1787/inf -mort-table-2011-1-en (accessed June 1, 2011), table titled "Infant Mortality, Deaths per 1,000 Live Births."

3. UN Statistics Division, "Maternal Mortality Ratio per 100,000 Live Births," Millennium Development Goals Indicators, 2008, http://unstats.un.org/unsd/mdg/Series Detail.aspx?srid=553 (accessed June 1, 2011).

4. UN Department of Economic and Social Affairs Population Division (2007), "World Population Prospects: The 2006 Revision, Highlights," http://www.un.org/esa/ population/publications/wpp2006/WPP2006_Highlights_rev.pdf (accessed June 1, 2011). Life expectancy at birth data extracted from table A.17 for 2005–2010.

5. World Health Organization (WHO), "World Health Report 2002," http:// www.who.int/whr/2002/en/ (accessed August 3, 2011). Countries were grouped by WHO mortality stratum, with developing countries representing regions with high and very high mortality, and developed countries representing regions with low and very low mortality.

6. Centers for Disease Control and Prevention (CDC), "Ten Great Public Health Achievements—United States, 1900–1999," *Morbidity and Mortality Weekly Report* 48, no. 12 (1999): 241–43, http://cdc.gov/mmwr/preview/mmwrhtml/00056796.htm (accessed August 3, 2011); reprinted in the *Journal of the American Medical Association* 281, no. 16 (1993): 1481.

7. OECD, "Health: Key Tables from OECD," table titled "Life Expectancy at Birth, Total Population 2011."

8. Kristen Lewis and Sarah Burd-Sharps, *The Measure of America 2010–2011* (New York: New York University Press, 2010), p. 63.

9. C. J. L. Murray et al., "Eight Americas: Investigating Mortality Disparities across Races, Counties, and Race-Counties in the United States," *Public Library of Science Med* 3, no. 9 (2006): e260.

10. Lewis and Burd-Sharps, *Measure of America*, p. 63.

11. OECD, "Health: Key Tables from OECD," http://dx.doi.org/10.1787/lifexpy -fe-table-2011-1-en (accessed June 3, 2011), table titled "Life Expectancy at Birth, Females, 2011"; OECD, "Health: Key Tables from OECD," table titled "Life Expectancy at Birth, Total Population 2011."

12. Mabel C. Buer, *Health, Wealth, and Population in the Early Days of the Industrial Revolution* (London: George Routledge and Sons, 1926), p. 30.

13. Myron E. Wegman, "Infant Mortality in the 20th Century, Dramatic but Uneven Progress," *Journal of Nutrition* 131 (2001): 401S–408S.

14. UNICEF, "State of the World's Children 2003 Report," http://www.unicef.org/ sowc03/tables/table1.html (accessed August 1, 2011), table 1 "Basic Indicators: Infant Mortality Rate."

15. OECD, "Health: Key Tables from OECD," http://dx.doi.org/10.1787/inf-mort-table-2011-1-en (accessed June 11, 2011), table titled "Infant Mortality, 2011."

16. H. C. Kung et al., "E-stat Deaths: Preliminary Data for 2005 Health E-stats," US Department of Health and Human Services, CDC, 2007, http://www.cdc.gov/nchs/data/hestat/prelimdeaths05/prelimdeaths05.htm (accessed August 3, 2011).

17. "State of the World's Mothers 2006: Saving the Lives of Mothers and Newborns," Save the Children, 2006, http://www.savethechildren.org/atf/cf/{9def2ebe-10ae-432c-9bd0-df91d2eba74a}/SOWM_2006_FINAL.PDF (accessed August 3, 2011).

18. "The Measure of America: American Human Development Report 2008–2009," American Human Development Project, July 16, 2008, http://www.measureofamerica.org/file/FACT_SHEET_-_US_AND_ITS_PEER_GROUP.pdf (accessed August 31, 2011).

19. Marian F. MacDorman and T. J. Mathews, "Recent Trends in Infant Mortality in the United States," US Department of Health and Human Services, CDC, 2008, http://www.cdc.gov/nchs/data/databriefs/db09.htm (accessed August 3, 2011).

20. UNICEF, "Low Birthweight Incidence by Country (2000–2007)," January 2009, http://www.childinfo.org/low_birthweight_profiles.php (accessed August 3, 2011).

21. Donna L. Hoyert et al., "Deaths: Final Data for 1999," *National Vital Statistics Report* 49, no. 8 (2001): 1–114, http://www.cdc.gov/nchs/data/nvsr/nvsr49/nvsr49_08.pdf (accessed August 3, 2011).

22. Joyce A. Martin et al., "Births: Final Data for 2000," *National Vital Statistics Reports* 50 (2002): 1–102, http://www.cdc.gov/nchs/data/nvsr/nvsr50/nvsr50_05.pdf (accessed August 3, 2011).

23. Computed based on data from T. J. Mathews and Marian F. MacDorman, "Infant Mortality Statistics from the 2004 Period Linked Birth/Infant Death Data Set," *National Vital Statistics Reports* 55, no. 14 (2007), http://www.cdc.gov/nchs/data/nvsr/nvsr55/nvsr55_14.pdf (accessed August 3, 2010).

24. Data from other competitor countries not available.

25. Stanley K. Henshaw, Susheela Singh, and Taylor Haas, "Research Note Recent Trends in Abortion Rates," *International Family Planning Perspectives* 25, no. 1 (March 1999), http://www.guttmacher.org/pubs/journals/2504499.html (accessed August 3, 2011).

26. Margaret Hogan et al., "Maternal Mortality for 181 Countries, 1980–2008: A Systematic Analysis of Progress towards Millennium Development Goal 5" *Lancet* 375, no. 9726 (May 8, 2010): 1609–23.

27. Ibid.

28. UN Department of Economic and Social Affairs, "World Population Prospects: The 2006 Revision," http://www.un.org/esa/population/publications/wpp2006/wpp2006.htm (accessed August 3, 2011).

29. John Wilmoth, "The Lifetime Risk of Maternal Mortality: Concept and Measurement," *Bulletin of the World Health Organization* 87, no. 4 (2009): 256–62, http://www.who.int/bulletin/volumes/87/4/07-048280/en/ (accessed August 3, 2011).

30. M. Brettingham, "Depression and Obesity Are Major Causes of Maternal Death in Britain." *British Medical Journal*, 329, no. 7476 (November 20, 2004): 1205; "Obesity and Maternal Death in Virginia 1999–2002," Virginia Department of Health, March 2009, http://www.vdh.virginia.gov/medExam/documents/2009/pdfs/MMRT_obesity _final.pdf (accessed August 3, 2011).

31. UNICEF, "A League Table of Teenage Births in Rich Nations," *Innocenti Report Card* no. 3 (July 2001), http://www.unicef-irc.org/publications/pdf/repcard3e.pdf (accessed August 3, 2011).

32. UNICEF, "State of the World's Children 2009: Maternal and Newborn Health," http://www.unicef.org/sowc09/ (accessed August 3, 2011).

33. "U.S. Teenage Pregnancies, Births and Abortions: National and State Trends and Trends by Race and Ethnicity," Guttmacher Institute, January 2010, http://www .guttmacher.org/pubs/USTPtrends.pdf (accessed August 4, 2011).

34. Jacqueline Darroch, David Landry, and Susheela Singh, "Changing Emphases in Sexuality Education in U.S. Public Secondary Schools, 1988–1999," *Family Planning Perspectives* 32, no. 6 (September/October 2000), http://www.guttmacher.org/pubs/ journals/3220400.html (accessed August 3, 2011).

35. John Santelli et al., "Abstinence and Abstinence-Only Education: A Review of U.S. Policies and Programs," *Journal of Adolescent Health* 38 (2006): 72–81, http://www .moappp.org/Documents/articles/2006/SantelliAbstinenceonlyEducationReviewPaper .pdf (accessed August 3, 2011).

36. Guss Valk, "The Dutch Model," *UNESCO Courier* July/August 2000, http:// unesdoc.unesco.org/images/0012/001201/120152e.pdf (accessed August 3, 2011).

37. Ibid.

38. Ellen Nolte and C. Martin McKee, "Measuring the Health of Nations: Updating an Earlier Analysis," *Health Affairs* 27, no. 1 (January/February 2008): 58–71, http:// content.healthaffairs.org/content/27/1/58.full.pdf+html (accessed August 3, 2011).

39. The American life expectancy would be expected to increase by at most about 0.5 years if the infant mortality rate were reduced to levels below that of Japan based on calculations using the life expectancy and infant mortality rates.

40. Eric Eckholm, "U.S. Hospitals Try to Stem Losses with Free Care," *New York Times*, October 25, 2009, http://www.nytimes.com/2006/10/25/business/world business/25iht-hospital.3285178.html (accessed August 30, 2011).

41. OECD, "Health: Key Tables from OECD," http://dx.doi.org/10.1787/hlthxp -cap-table-2011-1-en (accessed August 3, 2011), table titled "Total Expenditure on Health per Capita, 2011."

42. Ibid.

43. CIA, "World," Central Intelligence Agency World Factbook, https://www.cia
.gov/library/publications/the-world-factbook/geos/xx.html (accessed August 3, 2011).

44. Ibid.

45. Diana Farrell et al., "Accounting for the Cost of U.S. Healthcare," McKinsey
Global Institute, December 2008, http://www.mckinsey.com/mgi/publications/us
_healthcare/index.asp (accessed August 3, 2011).

46. *Merriam-Webster Online*, s.v. "defensive medicine," http://www.merriam
-webster.com/dictionary/defensive%20medicine (accessed November 1, 2009).

47. Susan Taylor Martin, "Canada Keeps Malpractice Cost in Check," *St. Petersburg
Times*, July 27, 2009, http://www.tampabay.com/news/article1021977.ece (accessed
November 1, 2009).

48. Dee Mahan, "Falling Short: Medicare Prescription Drug Plans Offer Meager Savings," Families USA, December 2005, http://www.familiesusa.org/assets/pdfs/PDP-vs
-VA-prices-special-report.pdf (accessed August 20, 2011); "Rhetoric versus Reality: Comparing Medicare Part D Prices to VA Prices," Families USA, April 2007, http://www
.familiesusa.org/assets/pdfs/rhetoric-vs-reality.PDF (assessed August 20, 2011).

49. United States General Accounting Office, "Medical Malpractice Insurance: Multiple Factors Have Contributed to Increased Premium Rates," June 2003, http://www
.gao.gov/new.items/d03702.pdf (accessed August 3, 2011).

50. T. R. Reid, *The Healing of America: A Global Quest for Better, Cheaper, and Fairer
Health Care* (New York: Penguin Press, 2009).

51. Ibid.

52. Robin Cohen and Michael Martinez, "Health Insurance Coverage: Early Release
of Estimates from the National Health Interview Survey," CDC, http://www.cdc.gov/
nchs/data/nhis/earlyrelease/insur200706.pdf (accessed August 3, 2011).

53. The Emergency Medical Treatment and Active Labor Act (EMTALA) was
passed in 1986. It ensures public access to emergency services regardless of ability to pay.
More information is available about the Emergency Medical Treatment and Active Labor
Act, 42 U.S.C. 1395dd at https://www.cms.gov/emtala/ (accessed August 3, 2011).

54. Gerard Anderson, "From 'Soak the Rich' to 'Soak the Poor': Recent Trends in
Hospital Pricing," *Health Affairs* 26 (2007).

55. CDC, "Health, United States, 2007: With Chartbook on Trends in the Health of
Americans," US Department of Health and Human Services, http://www.cdc.gov/nchs/
data/hus/hus07.pdf (accessed August 3, 2011).

56. Stan Dorn, "Uninsured and Dying Because of It: Updating the Institute of Medicine Analysis on the Impact of Uninsurance on Mortality," Urban Institute, 2008,
http://www.urban.org/UploadedPDF/411588_uninsured_dying.pdf (accessed August 3,
2011).

57. E. Ward et al., "Association of Insurance with Cancer Care Utilization and Outcomes," *CA Cancer Journal for Clinicians* 58, no. 1 (January–February 2008): 9–31.

58. Mark Pearson, "Disparities in Health Expenditure across OECD Countries: Why Does the United States Spend So Much More Than Other Countries?" Written Statement to Senate Special Committee on Aging, September 30, 2009, http://www.oecd.org/dataoecd/5/34/43800977.pdf (accessed August 3, 2011).

59. Gary Claxton et al., "Employer Health Benefits: 2009 Annual Survey," Kaiser Family Foundation and Health Research and Educational Trust, September 2009, http://ehbs.kff.org/pdf/2009/7936.pdf (accessed August 3, 2011).

60. Ibid.

61. Karyn Schwartz, "Spotlight on Uninsured Parents: How Lack of Coverage Affects Parents and Their Families," Kaiser Commission on Medicaid and the Uninsured, June 2007, http://www.kff.org/uninsured/upload/7662.pdf (accessed August 3, 2011).

62. Robin A. Cohen and Michael E. Martinez, "Health Insurance Coverage: Early Release of Estimates from the National Health Interview Survey, January–June 2006," CDC, December 2006, http://www.cdc.gov/nchs/data/nhis/earlyrelease/insur200612.pdf (accessed August 3, 2011).

63. Lewis and Burd-Sharps, *Measure of America*, p. 211.

64. Philip Musgrove et al., "The World Health Report 2000; Health Systems: Improving Performance," WHO, 2000, http://www.who.int/whr/2000/en/whr00_en.pdf (accessed August 3, 2011).

65. WHO, "World Health Statistics 2011," http://www.who.int/whosis/whostat/2011/en/index.html (accessed August 3, 2011).

66. Ibid.

67. Jiaquan Xu et al., "Deaths: Final Data for 2007," *National Vital Statistics Reports* 58, no. 19 (May 2010), http://www.cdc.gov/nchs/data/nvsr/nvsr58/nvsr58_19.pdf (accessed August 3, 2011).

68. Linda Kohn, Janet Corrigan, and Molla Donaldson, *To Err Is Human: Building a Safer Health System* (Washington, DC: National Academy Press, 2000).

69. OECD, "Organisation for Economic Co-operation and Development Health Data 2011," http://www.oecd.org/dataoecd/52/42/48304068.xls (accessed August 3, 2011).

70. A. Mokdad et al., "Actual Causes of Death in the United States, 2000," *Journal of the American Medical Association* 291 (2004) 1238–45.

71. OECD, "Organisation for Economic Co-operation and Development Health Data 2011." Note that adult here is defined as age fifteen or older.

72. CDC, "Behavioral Risk Factor Surveillance System," http://www.cdc.gov/brfss/ (accessed August 3, 2011).

73. A. A. de Lorimier, "Alcohol, Wine, and Health," *American Journal of Surgery* 180, no. 5 (November 2000): 357–61.

74. CDC, "Unintentional Poisoning Deaths—United States, 1999–2004," *Morbidity and Mortality Weekly Report* 56, no. 5 (February 9, 2007): 93–96, http://www.cdc.gov/mmwr/preview/mmwrhtml/mm5605a1.htm (accessed August 3, 2011).

75. J. P. Broderick et al., "Major Risk Factors for Aneurysmal Subarachnoid Hemorrhage in the Young are Modifiable," *Stroke* 34, no. 6 (June 2003): 1375–81.

76. Louisa Degenhardt et al., "Toward a Global View of Alcohol, Tobacco, Cannabis, and Cocaine Use: Findings from the WHO World Mental Health Surveys," *Public Library of Science Medicine* 5, no. 7 (June 1, 2008): e141.

77. "U.S. Cancer Statistics Working Group; United States Cancer Statistics: 1999–2005 Incidence and Mortality Web-Based Report," US Department of Health and Human Services, Centers for Disease Control and Prevention, and National Cancer Institute, 2009.

78. Ahmedin Jemal et al., "Annual Report to the Nation on the Status of Cancer, 1975–2005, Featuring Trends in Lung Cancer, Tobacco Use, and Tobacco Control," *Journal of the National Cancer Institute* 100, no. 23 (December 3, 2008): 1672–94, http://jnci.oxfordjournals.org/content/100/23/1672.full (accessed August 3, 2011).

79. Hanspeter Witschi, "A Short History of Lung Cancer," *Toxicological Sciences* 64, no. 1 (2001): 4–6, http://toxsci.oxfordjournals.org/content/64/1/4.full (accessed August 3, 2011).

80. OECD, "Organisation for Economic Co-operation and Development Health Data 2011." Note that adult here is defined as age fifteen or older.

81. Shirish M. Gadgeel et al., "Impact of Race in Lung Cancer," *Chest* 120, no. 1 (2001): 55–63, http://chestjournal.chestpubs.org/content/120/1/55.full (accessed August 3, 2011).

82. CDC, "The Health Consequences of Smoking: A Report of the Surgeon General," US Department of Health and Human Services, 2004, http://www.surgeongeneral.gov/library/smokingconsequences/ (accessed August 3, 2011).

83. OECD, "Organisation for Economic Co-operation and Development Health Data 2011." Note that adult here is defined as age fifteen or older.

84. CDC, "Cigarette Smoking among Adults—United States, 2006," *Morbidity and Mortality Weekly Report*, 56, no. 44 (November 2007): 1157–61, http://www.cdc.gov/mmwr/preview/mmwrhtml/mm5644a2.htm (accessed August 3, 2011).

85. Michel P. Coleman et al., "Cancer Survival in Five Continents: A Worldwide Population-Based Study (CONCORD)," *The Lancet Oncology* 9, no. 8 (August 2008): 730–56, http://healthcare.procon.org/sourcefiles/CONCORDCancerSurvivalStudy.pdf (accessed August 3, 2011).

86. WHO, "World Health Statistics 2011."

87. Ibid.

88. "FastStats: Accidents or Unintentional Injuries," Centers for Disease Control and Prevention, http://www.cdc.gov/nchs/fastats/acc-inj.htm (accessed August 3, 2011).

89. Margie Peden et al., "World Report on Road Traffic Injury Prevention," World Health Organization, 2004, http://whqlibdoc.who.int/publications/2004/9241562609 .pdf (accessed August 3, 2011).

90. "World Health Report 2002—Reducing Risks, Promoting Healthy Life," World Health Organization, 2002, http://www.who.int/whr/2002/en/ (accessed August 3, 2011).

91. J. Tiihonen et al., "11-Year Follow-up of Mortality in Patients with Schizophrenia: A Population-Based Cohort Study (FIN11 Study)," *Lancet* 374, no. 22 (August 22, 2009): 620–27.

92. K. Demyttenaere et al., "Prevalence, Severity, and Unmet Need for Treatment of Mental Disorders in the World Health Organization World Mental Health Surveys," *Journal of the American Medical Association* 291 (June 2004): 2581–90; World Health Organization International Consortium in Psychiatric Epidemiology, "Cross-National Comparisons of the Prevalances and Correlates of Mental Disorders," *Bulletin of the World Health Organization* 78, no. 4 (2000), http://www.who.int/bulletin/archives/78(4) 413.pdf (accessed August 3, 2011).

93. Ruut Veenhoven, "World Database of Happiness," Erasmus University Rotterdam, http://worlddatabaseofhappiness.eur.nl/ (accessed August 3, 2011).

94. Centers for Disease Control and Prevention, "Injury Prevention and Control: Data and Statistics (WISQARS™)," http://www.cdc.gov/injury/wisqars/index.html (accessed October 8, 2011).

95. E. R. Dorsey et al., "Funding of US Biomedical Research, 2003–2008," *Journal of the American Medical Association* 303, no. 2 (2010): 137–43.

96. "World Patent Report: A Statistical Review (2008)," World Intellectual Property Organization, http://www.wipo.int/ipstats/en/statistics/patents/wipo_pub_931.html (accessed August 3, 2011).

97. Calculation based on data extracted from http://www.uspto.gov/ (accessed August 3, 2011).

98. J. Banks et al., "Disease and Disadvantage in the United States and in England," *Journal of the American Medical Association* 295, no. 17 (2006): 2037–45.

99. Research groups led by Robert Gallo (United States) and Luc Montagnier (France) independently identified the retrovirus responsible for infecting AIDS patients. They published their findings in separate articles in the same issue of the journal *Science* in 1983.

100. Susan Sharon, "Ban Lifted on Federal Funding for Needle Exchange," National Public Radio, December 18, 2009, http://www.npr.org/templates/story/story.php ?storyId=121511681 (accessed August 19, 2011).

101. OECD, "Organisation for Economic Co-operation and Development Health Data 2011."

102. "Agriculture and Health Policies in Conflict: How Food Subsidies Tax Our Health," Physicians Committee for Responsible Medicine, http://www.pcrm.org/health/reports/agriculture-and-health-policies-intro (accessed August 3, 2011).

103. Nutritional facts from Wendy's menu extracted from "Nutrition Information," Wendy's International, Inc., http://www.wendys.com/food/pdf/us/nutrition.pdf (accessed August 27, 2011).

104. Melonie Heron et al., "Deaths: Final Data for 2006," *National Vital Statistics Reports* 57, no 14 (2009), http://www.cdc.gov/nchs/data/nvsr/nvsr57/nvsr57_14.pdf (accessed August 3, 2011).

105. Amy Goldstein, "Some Say Government's New Strategy to Fight Drug Addiction Needs More Funding," *Washington Post*, May 24, 2010, http://www.washingtonpost.com/wp-dyn/content/article/2010/05/23/AR2010052304010.html (accesses August 23, 2011).

106. "Cigarette Use among High School Students—United States, 1991–2007," *Morbidity and Mortality Weekly Report* 57, no. 25 (June 27, 2008): 689–91, http://www.cdc.gov/mmwr/preview/mmwrhtml/mm5725a3.htm (accessed August 30, 2011).

107. W. Orzechowski and R. C. Walker, "The Tax Burden on Tobacco," 44 (2009), http://www.nocigtax.com/upload/file/1/Tax_Burden_on_Tobacco_vol._44_FY2009.pdf (accessed August 3, 2011).

108. OpenSecrets.org, Center for Responsive Politics, http://www.opensecrets.org/index.php (accessed August 3, 2011).

109. Phillip Longman, *Best Care Anywhere: Why VA Health Care Is Better Than Yours* (San Francisco: Polipoint Press, 2007).

110. Steven Hill, *10 Steps to Repair American Democracy* (San Francisco: Polipoint Press, 2008), p. 178.

111. Milton Friedman and Rose Friedman, *Free to Choose* (New York: Mariner Books, 1980).

112. Marie McCullough, "No Deliveries Due at Mercy Fitzgerald, Mercy Fitzgerald Hospital No Longer Delivering Babies," *Philadelphia Inquirer*, June 3, 2003, http://articles.philly.com/2003-06-03/news/25447881_1_maternity-unit-delaware-valley-health care-council-deliveries/2 (accessed August 3, 2011).

113. American Congress of Obstetricians and Gynecologists, "Medical Liability Survey," July 16, 2004, http://www.acog.org/from_home/publications/press_releases/nr07-16-04.cfm (accessed August 3, 2011).

114. Brooke J. Doran, ed., *Medical Malpractice: Verdicts, Settlements, and Statistical Analysis* (Horsham, PA: Jury Verdict Research, 2005).

115. "Congressional Revolving Doors: The Journey from Congress to K Street," Public Citizen: Congress Watch, July 2005, http://www.cleanupwashington.org/documents/RevolveDoor.pdf (accessed August 3, 2011).

116. OpenSecrets.org, Center for Responsive Politics, http://www.opensecrets .org/index.php (accessed August 3, 2011).

CHAPTER 2. LOCKING OUR DOORS: SAFETY

1. Dictionary.com, s.v. "fear," http://dictionary.reference.com/browse/fear (accessed April 15, 2011).

2. For an overview of this issue, please see C. Coleman and J. Moynihan, *Understanding Crime Data: Haunted by the Dark Figure* (United Kingdom: Open University Press, 1996).

3. The British Crime Survey measures the amount of crime in England and Wales. More information may be found at http://www.statistics.gov.uk/ssd/surveys/british _crime_survey.asp (accessed August 1, 2011).

4. The National Crime Victimization Survey, conducted by the Office of Justice Programs, contains annual data from a nationally representative sample of seventy-six thousand households. More information is available at http://bjs.ojp.usdoj.gov/index.cfm ?ty=dcdetail&iid=245 (accessed August 1, 2011).

5. Home Office, "Crime in England and Wales 2009/10," British Crime Survey, April 5, 2011, http://data.gov.uk/dataset/crime-in-england-and-wales-bcs (accessed April 17, 2011).

6. Analysis from Australia Bureau of Statistics based on data from National Crime and Safety Survey, 2002. See "1301.0 - Year Book Australia, 2006: Likelihood of Victims Reporting Crimes to Police," January 20, 2006, http://www.abs.gov.au/ausstats/abs @.nsf/Previousproducts/1301.0Feature%20Article192006?opendocument&tabname =Summary&prodno=1301.0&issue=2006&num=&view= (accessed August 1, 2011).

7. Shannon M. Catalano, *Criminal Victimization, 2005* (Washington, DC: Bureau of Justice Statistics, 2006).

8. Raymond Blaine Fosdick, *American Police Systems* (New York: Century Company, 1920), p. 13.

9. World Values Survey Association, "World Values Survey 2005," http://wvsevsdb .com/wvs/WVSAnalize.jsp?Idioma=I (accessed April 24, 2011).

10. The Federal Assault Weapons Ban was signed into law in 1994, expired in 2004, and has not been renewed.

11. Russ Thurman, ed., "Business Hits Robust Level: An Energized Industry Enjoys Brisk Sales," *Shooting Industry*, July 2007, http://www.shootingindustry.com/Pages/ 07FAReport.pdf (accessed May 1, 2011).

12. Alexander Deconde, Fredrik Logevall, and Richard Dean Burns, *Encyclopedia of American Foreign Policy*, 2nd ed. (New York: Charles Scribner's Sons, 2001).

13. Joyce Lee Malcolm, *To Keep and Bear Arms: The Origins of an Anglo-American Right* (Cambridge, MA: Harvard University Press, 1996).

14. Geneva Graduate Institute of International Studies, *Small Arms Survey 2007: Guns and the City* (Cambridge: Cambridge University Press, 2007).

15. US Department of Justice, "Crime in the United States, 2006," September 2007, http://www.fbi.gov/ucr/cius2006/index.html (accessed August 1, 2011).

16. Philip J. Cook and Jens Ludwig, *Gun Violence: The Real Costs* (Oxford: Oxford University Press, 2000).

17. Linda Saltzman et al., "Weapon Involvement and Injury Outcomes in Family and Intimate Assaults," *Journal of the American Medical Association* 267, no. 22 (1992): 3043–47.

18. Douglas J. Wiebe, "Homicide and Suicide Risks Associated with Firearms in the Home: A National Case-Control Study," *Annals of Emergency Medicine* 41 (2003): 771–82.

19. E. G. Krug, K. E. Powell, and L. L. Dahlberg, "Firearm-Related Deaths in the United States and 35 Other High- and Upper-Middle-Income Countries," *International Journal of Epidemiology* 27 (1998): 214–21.

20. The Firearms (Amendment) (No. 2) Act 1997 allowed only the following guns to still be in private possession: antique and muzzle-loading black powder guns, guns of historic interest whose ammunition is no longer available, guns of historic interest with current calibers, air pistols, and guns which fall outside the Home Office definition of handguns. Information about the Firearms Act of 1997 is available at http://www.legislation.gov.uk/ukpga/1997/64/contents (accessed August 1, 2011).

21. Abraham Lincoln in 1865; James Garfield in 1881; William McKinley in 1901; John F. Kennedy in 1963.

22. Theodore Roosevelt in 1912 (former president running for election); Ronald Reagan in 1981.

23. Federal Bureau of Investigation, "Crime in the United States: Expanded Homicide Data," 2009, http://www.fbi.gov/ucr/cius2009/offenses/expanded_information/data/shrtable_07.html (accessed August 1, 2011), table 7 "Murder, Types of Weapons Used."

24. United Nations Office on Drugs and Crime, "Homicide Statistics, Criminal Justice Sources—Latest Available Year 2003–2008," http://www.unodc.org/documents/data-and-analysis/Crime-statistics/Criminal_justice_latest_year_by_country.20100201.xls (accessed August 4, 2011).

25. Kate Pickett and Richard Wilkinson, *The Spirit Level* (New York: Penguin Books, 2009), pp. 134–37.

26. Christopher Snowdon, *The Spirit Level Delusion: Fact-Checking the Left's New Theory of Everything* (Ripton, North Yorkshire, UK: Democracy Institute/Little Dice, 2010), pp. 71–83.

27. Steven D. Levitt, "Understanding Why Crime Fell in the 1990s: Four Factors That Explain the Decline and Six That Do Not," *Journal of Economic Perspectives* 18, no. 1 (Winter 2004): 163–90, http://pricetheory.uchicago.edu/levitt/Papers/LevittUnderstandingWhyCrime2004.pdf (accessed August 20, 2011).

28. US Census Bureau, "Law Enforcement, Courts, and Prisons: Crimes and Crime Rates," http://www.census.gov/compendia/statab/cats/law_enforcement_courts_prisons/crimes_and_crime_rates.html (accessed May 1, 2011).

29. Amnesty International, "Death Sentences and Executions 2010," http://www.amnesty.org/en/library/asset/ACT50/001/2011/en/ea1b6b25-a62a-4074-927d-ba51e88df2e9/act500012011en.pdf (accessed April 22, 2011).

30. United Nations Office on Drugs and Crime, "Homicide Statistics, Criminal Justice Sources."

31. International Centre for Prison Studies, "World Prison Brief," School of Law, King's College London, http://www.prisonstudies.org/info/worldbrief/ (accessed August 1, 2011).

32. Nils Christie, *Crime Control as Industry* (Oxford: Routledge, 2000).

33. Bureau of Justice Statistics, "Publications and Products: Prisoners," http://bjs.ojp.usdoj.gov/index.cfm?ty=pbse&sid=40 (accessed May 7, 2011).

34. Heather West, William Sabol, and Sarah Greenman, "Prisoners in 2009," *Bureau of Justice Statistics Bulletin* (Washington, DC: US Department of Justice, December 2010). This information can also be found online in the *Bureau of Justice Statistics Bulletin*, NCJ 231675, http://bjs.ojp.usdoj.gov/content/pub/pdf/p09.pdf (accessed August 1, 2011), appendix table 18, 33.

35. "Prison and Jail Inmates at Midyear 2005," *Bureau of Justice Statistics Bulletin* (Washington, DC: US Department of Justice, May 2006). This information can also be found online at http://bjs.ojp.usdoj.gov/content/pub/ascii/pjim05.txt (accessed August 4, 2011).

36. D. Farrington and P. A. Langdan, "Changes in Crime and Punishment in America in the 1980s," *Justice Quarterly* 9, no. 1 (March 1992): 5–18.

37. American College of Trial Lawyers, "United States Sentencing Guidelines 2004: An Experiment That Has Failed," September 2004, http://www.actl.com/AM/Template.cfm?Section=All_Publications&Template=/CM/ContentDisplay.cfm&ContentFileID=58 (accessed August 1, 2011).

38. US Sentencing Commission, "2002 Sourcebook of Federal Sentencing Statistics," http://ftp.ussc.gov/ANNRPT/2002/SBTOC02.htm (accessed April 17, 2011), figure C and table 10. Also referred to in *Testimony: United States Senate Committee on the Judiciary,* Blakely v. Washington *and the Future of the Federal Sentencing Guidelines, 13 July 2004* (2004) (joint prepared testimony of Commissioner John R. Steer and Judge William K. Sessions, III), http://www.ussc.gov/Legislative_and_Public_Affairs/Congressional_Testimony

_and_Reports/Testimony/20040716_Sessions_Steer_Testimony.pdf (accessed April 17, 2011).

39. Michael Jackson, "The Sentencing of Dangerous and Habitual Offenders in Canada," *Federal Sentencing Reporter* 9, no. 55 (March 1997): 256–61.

40. The University of California, Los Angeles (UCLA) was contracted to evaluate the impact of the program, and it regularly publishes the results of this analysis. See, for example, UCLA, "Evaluation of the Substance Abuse and Crime Prevention Act: Final Report," Integrated Substance Abuse Programs, April 13, 2007, http://www.uclaisap.org/prop36/documents/SACPAEvaluationReport.pdf (accessed May 1, 2011).

41. *Brown v. Plata*, 563 U.S. (2011). This information can be found at http://www.supremecourt.gov/opinions/10pdf/09-1233.pdf (accessed August 23, 2011).

42. Rose Heyer and Peter Wagner, "Too Big to Ignore: How Counting People in Prisons Distorted Census 2000," *Prison Policy Initiative* (April 2004), http://www.prisonersofthecensus.org/toobig/ (accessed April 22, 2011).

43. Peter Wagner, "Importing Constituents: Prisoners and Political Clout in New York," Prison Policy Initiative, last modified May 20, 2002, http://www.prisonpolicy.org/importing/importing.html#_ftn2 (accessed April 22, 2011).

44. Malcolm Feeley, "The Privatization of Prisons in Historical Perspective," *Criminal Justice Research Bulletins* 6, no. 2 (1991): 1–10.

45. Laura Sullivan, "Prison Economics Help Drive Ariz. Immigration Law," *Morning Edition*, October 28, 2010, http://www.npr.org/templates/story/story.php?storyId =130833741 (accessed May 1, 2011).

46. Thomas Frank, "Lock 'Em Up: Jailing Kids Is a Proud American Tradition," *Wall Street Journal*, April 1, 2009, http://online.wsj.com/article/SB123854010220075533 .html (accessed August 19, 2011).

47. US General Accounting Office, "Private and Public Prisons Studies Comparing Operational Costs and/or Quality of Service," August 1996, http://www.gao.gov/archive/1996/gg96158.pdf (accessed August 1, 2011).

48. Peter Wagner, *The Prison Index: Taking the Pulse of the Crime Control Industry* (Springfield, MA: Prison Policy Initiative, 2003). An excerpt of this book is available at http://www.prisonpolicy.org/prisonindex/toc.html (accessed August 1, 2011).

49. Tara Herivel and Paul Wright, *Prison Nation: The Warehousing of America's Poor* (London: Taylor and Francis Books, 2003), p. 122.

50. *Statement for the Record: Hearing on the Role of Social Security Numbers in Identity Theft and Options to Guard Their Privacy* (April 13, 2011) (statement of the Honorable Patrick P. O'Carroll Jr., Inspector General of the Social Security Administration), http://oig.ssa.gov/sites/default/files/testimony/04132011testimony_1.pdf (accessed November 30, 2011). This report states that prisons in thirteen states allowed inmates access to social security numbers through various work programs as of 2006. Further infor-

mation on the risks of prisoners working with social security numbers is available from the Social Security Administration itself, http://www.ssa.gov/oig/ADOBEPDF/A-08-06 -16082.pdf (accessed May 7, 2011).

51. William J. Sabol, Todd D. Minton, and Paige M. Harrison, "Prison and Jail Inmates at Midyear 2006," *Bureau of Justice Statistics Bulletin* (Washington, DC: US Department of Justice, June 2007). This information can also be found online at http://bjs.ojp.usdoj.gov/content/pub/pdf/pjim06.pdf (accessed August 1, 2011).

52. Marc Mauer and Ryan S. King, *Uneven Justice: State Rates of Incarceration by Race and Ethnicity* (Washington, DC: Sentencing Project, July 2007), http://www.sentencing project.org/doc/publications/rd_stateratesofincbyraceandethnicity.pdf (accessed August 2, 2011).

53. Elliot Currie, *Crime and Punishment in America* (New York: Picador Books, 1998).

54. Marc Mauer, *Comparative International Rates of Incarceration: An Examination of Causes and Trends,*" (Washington, DC: Sentencing Project 2003), http://www.sentencing project.org/doc/publications/inc_comparative_intl.pdf (accessed October 8, 2011).

55. Sasha Abramsky, *Hard Time Blues* (New York: Thomas Dunne, 2002).

56. GovTrack.us, "Fair Sentencing Act of 2010," Civic Impulse, http://www.govtrack .us/congress/bill.xpd?bill=s111-1789 (accessed August 21, 2011).

57. World Values Survey Association, "World Values Survey 2005."

58. Office of Management and Budget, "Defense Manpower Data Center," http:// www.fedstats.gov/key_stats/index.php?id=DMDC (accessed April 16, 2011).

59. Defense Manpower Data Center, "Active Duty Military Personnel Strengths by Regional Area and by Country (309A)," US Department of Defense, September 30, 2008, http://siadapp.dmdc.osd.mil/personnel/MILITARY/history/hst0809.pdf (accessed April 16, 2011).

60. North Atlantic Treaty Organization's relations with contact countries, which are referred to as "partners across the globe," are explained on the organization's website at http://www.nato.int/cps/en/natolive/topics_48899.htm (accessed February 28, 2012).

61. North Atlantic Treaty Organization (NATO) official website, http://www .nato.int (accessed April 16, 2011).

62. Stockholm International Peace Research Institute (SIPRI), "SIPRI Yearbook 2010," http://www.sipri.org/yearbook/2010 (accessed May 2, 2011).

63. Office of Management and Budget, http:/www.fedspending.org (accessed April 23, 2011).

64. World Bank, "Data," http://data.worldbank.org/ (accessed August 1, 2011).

65. International Institute for Strategic Studies, *The Military Balance*, ed. James Hackett (London: Routledge, 2010).

66. US General Accounting Office, "Military Personnel Reporting Additional Ser- vicemember Demographics Could Enhance Congressional Oversight," September 2005,

http://www.gao.gov/new.items/d05952.pdf (accessed August 4, 2011).

67. *Hamdi v. Rumsfeld*, No. 03-6696, 542 U.S. 507 (2004), http://www.law
.cornell.edu/supct/html/03-6696.ZO.html (accessed October 8, 2011).

68. *Boumediene v. Bush*, Nos. 06-1195 and 06-1196, 476 F.3d 981 (2007), http://
www.law.cornell.edu/supct/html/06-1195.ZS.html (accessed October 8, 2011).

69. T. R. Reid, *The United States of Europe: The New Superpower and the End of
American Supremacy* (New York: Penguin Press, 2004), p. 180.

70. SIPRI, "SIPRI Database," http://armstrade.sipri.org/armstrade/html/export
_toplist.php (accessed April 23, 2011).

71. Robert S. Norris and Hans M. Kristensen, "Global Nuclear Stockpiles,
1945–2006," *Bulletin of the Atomic Scientists* 62, no. 4 (July/August 2006): 64–66.

72. Hans M. Kristensen, "Status of World Nuclear Forces," Federation of American
Scientists, http://www.fas.org/programs/ssp/nukes/nuclearweapons/nukestatus.html
(accessed April 22, 2011). More generally, information about nuclear weapons may be
found at the SIPRI database located at http://www.sipri.org/databases (accessed August 2,
2011).

73. Hans M. Kristensen, "U.S. Nuclear Weapons in Europe," Natural Resources
Defense Council, February 2005, http://www.nrdc.org/nuclear/euro/euro.pdf (accessed
April 22, 2011).

74. Martin Butcher, et al., *NATO Nuclear Sharing and the NPT—Questions to Be
Answered* (Berlin Information-center for Transatlantic Security, June 1997), http://
www.bits.de/public/researchnote/rn97-3.htm (accessed April 22, 2011).

75. Susi Snyder and Wilbert van der Zeijden, *Withdrawal Issues: What NATO Countries Say about the Future of Tactical Nuclear Weapons in Europe* (IKV Pax Christi, March
2011), http://www.nonukes.nl/media/files/withdrawal-issues-report-nospread.pdf (accessed April 22, 2011).

76. *Hearing Before the Committee on Oversight and Government Reform*, H.R. 89,
110th Cong. (October 2, 2007). This information is available at https://house.resource
.org/110/org.c-span.201290-1.1.pdf (accessed August 30, 2011).

77. Spencer Ackerman, "Two More Merc Firms Get Big Iraq Contracts," *Wired*, May
4, 2011, http://www.wired.com/dangerroom/2011/05/two-more-merc-firms-get-big
-iraq-contracts/ (accessed June 2, 2011).

78. Vision of Humanity, "Global Peace Index: Methodology, Results and Findings,"
Institute for Economics and Peace, 2007, http://www.visionofhumanity.org/wp
-content/uploads/PDF/2007/2007%20%20%20%20Results%20Report.pdf (accessed
April 23, 2011).

79. Vision of Humanity, "About the GPI," Institute for Economics and Peace,
http://www.visionofhumanity.org/about/ (accessed February 28, 2012).

80. Vision of Humanity, "U.S. Peace Index 2011—Correlations," Institute for Eco-

nomics and Peace, http://www.visionofhumanity.org/wp-content/uploads/2011/04/U.S. -Peace-Index-Spider-chart-correlation-1.pdf (accessed August 1, 2011).

81. SIPRI, "SIPRI Yearbook 2010."

82. "Canadian Firearms Safety Course," Royal Canadian Mounted Police, February 13, 2004, http://www.rcmp-grc.gc.ca/cfp-pcaf/safe_sur/cour-eng.htm (accessed May 2, 2011).

83. Information available from the Citizens Research Council of Michigan, http://www.crcmich.org/ (accessed August 1, 2011).

84. Louisa Degenhart et al., "Towards a Global View of Alcohol, Tobacco, Cannibis and Cocaine Use: Findings from the WHO World Mental Health Surveys," *Public Library of Science Medicine* 5, no. 7 (June 1, 2008): 1057.

85. European Monitoring Centre for Drugs and Drug Addiction, *2007 Annual Report: The State of the Drugs Problem in Europe* (Lisbon: EMCDDA, 2007), pp. 12–13, http://www.emcdda.europa.eu/publications/annual-report/2007 (accessed August 1, 2011).

86. Donald Riddle, *The Truman Committee: A Study in Congressional Responsibility* (New Brunswick, NJ: Rutgers University Press, 1964).

CHAPTER 3. THE RIGHT TO THE THREE RS: EDUCATION

1. UN Development Program, "Technical Notes," *Human Development Report 2010* (New York: Palgrave Macmillan, 2010). This information is also available at http://hdr.undp.org/en/media/HDR_2010_EN_TechNotes_reprint.pdf (accessed May 24, 2011).

2. UN Development Program, "Human Development Index and Its Components," *Human Development Report 2010* (New York: Palgrave Macmillan, 2010), table 1. This information is also available at http://hdr.undp.org/en/media/HDR_2010_EN_Table1 _reprint.pdf (accessed May 24, 2011).

3. Claudia Goldin and Lawrence Katz, *The Race between Education and Technology* (Cambridge, MA: Belknap Press, 2008).

4. Ibid.

5. National Commission on Excellence in Education, *A Nation at Risk: The Imperative for Educational Reform* (Washington, DC: US Government Printing Office, April 1983). This information is also available online at http://www2.ed.gov/pubs/NatAtRisk/index.html (accessed May 31, 2011).

6. Organisation for Economic Co-operation and Development (OECD), *Education at a Glance 2010: OECD Indicators* (Paris: OECD, 2010), table A1.2. This information is also available online at http://www.oecd.org/document/52/0,3746,en_2649 _39263238_45897844_1_1_1_1,00.html (accessed May 31, 2011).

7. OECD, *PISA 2009 Results: What Students Know and Can Do* (Paris: OECD, 2010). This information is also available online at http://www.oecd.org/document/61/ 0,3746,en_32252351_32235731_46567613_1_1_1_1,00.html (accessed May 31, 2011).

8. Shawn Fremstad and Andy Van Kleunan, "Redefining Public Education for the 21st Century: Toward a Federal Guarantee of Education and Training for America's Workers," *Clearinghouse Review Journal of Poverty Law and Policy* 40, no. 1/2 (May–June 2006).

9. Ina V. S. Mullis et al., "Chapter 4: Students' Backgrounds and Attitudes Towards Mathematics," *TIMSS 1999 International Mathematics Report: Findings from IEA's Repeat of the Third International Mathematics and Science Study at the Eighth Grade* (Chestnut Hill, MA: International Study Center, Boston College, Lynch School of Education, 2000). Chapter 4 is also available at http://timss.bc.edu/timss1999i/pdf/T99i_Math_4.pdf (accessed May 25, 2011).

10. OECD, "A Family Affair: Intergenerational Social Mobility across OECD Countries," *Economic Policy Reforms: Going for Growth* (Paris: OECD, 2010). This chapter is also available at http://www.oecd.org/dataoecd/3/62/44582910.pdf (accessed August 21, 2011).

11. Linda Darling-Hammond, *The Flat World and Education* (New York: Teachers College Press, 2010), p. 20.

12. Programme for International Student Assessment (PISA), "PISA 2009: Data Tables, Figures, and Exhibits," http://nces.ed.gov/pubs2011/2011004_1.pdf (accessed May 27, 2011).

13. Darling-Hammond, *Flat World and Education*, p. 3.

14. Kristen Lewis and Sarah Burd-Sharps, *The Measure of America 2010–2011* (New York: New York University Press, 2010).

15. National Center for Education Statistics, "Fast Facts," US Department of Education, http://nces.ed.gov/fastfacts/display.asp?id=66 (accessed July 7, 2011). Information presented on this webpage found in the US Department of Education, National Center for Education Statistics, *Digest of Education Statistics, 2010* (NCES 2011 015), table 188 and chapter 2, 2011.

16. OECD, *Education at a Glance 2010*, table B1.1a.

17. Ibid.

18. Public expenditure on education consists of current and capital public expenditure on education, including government spending on educational institutions (both public and private), education administration, and subsidies for private entities (students/households and other privates entities). For more information, see World Bank, "Expenditure per Student, Primary (% of GDP per Capita)," United Nations Educational, Scientific, and Cultural Organization (UNESCO) Institute for Statistics, http://data.worldbank.org/ indicator/SE.XPD.PRIM.PC.ZS/countries (accessed March 2, 2012); World Bank, "Expenditure per Student, Secondary (% of GDP per Capita)," UNESCO Institute for Sta-

tistics, http://data.worldbank.org/indicator/SE.XPD.SECO.PC.ZS/ countries (accessed March 2, 2012).

19. Ibid.

20. Michael Barber, Mona Mourshed, and McKinsey and Company, *How the World's Best School Systems Come Out on Top* (New York: McKinsey, September 2007). This information is also available for download at http://www.mckinsey.com/clientservice/social_sector/our_practices/education/knowledge_highlights/best_performing_school.as px (accessed May 25, 2011).

21. Brian August, Paul Kihn, and Matt Miller *Closing the Talent Gap: Attracting and Retaining Top-Third Graduated to Careers in Teaching* (New York: McKinsey, September 2010). This information is also available for download at http://www.mckinsey.com/clientservice/Social_Sector/our_practices/Education/Knowledge_Highlights/Closing_the_talent_gap.aspx (accessed May 26, 2011).

22. Darling-Hammond, *Flat World and Education*, p. 47.

23. Diane Ravitch, *The Death and Life of the Great American School System* (New York: Basic Books, 2010).

24. National Commission on Teaching and America's Future, *No Dream Denied: A Pledge to America's Children* (Washington, DC: National Commission on Teaching and America's Future, January 2003), figure 5.

25. August, Kihn, and Miller, "Closing the Talent Gap."

26. OECD, *Education at a Glance 2010*, table D3.1.

27. Lisa Lambert, "Half of Teachers Quit in 5 Years," *Washington Post*, May 9, 2006, http://www.washingtonpost.com/wp-dyn/content/article/2006/05/08/AR2006050801344.html (accessed May 25, 2011).

28. August, Kihn, and Miller, "Closing the Talent Gap."

29. Center for Public Education, "Pre-kindergarten: What the Research Shows," March 2007, http://www.centerforpubliceducation.org/Main-Menu/Pre-kindergarten/Pre-Kindergarten/Pre-kindergarten-What-the-research-shows.html (accessed August 20, 2011).

30. Lewis and Burd-Sharps, *Measure of America 2010–2011*, p. 135.

31. Darling-Hammond, *Flat World and Education*, p. 34.

32. James J. Heckman and Dimitriy V. Masterov, "The Productivity Argument for Investing in Young Children" (working paper series, no. 13016, National Bureau of Economic Research, Cambridge, MA, 2007). This information is also available at http://jenni.uchicago.edu/human-inequality/papers/Heckman_final_all_wp_2007-03-22c_jsb.pdf (accessed June 2, 2011).

33. Elliot Currie, *Crime and Punishment in America* (New York: Picador, 1998), p. 92.

34. Paul Tough, "What It Takes to Make a Student," *New York Times*, November 26, 2006, http://www.nytimes.com/2006/11/26/magazine/26tough.html (accessed May 25, 2011).

35. Lewis and Burd-Sharps, *Measure of America 2010–2011*, p. 137.

36. The enrollment ratio for preprimary education was defined as the ratio of total enrollment, regardless of age, to the population of the primary school age. Data extracted from Lewis and Burd-Sharps, *Measure of America 2010–2011*, p. 134.

37. National Center for Education Statistics, "Fast Facts," US Department of Education, http://nces.ed.gov/fastfacts/display.asp?id=516 (accessed August 19, 2011). Information presented on this webpage found in US Department of Education, National Center for Education Statistics, *Digest of Education Statistics, 2010* (NCES 2011-015), table 52.

38. Correlation computed between the average PISA score for each country where the data was extracted from PISA, "PISA 2009: Data Tables, Figures, and Exhibits" and the number of days per year of primary school education taken from OECD, *Education at a Glance 2010*, table D4.1. Table D4.1 is also available at http://dx.doi.org/10.1787/888932310529.

39. Jeffrey Tomlinson, *Number of Instructional Days/Hours in the School Year* (Denver: Education Commission of the States, July 2004), http://www.ecs.org/clearing house/55/26/5526.doc (accessed May 25, 2011).

40. OECD, *Education at a Glance 2010*, table D4.1. Note that Japan had 223 days reported in Mullis et al., *TIMSS 1999 International Mathematics Report*. The TIMSS 1999 report is also available for download at http://timss.bc.edu/timss1999i/math _achievement_report.html (accessed May 25, 2011).

41. For example, the New York City school calendar had the last class of the school year on June 28, 2011, and the first class of the fall on September 7, 2011. New York City Department of Education, "2011–2012 School Year Calendar," January 24, 2011, http:// schools.nyc.gov/NR/rdonlyres/498AE989-7C83-49CE-A90F-8BDEB72E2109/0/Final 320112012SchoolYearCalendar20110126.pdf (accessed May 28, 2011).

42. Hermann Ebbinghaus, *Memory: A Contribution to Experimental Psychology*, trans. Henry A. Ruger and Clara E. Bussenius (New York: Teachers College,1913).

43. Oxnard School District (CA), *What YRE Can Do to Enhance Academic Achievement and to Enrich the Lives of Students That the Traditional Calendar Cannot Do* (Washington, DC: ERIC Clearinghouse, 1992).

44. "The Underworked American: Children Are Exceptions to the Country's Work Ethic," *Economist*, June 11, 2009, http://www.economist.com/world/unitedstates/dis playstory.cfm?story_id=13825184 (accessed May 25, 2011).

45. Ravitch, *Death and Life of the Great American School System*, p. 281.

46. National Governors Association, Council of Chief State School Officers, and Achieve, Inc., *Benchmarking for Success: Ensuring U.S. Students Receive a World-Class Education* (Washington, DC: National Governors Association, 2008), http://www.core standards.org/assets/0812BENCHMARKING.pdf (accessed May 28, 2011).

47. "What Matters Most: Teaching for America's Future," National Commission on

Teaching and America's Future, 1996, http://www.nctaf.org/resources/research_and
_reports/nctaf_research_reports/rr_96_what-matters-most.htm (accessed May 31, 2011).

48. National Center for Education Statistics, Institute of Education Sciences, August
2010, http://nces.ed.gov/programs/digest/d10/tables/dt10_188.asp (accessed August 20,
2011), table 188 "Total Expenditures for Public Elementary and Secondary Education, by
Function and Subfunction: Selected Years, 1990–91 through 2007–08." Information presented in this table found in US Department of Education, *Common Core of Data National
Public Education Financial Survey* (Ann Arbor, MI: Inter-University Consortium for Political and Social Research [distributor], 1990–1991 through 2007–2008).

49. Lewis and Burd-Sharps, *Measure of America 2010–2011.*

50. Goodwin Liu et al., *Funding Gaps 2006* (Washington, DC: Education Trust,
2006), http://www.edtrust.org/sites/edtrust.org/files/publications/files/FundingGap
2006.pdf (accessed May 26, 2011).

51. Darling-Hammond, *Flat World and Education*, p. 29.

52. Barbara Kridl et al., *The Condition of Education 2003* (Washington, DC: US
Department of Education, National Center for Education Statistics, 2003), http://nces
.ed.gov/pubs2003/2003067.pdf (accessed May 31, 2011).

53. Margaret Goertz and Michael Weiss, *Assessing Success in School Finance Litigation: The Case of New Jersey. Education, Equity, and the Law. No 1* (New York: Campaign
for Educational Equity, Teachers College, Columbia University, November 2009), http://
www.equitycampaign.org/i/a/document/11775_EdEquityLawNo1.pdf (accessed May 26,
2011).

54. The US Supreme Court case is referred to as *San Antonio Independent School District v. Rodriguez*, 411 U.S. 1 (1973). The transcript may be read at http://supreme.justia
.com/us/411/1/case.html (accessed June 16, 2011).

55. Darling-Hammond, *Flat World and Education*, p. 111.

56. Lewis and Burd-Sharps, *Measure of America 2010–2011*, p. 142.

57. N. H. Kang and M. Hong, "Achieving Excellence in Teacher Workforce and
Equity in Learning Opportunities in South Korea," *Educational Researcher* 37, no. 4
(2008): 200–207.

58. Darling-Hammond, *Flat World and Education*, p. 16.

59. Fernanda Santos, "A Class Action: Illiterate Student Sues, Gets City to Pay for
Tutor," *New York Daily News*, September 26, 2003, http://www.nydailynews.com/
archives/news/2003/09/26/2003-09-26_a_class_action__illiterate_s.html (accessed
October 8, 2011).

60. OECD, *Education at a Glance 2010*, table A1.3.

61. John Aubrey Douglass, *The Waning of America's Higher Education Advantage:
International Competitors Are No Longer Number Two and Have Big Plans in the Global
Economy* (Berkeley: University of California, Center for Studies in Higher Education, June

2006), http://cshe.berkeley.edu/publications/publications.php?id=226 (accessed May 27, 2011).

62. Computed based on the data from OECD, *Education at a Glance 2010*, tables 1.2 and 1.3.

63. Lewis and Burd-Sharps, *Measure of America 2010–2011*, p. 212.

64. National Center for Public Policy and Higher Education, *Measuring Up 2008: The National Report Card on Higher Education* (San Jose: National Center for Public Policy and Higher Education, 2008). This information is also available at http://measuringup2008.highereducation.org/print/NCPPHEMUNationalRpt.pdf (accessed June 16, 2010).

65. Jay Greene, Brian Kisida, and Jonathan Mills, *Administrative Bloat at American Universities: The Real Reason for High Costs in Higher Education* (Phoenix, AZ: Goldwater Institute, August 17, 2010).

66. Lewis and Burd-Sharps, *Measure of America 2010–2011*, p. 146.

67. John A. Boehner et al., *The College Cost Crisis: A Congressional Analysis of College Costs and Implications for America's Higher Education System* (Washington, DC: US House Committee on Education and the Workforce, September 4, 2003).

68. Computed from OECD, *Education at a Glance 2010*, table B2.1.

69. Ibid.

70. OECD, "Glossary," in *Education at a Glance 2009*. This information is also available at http://www.oecd.org/dataoecd/44/7/43642148.pdf (accessed August 20, 2011).

71. OECD, *Education at a Glance 2010*, table B5.1.

72. OECD, *Education at a Glance 2010*, table B5.2.

73. Darling-Hammond, *Flat World and Education*.

74. OECD, *Education at a Glance 2010*, table B4.1.

75. Ann Marie Chaker, "Students Borrow More Than Ever for College," *Wall Street Journal*, September 4, 2009, http://online.wsj.com/article/SB10001424052970204731804574388682129316614.html (accessed August 20, 2011).

76. For further information on the ongoing issues of segregation and inequality in American education, I suggest reading Jonathan Kozol, *The Shame of the Nation: The Restoration of Apartheid Schooling in America* (New York: Crown Publishers, 2005).

77. Fulfilling the Dream, "Segregation in Chicago 2006: Executive Summary," Center for Urban Research and Learning at Loyola University Chicago, http://www.luc.edu/curl/cfm40/data/minisynthesis.pdf (accessed August 21, 2011).

78. Robert K. Merton, "The Unanticipated Consequences of Purposive Social Action," *American Sociological Review* 1, no. 6 (December 1936): 894–904.

79. Ravitch, *Death and Life of the Great American School System*, p. 76.

80. Ibid., p. 79.

81. Stanford University, *Multiple Choice: Charter School Performance in 16 States*

(Stanford, CA: Center for Research on Education Outcomes (CREDO), Stanford University, 2009). This information is also available at http://credo.stanford.edu/reports/ MULTIPLE_CHOICE_CREDO.pdf (accessed May 26, 2011).

82. Katrina Woodworth et al., *San Francisco Bay Area KIPP Schools: A Study of Early Implementation and Achievement, Final Report* (Menlo Park, CA: SRI International, 2008). This information is also available at http://policyweb.sri.com/cep/publications/ SRI_ReportBayAreaKIPPSchools_Final.pdf (accessed August 24, 2011).

83. Cecilia E. Rouse and Lisa Barrow, "School Vouchers and Student Achievement: Recent Evidence and Remaining Questions," *Annual Review of Economics* 1 (2009): 17–42, http://www.ers.princeton.edu/workingpapers/28ers.pdf (accessed May 31, 2011).

84. Barber, Mourshed, and McKinsey and Company, *How the World's Best School Systems Come Out on Top.*

85. Ibid.

86. G. W. Bohrnstedt and B. M. Stecher, eds., *What We Have Learned about Class Size Reduction in California* (Sacramento: California Department of Education, 2002). This information is also available at http://www.classize.org/techreport/CSRYear4 _final.pdf (accessed May 31, 2011).

87. Kozol, *Shame of the Nation*, p. 201.

88. Arthur J. Rolnick and Rob Grunewald, "Early Childhood Development: Economic Development with a High Public Return," Federal Reserve Bank of Minneapolis, December 2003, http://www.minneapolisfed.org/publications_papers/studies/early- child/abc-part2.pdf (accessed June 2, 2011).

89. Center on the Developing Child, Harvard University, "Understanding the Head Start Impact Study," National Forum on Early Childhood Policy and Programs, 2010, http://www.nhsa.org/files/static_page_files/0BF4EB6E-1D09-3519-ADBFF989BFF 11535/2-10ForumEvalScienceBrief_HeadStart.pdf (accessed March 2, 2012).

90. Ibid.

91. Head Start Research, *Head Start Impact Study: Final Report* (Washington, DC: US Department of Health and Human Services, January 2010). This information is also available at http://www.acf.hhs.gov/programs/opre/hs/impact_study/reports/impact _study/hs_impact_study_final.pdf (accessed June 15, 2011).

92. Darling-Hammond, *Flat World and Education*, p. 201.

93. National Commission on Time and Learning, *Prisoners of Time* (Washington, DC: US Department of Education, April 1994). This information is also available online at http://www2.ed.gov/pubs/PrisonersOfTime/index.html (accessed May 25, 2011).

94. Darling-Hammond, *Flat World and Education*, pp. 300–308.

CHAPTER 4. WE THE PEOPLE: DEMOCRACY

1. Charles L. Mee Jr., *The Genius of the People* (New York: Harper and Row, 1987), p. 237. Further information is available from the US Senate, S. Res. 331, 100th Cong. (October 21, 1988), http://www.senate.gov/reference/resources/pdf/hconres331.pdf (accessed April 21, 2011).

2. Pauline Maier, *Ratification: The People Debate the Constitution, 1787–1788* (New York: Simon and Schuster, 2010).

3. International Institute for Democracy and Electoral Assistance (IDEA), "Voter Turnout Database," http://www.idea.int/vt/viewdata.cfm (accessed November 14, 2010).

4. Dictionary.com, s.v. "democracy," http://dictionary.reference.com/browse/democracy (accessed November 6, 2010).

5. National Conference of State Legislatures, "Recall of State Officials," http://www.ncsl.org/default.aspx?tabid=16581(accessed August 2, 2011). This website reports that nineteen states permit the recall of state officials.

6. David B. Magleby, *Direct Legislation: Voting on Ballot Propositions in the United States* (Baltimore: Johns Hopkins University Press, 1984); Thomas E. Cronin, *Direct Democracy: The Politics of Initiative, Referendum, and Recall* (Cambridge, MA: Harvard University Press, 1989).

7. Paraphrased from the online definition, US Legal, s.v. "Representative Democracy Law and Legal Definition," http://definitions.uslegal.com/r/representative-democracy/ (accessed March 5, 2012).

8. "Antony Green's Election Guide," ABC News (Australia), http://www.abc.net.au/elections/federal/2007/guide/ (accessed August 2, 2011).

9. Arend Lijphart, *Patterns of Democracy: Government Forms and Performance in Thirty-Six Countries* (New Haven, CT: Yale University Press, 1999).

10. Some models of democracy focus on the concept of inclusion, that is, who is eligible to vote, rather than participation. As will be discussed later in this chapter, the countries on our list have generally addressed the issues of inclusion that plagued them historically and so participation is a more relevant metric. For more details, see Robert Dahl, *Polyarchy: Participation and Opposition* (New Haven, CT: Yale University Press, 1971).

11. Gerardo L. Munck and Jay Verkuilen, "Conceptualizing and Measuring Democracy: Evaluating Alternative Indices," *Comparative Political Studies* 35 (2002): 5–34; Axel Hadenius and Jan Teorell, "Assessing Alternative Indices of Democracy," (working paper, Committee on Concepts and Methods, International Political Science Association, August 2005), http://www.concepts-methods.org/Files/WorkingPaper/PC%206%20Hadenius%20Teorell.pdf (accessed August 2, 2011).

12. Polyarchy data set published in Tatu Vanhanen, "A New Dataset for Measuring Democracy, 1810–1998," *Journal of Peace Research* 37 (2000): 251–65, http://www.nsd.uib.no/macrodataguide/set.html?id=34&sub=1 (accessed August 2, 2011).

13. IDEA, "Voter Turnout Database." For specific data related to this discussion, follow steps one through three by selecting a country, then choosing the Congress/Parliamentary section, and then filtering the election-year range to 2005–2008 elections, depending on the selected country.

14. Ibid.

15. Computed from data provided by Michael McDonald, "Voter Turnout," US Elections Project, http://elections.gmu.edu/voter_turnout.htm (accessed December 27, 2010), graph titled "Presidential Voter Turnout Rates, 1948–2008."

16. Australia first introduced compulsory voting in 1924, according to the Department of Parliamentary Services, *Compulsory Voting in Australian National Elections* ([Canberra]: Department of Parliamentary Services report titled October 31, 2005), http://users .polisci.wisc.edu/kmayer/Comparative%20Electoral%20Systems/Compulsary%20Voting %20Parliamentary%20Report.pdf (accessed March 2, 2012).

17. IDEA, "Voter Turnout Database."

18. Michael McDonald, " 2008 General Election Turnout Rates," US Elections Project, http://elections.gmu.edu/Turnout_2008G.html (accessed April 9, 2011).

19. G. Bingham Powell, "American Voter Turnout in Comparative Perspective," *American Political Science Review* 80, no. 1 (1986): 17–43, http://www.nonprofitvote .org/download-document/141-american-voter-turnout-in-comparative-perspective.html (accessed August 2, 2011).

20. US Census Bureau, "Voting and Registration in the Election of November 2008—Detailed Tables," November 2008, http://www.census.gov/hhes/www/socdemo/ voting/publications/p20/2008/tables.html (accessed August 2, 2011).

21. North Dakota Secretary of State, "Voter Registration in North Dakota," August 1999, http://www.nd.gov/sos/electvote/voting/vote-history.html (accessed August 4, 2010).

22. Elections Canada, http://www.elections.ca/home.aspx (accessed December 23, 2010). Elections Canada is an independent, nonpartisan agency that reports directly to Parliament.

23. Raymond E. Wolnger and Steven J. Rosenstone, *Who Votes?* (New Haven, CT: Yale University Press. 1980).

24. For simplicity, Washington, DC, is included as a state in this discussion. *Wikipedia*, s.v. "Election Day voter registration," http://en.wikipedia.org/wiki/Election _Day_voter_registration (accessed December 27, 2010).

25. McDonald, "Voter Turnout," graph titled "Presidential Voter Turnout Rates, 1948–2008."

26. Jan Leighley and Jonathan Nagler, "The Effects of Non-precinct Voting Reforms on Turnout, 1972–2008," *Pew Charitable Trusts*, January 15, 2009, http://www.pew centeronthestates.org/report_detail.aspx?id=58252 (accessed December 27, 2010).

27. Jeffrey A. Karp and Susan A. Banducci, "Going Postal: How All-Mail Elections Influence Turnout," *Political Behavior* 22 (2000): 223–29; Adam J. Berinsky, Nancy Burns,

and Michael W. Traugott, "Who Votes by Mail? A Dynamic Model of the Individual-Level Consequences of Vote-by-Mail Systems," *Public Opinion Quarterly* 65 (2001): 178–97; Priscilla L. Southwell and Justin Burchett, "The Effect of All-Mail Elections on Voter Turnout," *American Politics Research* 28 (2000): 72–79.

28. Maya Harris, "Slavery to Prison, Disenfranchisement Plagues America's Ballot Box," American Civil Liberties Union of Northern California, December 1, 2005, http://www.aclunc.org/news/opinions/slavery_to_prison,_disenfranchisement_plagues_americas_ballot_box.shtml (accessed August 2, 2011).

29. Michael Alvarez et al., "Classifying Political Regimes," *Studies in Comparative International Development* 31 (1996): 1–37.

30. Douglas Rae, "A Note on the Fractionalization of Some European Party Systems," *Comparative Political Studies* 1 (1968): 413–18. Definition ranges from 0–1, where if all representation resides in one party then the fractionalization equals 1, and fractionalization increases as representation is more widely distributed.

31. G. Casper and C. Tufis, "Correlation versus Interchangeability: The Limited Robustness of Empirical Findings on Democracy Using Highly Correlated Datasets," *Political Analysis* 11, no. 2 (2002), http://www.personal.psu.edu/ggc3/caspertufisPAweb.pdf (accessed August 2, 2011).

32. This is discussed extensively in Steven Hill, *Fixing Elections: The Failure of America's Winner Take All Politics* (New York: Routledge, 2003).

33. Ibid.

34. Connecticut Judicial Branch Law Libraries, "Roger Sherman and the Connecticut Compromise," http://www.jud.ct.gov/lawlib/History/Sherman.htm (accessed April 4, 2010).

35. James Madison, "Objection That the Number of Members Will Not Be Augmented as the Progress of Population Demands Considered," *The Federalist* no. 58 (February 20, 1788), http://www.constitution.org/fed/federa58.htm (accessed August 2, 2011).

36. The cap of 435 seats in the House of Representatives was introduced by the Reapportionment Act of 1929. For more information, see Office of the Law Revision Counsel, "Title 2—The Congress," *U.S. Code*, http://uscode.house.gov/pdf/2001/2001usc02.pdf (accessed August 19, 2011).

37. For purposes of this calculation, both houses for bicameral systems have been combined. For the three unicameral systems, Greece, South Korea, and Portugal, the number of representatives from the single house were used. Population estimates were based on the most recent data available from May 2011. Number of representatives and population estimates were extracted from *Wikipedia*, s.v. "List of countries by population," http://en.wikipedia.org/wiki/List_of_countries_by_population (accessed May 1, 2011). Number of representatives were identified from individual country political descriptions. For example, for Korea the number of representatives was identified from *Wikipedia*, s.v.

"Politics of South Korea," http://en.wikipedia.org/wiki/Politics_of_South_Korea (accessed May 1, 2011).

38. Monty G. Marshall and Keith Jaggers, "Political Regime Characteristics and Transitions, 1800–2010," *Polity IV Project* (College Park: Center for International Development and Conflict Management at the University of Maryland, 2002). Dataset user's manual for time-series data and polity-case data available for download at http://www .systemicpeace.org/inscr/inscr.htm (accessed March 5, 2012).

39. Keith Jaggers and Ted Robert Gurr, "Tracking Democracy's Third Wave with the Polity III Data," *Journal of Peace Research* 32, no. 4 (1995): 469–82.

40. For more information about the World Bank, please see its homepage at http://www.worldbank.org/ (accessed August 4, 2011). While the president of the World Bank has traditionally been from the United States, it is assumed that this has not had any influence on the Worldwide Governance Indicators national estimates.

41. World Bank, "The Worldwide Governance Indicator (WGI) Project," http://info.worldbank.org/governance/wgi/index.asp (accessed November 28, 2010).

42. World Bank, "Voice and Accountability," (definition), http://info.worldbank .org/governance/wgi/pdf/va.pdf (accessed November 28, 2010).

43. "No Time to Vote: Challenges Facing America's Overseas Military Voter," Pew Charitable Trusts, January 2009, http://www.pewcenteronthestates.org/uploadedFiles/ NTTV_Report_Web.pdf (accessed March 6, 2012).

44. World Bank, "Political Stability and Absence of Violence," (definition), http://info.worldbank.org/governance/wgi/pdf/pv.pdf (accessed November 28, 2010).

45. World Bank, "Government Effectiveness," (definition), http://info.worldbank .org/governance/wgi/pdf/ge.pdf (accessed November 28, 2010).

46. Joe Eaton, M. B. Pell, and Aaron Mehta, "Washington Lobbying Giants Cash in on Health Reform Debate," NPR News Investigations, March 26, 2010. http://m.npr .org/news/Health/125170643 (accessed August 2, 2011).

47. World Bank, "Regulatory Quality," (definition), http://info.worldbank.org/ governance/wgi/pdf/rq.pdf (accessed November 28, 2010).

48. World Bank, "Rule of Law," (definition), http://info.worldbank.org/ governance/wgi/pdf/rl.pdf (accessed November 28, 2010).

49. World Bank, "Control of Corruption" (definition), http://info.worldbank .org/governance/wgi/pdf/cc.pdf (accessed November 28, 2010).

50. Economist Intelligence Unit, "The Economist Intelligence Unit's Index of Democracy 2008," http://graphics.eiu.com/PDF/Democracy%20Index%202008.pdf (accessed August 2, 2011).

51. Transparency International, *Corruptions Perceptions Index 2010* (Berlin: Transparency International, 2010). This information is also available at http://www .transparency.org/content/download/55725/890310 (accessed August 4, 2011).

52. For more information, visit the Freedom House homepage at http://www .freedomhouse.org/ (accessed November 27, 2010).

53. Gerardo L. Munck and Jay Verkuilen, "Conceptualizing and Measuring Democracy: Evaluating Alternative Indices," *Comparative Political Studies* 35 (2002): 5–34.

54. Michael Alvarez, Stephen Ansolabehere, and Catherine H. Wilson, "Election Day Voter Registration in the United States: How One-Step Voting Can Change the Composition of the American Electorate" (working paper, no. 5, California Institute of Technology, Pasadena, CA, and Massachusetts Institute of Technology, Cambridge, MA, June 2002), http:// www.vote.caltech.edu/drupal/files/working_paper/vtp_wp5.pdf (accessed August 2, 2011).

55. Bev Harris, *Black Box Voting in the 21st Century* (Renton, WA: Talion, 2004).

56. Office for Democratic Institutions and Human Rights, *United States of America 2 November 2004 Elections: OSCE/ODIHR Election Observation Mission Final Report* (Warsaw: OSCE/ODIHR, March 31, 2005). This information is also available at http:// www.osce.org/odihr/elections/usa/14028 (accessed August 2, 2011).

57. The court case is known as *League of United Latin American Citizens v. Perry*, 548 U.S. 399 (2006). Details of this court case are available for download at http:// www.law.cornell.edu/supct/html/05-204.ZS.html (accessed August 2, 2011).

58. For more information, see the Washington State Redistricting Commission website at http://www.redistricting.wa.gov (accessed August 2, 2011).

59. For more information, see the Arizona Independent Redistricting Commission website at http://www.azredistricting.org (accessed August 2, 2011).

60. Proposition 11 passed in 2008; Proposition 20 passed in 2010. For more information, see Kathay Feng, Jeannine English, and David Flemming, letter to Patricia Galvan (initiative coordinator, Attorney General's Office, Sacramento, CA), October 22, 2007, http:// ag.ca.gov/cms_pdfs/initiatives/i746_07-0077_Initiative.pdf (accessed August 2, 2011).

61. Steven Hill, personal communication with the author, August 9, 2011.

62. Robert J. Kolesar, *Communism, Race, and the Defeat of Proportional Representation in Cold War America* (paper presented at the New England Historical Association Conference, John Carroll University, University Heights, OH, 1996).

63. Election Center 2008, "Election Tracker: Ad Spending," CNN, http://www.cnn .com/ELECTION/2008/map/ad.spending/ (accessed June 19, 2011).

64. For an online version of the US Constitution, see http://www.house.gov/house/ Constitution/Constitution.html (accessed August 21, 2011).

CHAPTER 5. EQUALITY: A BALANCING ACT

1. Abraham Lincoln to Colonel William F. Elkins, November 21, 1864, in *The Lincoln Encyclopedia: The Spoken and Written Words of A. Lincoln Arranged for Ready Reference* by Archer H. Shaw (New York: Macmillan, 1950).

2. Plutarch quotes extracted from Inequality.org, "Inequality Quotes by Plutarch," Program on Inequality and the Common Good, http://inequality.org/quotes/plutarch/ (accessed July 12, 2011).

3. Corrado Gini, *Variabilità e mutabilità* [*Variability and Mutability*] (Bologna: C. Cuppini, 1912). Reprinted in *Memorie di metodologica statistica*, E. Pizetti and T. Salvemini, eds. (Rome: Libreria Eredi Virgilio Veschi, 1955).

4. Organisation for Economic Co-operation and Development (OECD), "Income Distribution—Inequality," http://stats.oecd.org/Index.aspx?DataSetCode=INEQUALITY (accessed July 2, 2011).

5. United Nations Development Programme (UNDP), "Human Development Report 2009: Overcoming Barriers; Human Mobility and Development," http://hdr.undp .org/en/media/HDR_2009_EN_Complete.pdf (accessed August 20, 2011), table m, "Economy and Inequality," pp. 195–98.

6. OECD, "Equity Indicators," *Society at a Glance 2009: OECD Social Indicators* (Paris: OECD, 2009). This information is also available at http://dx.doi.org/ 10.1787/550365522422 (accessed August 21, 2011).

7. OECD, "Income Distribution—Inequality."

8. The fact that the United States has a much higher level of income inequality is one of the rare points of agreement in the competing books Richard Wilkinson and Kate Pickett, *The Spirit Level: Why Greater Equality Makes Societies Stronger* (London: Bloomsbury, 2009) and Christopher Snowdon, *The Spirit Level Delusion: Fact-Checking the Left's New Theory of Everything* (Ripton, North Yorkshire, UK: Democracy Institute/Little Dice, 2010).

9. OECD, "Stat Extracts: Country Statistical Profiles—2010 Edition," http:// stats.oecd.org/Index.aspx?DataSetCode=CSP2010 (accessed August 2, 2011).

10. Kristen Lewis and Sarah Burd-Sharps, *The Measure of America 2010–2011* (New York: New York University Press, 2010), p. 211.

11. Ibid.

12. Sheila Block, *Ontario's Growing Gap: The Role of Race and Gender* (Ottawa: Canadian Centre for Policy Alternatives, June 2010), http://www.policyalternatives.ca/ sites/default/files/uploads/publications/reports/docs/The%20Role%20of%20Race%20 Ontario%20Growing%20Gap.pdf (accessed October 16, 2011).

13. Susan Aud et al., *Status and Trends in the Education of Racial and Ethnic Groups* (Washington, DC: US Department of Education, July 2010), http://nces.ed.gov/ pubs2010/2010015.pdf (accessed July 12, 2011).

14. Paul Krugman, *The Conscience of a Liberal* (New York: W. W. Norton, 2007), p. 178.

15. Data extracted from the provisional data from OECD, "Income Distribution— Inequality." Germany is not included in this graph on the change in inequality since the national data from the mid-1980s is based on West Germany and the data from the late 2000s is based on post-reunification with the considerably poorer former East Germany.

16. Lane Kenworthy and Jonas Pontusson, "Rising Inequality and the Politics of Redistribution in Affluent Countries," *Perspectives on Politics* 3 (2005): 449–71.

17. Allan H. Meltzer and Richard Scott, "A Rational Theory of the Size of Government," *Journal of Political Economy* 89 (1981): 914–27.

18. OECD, "Stat Extracts: Social Expenditure—Aggregated Data," http://stats .oecd.org/Index.aspx?DataSetCode=SOCX_AGG (accessed July 12, 2011).

19. Vincent A. Mahler and David K. Jesuit, "Fiscal Redistribution in the Developed Countries: New Insights from the Luxembourg Income Study," *Socio-Economic Review* 4 (2006): 483–511.

20. Krugman, *Conscience of a Liberal*, p. 21.

21. OECD, "Total Tax Revenue as Percentage of GDP," http://www.oecd.org/ dataoecd/13/38/46721091.xls (accessed July 10, 2011), table A.

22. World Values Survey (WVS), "Online Data Analysis," http://www.wvsevsdb .com/wvs/WVSAnalize.jsp (accessed June 30, 2011).

23. Michael I. Norton and Dan Ariely, "Building a Better America—One Wealth Quintile at a Time," *Perspectives on Psychological Science* 6 (2011): 9–12, http://www .people.hbs.edu/mnorton/norton%20ariely%20in%20press.pdf (accessed July 16, 2011).

24. Anthony B. Atkinson, Thomas Piketty, and Emmanuel Saez, "Top Incomes in the Long Run of History," *Journal of Economic Literature* 49, no. 1 (2011): 3–71, http://elsa .berkeley.edu/~saez/atkinson-piketty-saezJEL10 (accessed July 10, 2011).

25. Lane Kenworthy and Jonas Pontusson, "Rising Inequality and the Politics of Redistribution in Affluent Countries," *Perspectives on Politics* 3 (2005): 449–71.

26. John F. Kennedy, "Remarks in Heber Springs, Arkansas, at the Dedication of Greers Ferry Dam," American Presidency Project, October 3, 1963, http://www.presidency .ucsb.edu/ws/index.php?pid=9455 (accessed July 9, 2011).

27. Larry M. Bartels, *Unequal Democracy: The Political Economy of the New Gilded Age* (Princeton, NJ: Princeton University Press, 2008), p. 9.

28. Isabel Sawhill and John E. Morton, *Economic Mobility: Is the American Dream Alive and Well?* (Washington, DC: Economic Mobility Project, 2007), http://www .economicmobility.org/assets/pdfs/EMP%20American%20Dream%20Report.pdf (accessed July 9, 2011).

29. Paul Pierson and Jacob S. Hacker, *Winner-Take-All Politics: How Washington Made the Rich Richer—and Turned Its Back on the Middle Class* (New York: Simon and Schuster, 2010), p. 46.

30. Economic Policy Institute, "The State of Working America: Inequality; Wages & Compensation," http://stateofworkingamerica.org/inequality/wages-compensation/ (accessed July 10, 2011).

31. Robert Reich, *Supercapitalism: The Transformation of Business, Democracy, and Everyday Life* (New York: Albert Knopf, 2007), p. 108.

32. Computation based on OECD, "Stat Extracts: Real Hourly Minimum Wages," http://stats.oecd.org/Index.aspx?DataSetCode=RHMW (accessed July 16, 2011).

33. Chuck Collins, *Economic Apartheid in America: A Primer on Economic Inequality and Security* (New York: New Press, 2000), p. 111.

34. Pierson and Hacker, *Winner-Take-All Politics*, p. 188.

35. William H. Boyer, *Myth America: Democracy vs. Capitalism* (New York: Apex Press, 2003), p. 172.

36. Collins, *Economic Apartheid in America*, p. 57.

37. UN University World Institute for Development Economics Research, "Pioneering Study Shows Richest Two Percent Own Half World Wealth," 2006, http://www.wider.unu.edu/events/past-events/2006-events/en_GB/05-12-2006/ (accessed June 1, 2011).

38. Meizhu Lui, *Laying the Foundation for National Prosperity: The Imperative of Closing the Racial Wealth Gap* (n.p.: Insight Center for Community Economic Development, March 2009), http://www.newdeal20.org/wp-content/uploads/2009/11/executive-summary.pdf (accessed August 3, 2011).

39. Forbes, "The World's Billionaires," 2010, http://www.forbes.com/lists/2010/10/billionaires-2010_The-Worlds-Billionaires_CountryOfCitizen.html (accessed July 2, 2011). Population data extracted from CIA, "Field Listing: Population," Central Intelligence Agency World Factbook, https://www.cia.gov/library/publications/the-world-factbook/fields/2119.html (accessed July 2, 2011).

40. Bill Moyers and Julie Leininger Pycior, *Moyers on America: A Journalist and His Times* (New York: Anchor Books, 2005).

41. Lewis and Burd-Sharps, *Measure of America 2010–2011*, p. 159.

42. Reich, *Supercapitalism*, p. 113.

43. Tom Hertz, *Understanding Mobility in America* (Washington, DC: Center for American Progress, April 26, 2006), http://www.americanprogress.org/issues/2006/04/Hertz_MobilityAnalysis.pdf (accessed July 11, 2011).

44. WVS, "Online Data Analysis."

45. John Kingdon, *America the Unusual* (New York: St. Martin's/Worth, 1999), p. 34.

46. While similar analysis can also be performed for daughters, it introduces issues of gender equality into the discussion of income mobility, thus making the interpretation more challenging.

47. Jo Blanden, *How Much Can We Learn from International Comparisons of Intergenerational Mobility?* (London: Centre for the Economics of Education, London School of Economics, November 2009), http://cee.lse.ac.uk/ceedps/ceedp111.pdf (accessed July 10, 2011).

48. Jo Blanden, Paul Gregg, and Stephen Machin, *Intergenerational Mobility in Europe and North America: A Report Supported by the Sutton Trust* (London: Centre for

Economic Performance, April 2005), http://cep.lse.ac.uk/about/news/Intergenerational Mobility.pdf (accessed July 15, 2011).

49. Markus Jäntti et al., "American Exceptionalism in a New Light: A Comparison of Intergenerational Earnings Mobility in the Nordic Countries, the United Kingdom, and the United States" (research paper, no. 781, University of Warwick, Department of Economics, 2007), http://www2.warwick.ac.uk/fac/soc/economics/research/workingpapers/publications/twerp_781.pdf (accessed July 11, 2011).

50. James Lardner, *Inequality Matters: The Growing Economic Divide in America and Its Poisonous Consequences* (New York: New Press, 2006), p. 34.

51. John Wirt et al., *The Condition of Education 2003* (Washington, DC: US Department of Education, June 2003), http://nces.ed.gov/pubs2003/2003067.pdf (accessed July 12, 2011).

52. Hertz, *Understanding Mobility in America.*

53. W. O. Bae, "Sex Ratio at Birth in Korea," *Bogeon Sahoe Nonjib* 11 (1991): 114–31.

54. "Gender Inequality Index (GII)," Human Development Reports, http://hdr .undp.org/en/statistics/gii/ (accessed July 1, 2011).

55. Ibid.

56. OECD, *Education at a Glance 2009: OECD Indicators* (Paris: OECD, 2009). Information regarding some of the data tables is also available at http://statlinks.oecd code.org/962009061P1G002.XLS (accessed July 2, 2011).

57. UN Development Programme, *The Human Development Report: The Real Wealth of Nations; Pathways to Human Development* (New York: Palgrave Macmillan, 2010), http://hdr.undp.org/en/reports/global/hdr2010/ (accessed July 2, 2011).

58. Pamela Paxton and Sheri Kunovich, "Women's Political Presentation: The Importance of Ideology," *Social Forces* 82 (2003): 87–114.

59. Labor workforce participation rate extracted from *Human Development Report: The Real Wealth of Nations.* Gender gap in earnings extracted from OECD, *OECD Employment Outlook: Moving Beyond the Job Crisis* (Paris: OECD, 2010), http:// www.oecd.org/document/42/0,3746,en_2649_34747_40401454_1_1_1_1,00.html (accessed July 2, 2010).

60. Lewis and Burd-Sharps, *Measure of America 2010–2011*, p. 167.

61. Ibid., p. 170.

62. Ibid., p. 246.

63. Center for American Women and Politics, Eagleton Institute of Politics, "Facts on Women in Statewide Elected Executive Office," Rutgers University, http://www.cawp .rutgers.edu/fast_facts/levels_of_office/statewide.php (accessed August 31, 2011).

64. Norton and Ariely, "Building a Better America."

65. Pierson and Hacker, *Winner-Take-All Politics*, p. 36.

66. Krugman, *Conscience of a Liberal*, p. 136.

67. A recent article stated that in 2011, the New York securities firms will pay employees $19.7 billion in cash bonuses. Brett Philbin, "Wall Street Bonuses Shrink: New York Comptroller Says Pool Dropped 14 % in 'Difficult Year' for Industry," *Wall Street Journal*, March 6, 2012, http://online.wsj.com/article/SB10001424052970203986604577253111846696908.html?mod=googlenews_wsj (accessed March 12, 2012).

68. Tax Foundation, "Tax Data: U.S. Federal Individual Income Tax Rates History, 1913–2011 (Nominal and Inflation-Adjusted Brackets)," http://www.taxfoundation.org/publications/show/151.html (accessed July 11, 2011).

69. Alicia DeSantis et al., "Republican Presidential Candidates on the Issues: Taxes and Spending," *New York Times*, http://elections.nytimes.com/2012/primaries/issues#issue/taxes-spending (accessed March 12, 2012).

70. Krugman, *Conscience of a Liberal*, p. 250.

71. Romney for President, "Introduction," http://www.mittromney.com/learn/mitt/tax-return/main (accessed March 12, 2012).

72. Tax Foundation, "Tax Data."

73. Michael Health, "Warren Buffett Urges Congress to Increase Taxes on 'Coddled' Billionaires," *Bloomberg News*, August 15, 2011, http://www.bloomberg.com/news/2011-08-15/buffett-urges-congress-to-raise-taxes-on-coddled-billionaires.html (accessed October 16, 2011).

74. Bartels, *Unequal Democracy*, p. 240.

75. Collins, *Economic Apartheid in America*, p. 111.

76. David Card and Alan B. Krueger, *Myth and Measurement* (Princeton, NJ: Princeton University Press, 1997).

77. Donald B. Marron, Acting Director, Congressional Budget Office, to the Honorable Charles E. Grassley, Chairman of the Committee on Finance, US Senate, January 9, 2007, http://www.cbo.gov/ftpdocs/77xx/doc7721/01-09-MinimumWageEITC.pdf (accessed August 2, 2011).

78. Bartels, *Unequal Democracy*, p. 148.

79. Jo Blanden, "Big Ideas: Intergenerational Mobility," *CentrePiece* (Winter 2008/2009), http://cep.lse.ac.uk/pubs/download/cp270.pdf (accessed July 10, 2011).

80. Lawrence Mishel, Jared Bernstein, and Heidi Shierholz, *The State of Working America 2008/2009* (Ithaca, NY: Cornell University Press, 2009).

81. Wilma Rule, "Electoral Systems, Contextual Factors, and Women's Opportunities for Election to Parliament in Twenty-Three Democracies," *Western Political Quarterly* 40 (1987): 477–98.

82. Lane Kenworthy and Melissa Malami, "Gender Inequality in Political Representation: A Worldwide Comparative Analysis," *Social Forces* 78 (1999): 235–68.

83. Jelle Visser, "Union Membership Statistics in 24 Countries," *Monthly Labor*

Review (Washington, DC: US Department of Labor, January 2006), http://www
.bls.gov/opub/mlr/2006/01/art3full.pdf (accessed July 9, 2011).

84. For an extensive discussion of the work councils, codetermined boards, and
regional wage-setting institutions see Thomas Geoghegan, *Were You Born on the Wrong
Continent? How the European Model Can Help You Get a Life* (New York: New Press,
2010).

85. There is a detailed discussion of work councils at the European Trade Union Confederation (ETUC) website at ETUC, "European Work Councils," http://www.etuc
.org/r/57 (accessed August 2, 2011).

86. Paul Krugman, "For Richer," *New York Times*, October 20, 2002, http://www
.nytimes.com/2002/10/20/magazine/20INEQUALITY.html (accessed July 9, 2011).

87. Lewis and Burd-Sharps, *Measure of America 2010–2011*, p. 183.

88. Anne Marie Goetz, *Who Answers to Women? Gender and Accountability* (New
York: UN Development Fund for Women, 2008), http://www.unifem.org/progress/
2008/media/POWW08_Report_Full_Text.pdf (accessed July 12, 2011).

CHAPTER 6. WHAT THE DATA HAVE SHOWN US

1. The International Monetary Fund (IMF) lists Australia as having a higher nominal GDP per capita than the United States in 2010. The World Bank (2009) lists the
Netherlands as having a higher nominal GDP per capital than the United States.
Wikipedia, s.v. "List of countries by GDP (nominal) per capita," http://en.wikipedia.org/
wiki/List_of_countries_by_GDP_(nominal)_per_capita (accessed August 1, 2011).

2. *Wikipedia*, s.v. "List of countries by GDP (PPP) per capita," http://en
.wikipedia.org/wiki/List_of_countries_by_GDP_(PPP)_per_capita (accessed August 1,
2011).

3. Kristen Lewis and Sarah Burd-Sharps, *The Measure of America 2010–2011* (New
York: New York University Press, 2010), p. 171.

4. Susan Aud et al., *Status and Trends in the Education of Racial and Ethnic Groups*
(Washington, DC: US Department of Education, July 2010), http://nces.ed.gov/
pubs2010/2010015.pdf (accessed July 12, 2011).

5. Tom Hertz, *Understanding Mobility in America* (Washington, DC: Center for
American Progress, April 26, 2006), http://www.americanprogress.org/issues/2006/
04/Hertz_MobilityAnalysis.pdf (accessed July 11, 2011).

6. Lewis and Burd-Sharps, *Measure of America*, p. 75.

7. Donna L. Hoyert et al., "Deaths: Final Data for 1999," *National Vital Statistics
Report* 49, no. 8 (2001): 1–114, http://www.cdc.gov/nchs/data/nvsr/nvsr49/nvsr49
_08.pdf (accessed August 3, 2011).

8. Melonie Heron, "Deaths: Leading Causes for 2007," *National Vital Statistics Reports* 59, no. 8 (August 26, 2011), http://www.cdc.gov/nchs/data/nvsr/nvsr59/nvsr59_08.pdf (accessed March 12, 2012).

9. *Citizens United v. Federal Election Commission Appeal from the United States District Court for the District of Columbia*, No. 08-205 (2009), http://www.supremecourt .gov/opinions/09pdf/08-205.pdf (accessed March 12, 2012).

10. Larry M. Bartels, *Unequal Democracy: The Political Economy of the New Gilded Age* (Princeton, NJ: Princeton University Press, 2008), p. 254.

11. Organisation for Economic Co-Operation and Development (OECD), "Health Data 2011: Frequently Requested Data; Updated November 2011," last updated November 29, 2011, http://www.oecd.org/dataoecd/52/42/49188719.xls (accessed March 12, 2012).

12. Abraham Lincoln, "House Divided," (speech, Illinois Republican Convention, June 16, 1858), http://www.ushistory.org/documents/housedivided.htm (accessed July 24, 2011).

13. For a discussion of this parable, read James Fallows, "Peace on the Boiled Frog Front," *Atlantic*, July 13, 2009, http://jamesfallows.theatlantic.com/archives/2009/07/peace_on_the_boiled_frog_front.php (accessed August 1, 2011).

14. For more discussion on this subject see Robert Frank, *Richistan: A Journey through the American Wealth Boom and the Lives of the New Rich* (New York: Crown Business, 2007).

15. You can find further discussion in Paul Krugman, *The Conscience of a Liberal* (New York: W. W. Norton, 2007).

INDEX